HOW TO WRITE LIGHT NOVELS AND WEBNOVELS

*Your Key to Writing Addictive Stories
That Get Reads, Reviews and Sales*

R. A. Paterson

Cover designed by Pixelstudio
Cover Art: ©gow27 - stock.adobe.com

This book is a work of fiction. Names, characters, places, and incidents either are products of the author's imagination or are used fictitiously. Any resemblance to actual persons, living or dead, events, or locales is entirely coincidental.

Robyn Paterson
Visit my website at www.robynpaterson.com

Printed in the United States of America

First Printing: Aug 2019
Kung Fu Action Theatre

ISBN-978-1-989357-05-7

This book is dedicated to the writers of tomorrow.

With Special Thanks to...
Don Chisholm
Justus R. Stone
Jeremy Barwick
Jonathan Kinney
Richard Curtissmith
And the many translators who toil endlessly to bring us
webfiction from across the world.

And with love to my wife for putting up with my late nights
reading webfiction.

CONTENTS

INTRODUCTION: WINNING AT WRITING

Across Asia, writers just like you have been turning their hobby of writing into careers.

In China and South Korea, writers of online fiction (called webnovels in English) are churning out online serials that are making them rich and famous. Thanks to webfiction portals like *Qidian*, *Joara*, *Naver*, and others, they're able to build huge fan bases who flock to their every new release, and get media deals to turn their stories into comics, movies, TV series, online games, and more.

Meanwhile, in Japan, online fiction hubs like *Shōsetsuka ni Narō!* have become the greenhouses where publishers find the next hot young writers, turning their work into serialized young adult books called "light novels." These light novels have become the hottest media properties going, and every season fans around the world are treated to the newest anime, manga, and films based on light novel properties.

And now, it's your turn!

China's giant online publisher *Qidian* has created *Webnovel.com*, a site that is attracting millions of users and turning webfiction writers into profit-sharing authors. Meanwhile, other webfiction sites like *Wattpad*, *Radish*, *Tapas* have launched their own profit-sharing programs with their authors, letting writers like you convert millions of readers into steady income.

At the same time, major English publishers are watching the webfiction sites looking for the next great young writer and media companies are trying to find the source for their next hit movie or TV series. And, self-publishing is now 40%+ of the English book market, so anyone can publish their books online and get them in front of tens of millions of readers.

Anybody with a story can get it out there and show the world their creativity while making an income doing what they love- including you.

But writing webfiction isn't easy.

You can't just write- you need to know what's popular and how the top writers turn their stories and dreams into big audiences and big opportunities. You need to know the little tricks that will get your audience hooked and keep them reading, reviewing, and buying each new story you put out there. What are the top Chinese, Korean, and Japanese writers doing that are bringing in global audiences? How do they make stories so compelling that millions of people are willing to read bad machine translations just to get a taste of the stories?

This book will show you all of that, and more.

You don't want to just write- you want to win at writing.

So, turn the page, and let's get started in making your writing dreams come true.

HOW TO USE THIS BOOK

This book isn't meant to be read straight though.

You are welcome to read it that way, and will learn a lot if you do, but it's better to use it as a guidebook where you read about what you need when you need it.

It is divided into four sections:

1) What Popular Webfiction Has in Common
2) Asian Webfiction
3) Webfiction Genres
4) Writing Your Own Webfiction

And while the first section and the last section of the book are probably required reading, the middle two sections which make up most of the book cover a wide variety of topics and can be read as needed.

For example, perhaps you want to write a xianxia cultivator story you intend to serialize on a fiction site?

Then, you would only need to read the first and last sections, the chapter on Chinese Webnovels, the Rising Hero Story chapter, and perhaps the Fantasy chapter for good measure. Unless you also intended it to be a litRPG, in which case that chapter would be good reading too.

Or, let's say you want to write a romance light novel?

Then, besides the basics, the sections on Japanese Light Novels and the Romance genre notes would be all the things you'd need to focus on. Unless it's also about a girl building a clothing empire in a fantasy world, in which case the Fantasy and Task Story chapters might be worth a look.

As you can see, you can pick and choose your chapters as needed.

Most chapters are complete in themselves, and designed to be read without reading anything else except the first and last sections of the book. So, don't worry about missing something important by not reading everything.

That said, you might want to look at the other chapters sometime as well, since you never know what interesting tidbits are hiding in them that can produce story ideas or new takes on old genres.

Let's do it!

QUICK DEFINITIONS

If you picked up this book, you probably know what webnovels or light novels are, but just to make sure, let's do some quick definitions.

Light Novel – a style of young adult novels from Japan which is heavily influenced by anime and manga and usually includes illustrations. Light novels were usually (but not always) originally published online and then later acquired by publishers. They are often thinner than regular novels and can cover any genre.

Webnovel – the generally accepted English term for online fiction produced in China or South Korea. Webnovels are most often serialized stories written by amateurs and semi-professional writers and may run hundreds or thousands of chapters. They too can cover any genre, but fantasy and romance are the most popular genres.

Webfiction – a generic term for stories written for sharing on the internet. This book uses the term "webfiction" to describe both webnovels and light novels since the majority of them share this common beginning. Yes, not all light novels start as webfiction, but for the purposes of this book they're going to be lumped together as webfiction as a way to avoid saying "webfiction and light fiction" over and over again. Our apologies.

WHAT POPULAR WEBFICTION STORIES HAVE IN COMMON

With millions of writers churning out millions of chapters on Asian webfiction sites like *Qidian, Joara, Narō,* and others, it should be no surprise that people very quickly began to figure out what worked and what didn't when it came to building an audience. That isn't to say there is only one way to do it, but copying others who are more successful has always been one the fastest paths to the top. And, when you add that the people at the top can make a lot of money, that gave Asian writers a whole lot of incentive to zero in on the "best" ways to do things.

As a result, there are a number of tricks and approaches that Asian web fiction writers have developed to maximize their chances of success. They even work across cultures, since they're also what draw a lot of fans in other languages to translate and read web fiction on popular English, French, Spanish and Arabic sites. They don't work so well for romance, but that's because romance has its own rules.

Here are some of the most common traits of Asian web fiction. Feel free to follow them (or not) when planning your own online fiction adventures, and see if there's more you can add to the list!

THE SYSTEM

Characters in almost all popular webfiction stories live inside a system. It might be a literal system like in a litRPG where the characters exist inside a video game, it might be a system of magical forces and rules like in a xianxia novel, or it might be a social system like a structured society in a palace romance. In any case, this system gives the world that the characters live in structure, and there are rules that the people or world which exists inside this system follows.

The reason for this is fairly simple- characters navigating systems is automatically interesting to young readers who are trying to understand the real-world systems they live in. Systems exist around us in real life- social systems, mechanical systems, legal systems, biological systems, and our brains are wired to learn how to navigate these systems. Asian writers have caught on to this simple principle, and webnovels hack this by placing the story characters inside systems which they then need to figure out and overcome, just like we wish we could do in the systems we live inside in real life.

The Greek philosopher Aristotle once said that all stories can be broken down into central conflicts- man versus man, man versus himself, man versus nature, and a few others. Webfiction stories are "man versus system" stories where the main character finds themselves faced by a system they didn't create and must figure out the rules of this system and then overcome that system. This might mean climbing from the bottom of the power structure to the top, bringing peace to a disordered system, or even destroying a system and rebuilding it from scratch.

But, no matter what, there will almost always be a system involved somewhere.

This isn't a unique idea to Asian webfiction, many popular English young adult novels like *The Hunger Games*, *Divergent*, *The Maze Runner*, and many others, are also "(wo)man versus system" stories about characters who are thrust into a new world (system) and must find a way to survive and prosper inside that system. In fact, in most of these stories, the character must master the system in order to destroy it and rebuild a new one- which is the most popular ending to system stories in English. Asian stories, on the other hand, usually prefer an ending where the character becomes the new master of the system and changes it for the better rather than destroying the old one.

That said, sometimes the system just exists as a background element like the rules of physics that apply to that setting, and are as natural as air and water. In these cases, the system isn't the main conflict of the story, but merely a tool for the writer to explain different aspects of the character's world or create drama.

Either way, the main character will be someone who is rising up through the system in an unconventional way- thus defeating it.

CHEATS

If there is a system, there are ways to cheat it, and the main character of a successful webfiction story will almost always have a cheat of some kind that gives them an edge in the system they're navigating. Thanks to this cheat, they're able to do what normal people can't do and avoid the consequences that normal people might face when in difficult situations.

There are two kinds of cheats- controllable and uncontrollable.

Controllable cheats are ones which the character mostly has control over, and uncontrollable cheats are ones which the character has little to no control over.

Controllable cheats are basically ultimate superpowers that make the character almost unstoppable thanks to only being limited by the imagination of the character. Examples include...

- knowledge of the future
- access to all magical known spells
- being truly immortal
- being able to multitask many different things simultaneously
- having a perfect memory of everything
- being able to learn any skill by seeing in used once
- having access to collections of magical or high-tech equipment
- superspeed
- being able to copy any superpower they see perfectly after seeing it used
- having limitless growth ability

Characters who have controllable cheats usually start the story by gaining the cheat, and then spend the rest of the story learning how to use it in different ways as they slowly dominate their world.

On the other hand, there are also uncontrollable cheats, which are ones which aren't controlled by the character themselves, but someone else.

For example, one excellent (and very common) example of an uncontrollable cheat in Chinese xianxia novels is the "ghost master." This is the ghost of an ancient master who gets stuck in either the main character's body or is in an item that the character possesses and must now work with the main character in order to accomplish some unfinished goal the ghost has. Of course, the main character is too weak to accomplish what the ghost master needs them to do, so the ghost master must train them up, using ancient secret arts that let the main character level up faster than any other character could. (However, they can only give the character what they need to grow faster on their own, the character still has to do the work.)

They also act as a guide to the character, giving them someone to talk to as they enter the world of fierce martial arts battles, and providing secret knowledge that nobody else has. And, if the main character gets into trouble, the ghost master can often lend them their powers in times of need, keeping them safe.

However, the ghost master also comes with a set of disadvantages.

First, they are a character with their own needs and goals, and those needs and goals won't always match with the main character's goals. There will be times when the ghost master will force the character to do things they don't want to do, or refuse to help when the main character needs it most. Also, the ghost master must be kept a carefully guarded secret because usually the ghost master has powerful enemies, who are now the enemies of the young hero who has no chance against them if anyone finds out the ghost master is still around. Thus, the ghost master can't openly use their abilities to help the main character.

In addition, the ghost master will usually only help the main character in times of extreme emergencies to avoid "making them weak," and there will almost always be a cost to their help. It might be that the master only has enough power to help them once every few months, or it might be that the character will have to perform some task if they ask the master for help.

Finally, the ghost master's usefulness scales down with the main character as they go up in level, usually becoming less useful as the lead rises in level and can take care of themselves. This almost always leads to the main character losing the ghost master at some point in their development, forcing them to stand on their own while going on a quest to save the master they now feel deeply attached to from their enemies.

All of this combines together to produce a "cheat" which lets the main character level up and break the system while at the same time adding drama to the story and forcing the main character to unavoidably connect with the main plot.

And that's what a good cheat does, it acts as a double-edged sword which both makes the main character's life easier while adding complications that the main character has to deal with. In addition, the best cheats are usually not entirely under the main character's control, so they can't rely on them and still have to struggle and stand on their own two feet. They're not a magic sword that cuts through anything, but a magic sword that can sense other magic items of power and help the character find the things they need to make themselves better.

And they don't always have to be weapons...

Top 10 Fantasy Cheats List!
1. A ghost master
2. A sentient magic book
3. Knowledge from another world or life
4. A unique skill set/Special training
5. Magical jewels/items
6. A unique character class
7. A unique upbringing
8. A secret meditation technique
9. An imprisoned demon or spirit

10.   Magical weapons

Or even in fantasy settings...

Top 10 Modern Cheats List!
1.   A powerful mentor
2.   Access to special technology
3.   Special training/ Unique skill set
4.   A unique background
5.   A mysterious backer
6.   An extensive contact network
7.   Unique physical traits (extra strong, extra fast, heals quickly, etc.)
8.   A powerful family
9.   Unique family/friends
10. Access to special information

Each of these will let a character (with a little creativity) have a big advantage over the competition, and quickly progress through whatever system they're working within to reach the top. The right cheats must be matched with the right system, because they're only a cheat when the character is working within that system. A powerful family isn't a cheat when the character spends the story wandering a desert alone on the other side of the planet, unless they also have influence there too!

However, cheats are important because they don't just help the main character- they also help the writer!

You see, at some point, the character is going to get into trouble that the writer is going to have difficulty getting them out of without resorting to the dreaded "plot armor" that audiences hate so much. This is especially true if the character is in a serial adventure where every chapter is ending with newer and more dangerous situations to bring the reader back for more. Sooner or later, the readers are going to throw up their hands and say "this is ridiculous!"

But if the character already has a pre-established cheat right from the beginning the writer just needs to point to the cheat and say "this was established way back in chapter XX." And suddenly, the writer (who has been making it up as they went along) looks like a genius who was planning it out a hundred chapters ago instead of a desperate hack. Not only that, often the audiences will get excited because they predicted correctly that the cheat will come into play at the critical moment, feeling proud of themselves and happy with the story instead of unhappy with the writer.

Not only that, cheats also have several bigger advantages for writers.

First, they often provide one way for the main character to skip all the boring stuff they might have to do in the story. The cheat often enables them to learn things faster or in a different way than a normal character would, thus jumping over the dull parts and going from one major conflict to another. Or maybe it lets them heal faster than a normal person could, getting them back in the fight when they might have to wait weeks between big battles to recover. In any case, if the author wishes it, the cheat provides a way to keep the story moving at a brisk pace and not have to worry about downtime unless it's important for the plot.

Second, they create a natural way for the writer to push and pull the character in the directions they need them to go for the story. As with the ghost master above, a cheat often has story requirements that the character is forced to deal with as part of the story and these can happen at any time. For example, the character's guardian falls ill, and now they need to find an antidote. Or maybe the character just struck it rich, but the writer needs them to lose the money quickly, so then the cheat uses up their money in some way to return them to being poor. Cheat can be endless story complications and used in many different ways to keep a serial story flowing.

Third, cheats can help make a story unique. A swordsman wandering the landscape killing monsters is so cliché it's barely worth mentioning- unless that swordsman is wearing a mysterious gem that resets time by an hour every time they die! Then, suddenly this situation offers new and interesting story potentials that can tickle the imaginations of readers and provide a new spin on tired genre tropes that can lead to better sales. Just make sure the gem is "mysterious" and fails from time to time to keep the tension up, after all, a purely reliable cheat is no fun at all! This can become a great hook to hang a story on and sell it to audiences who will want to see how this changes the game.

And last, cheats boost the wish-fulfilment factor of the story...

WISH FULFILLMENT

Webfiction is pure escapist entertainment, and a big part of that is letting the audience escape their own mundane lives and be someone or something greater for a while. The characters in webfiction stories are stand-ins for the audience doing what the audience only wishes they could do- stand up to authority, beat down bullies, get the hottie, run the show, say witty lines, look cool, and most of all have control over their lives.

Even though characters in webfiction usually start under poor circumstances, it doesn't take them long to find their balance and begin working their way through the system. As they do, they will slowly gain confidence in their positions and abilities, being able to influence and control the world around them more and more. This will eventually reach the point where they are able to start reshaping the world/system itself and rebuild or remake it in their image.

Of course, the world isn't going to let itself be reshaped without a fight! There are always characters who benefit from the system, and they're going to strongly resist the main character's attempts to change things. These will usually be presented as selfish people who represent the bad side of this system, and glory in the power and positions the system gives them. Thus, they're the perfect opponents for the main character to slap around and soundly defeat, bringing justice to the fantasy world in a way that the audience only wishes they could.

To keep the wish-fulfillment flowing, two common patterns have popped up in webfiction- "the rising overlord" and "the forever underdog."

The rising overlord is a character who starts already powerful or gains power quickly after the start of the story due to their cheat or incredible abilities. After that, the story is about them encountering a long series of opponents who think they're stronger than the rising overlord, and get crushed like a frog on a highway by the passing overlord. This pattern is popular in Japanese light novels, where the hero is merrily marching along towards their goals and the system is just fighting a losing battle to try and stop them from changing everything.

The forever underdog, on the other hand, is a character who is also rising in power, but is always just a few steps below their opponents. They are still shaping the world, and still winning the competitions, but each battle they face is against seemingly superior opponents who force the hero to bring their a-game over and over again. Unlike the overlord, the underdog also faces opponents who often really are better than the main character, but thanks to skills, talents, connections, favors, and incredible luck, the lead keeps winning anyways. This gives the audience a nice roller-coaster ride of suspense, tension and then relief as the hero pulls off yet another miracle save, and is the reason why Chinese audiences can't seem to get enough of this kind of story.

Either way, these plots deliver a whole lot of wish fulfilment by letting the main character (and thus the audience) get to feel a sense of control and power over their lives and environment that only builds as the story goes on. And, along the way they will get tastes and glimpses of what it's like to enjoy being really powerful- trashing bullies, being chased by hotties, enjoying wealth and status, and feeling a sense of happiness and control in their lives – only to lose it when the next opponent comes up to remind them that they're not at the top yet and can lose everything if they don't keep fighting on.

Until, in the end, the character has remade the world/system in some way, and now enjoys what it's like to live the good life.

It's a nice dream!

ACTION ORIENTED WRITING

Webfiction is all about action- they're designed to be written fast and read faster.

Readers of webfiction aren't looking for novels with long paragraphs and deep introspective prose. They want simple, practical and cinematic stories that they can read during a quick 10-minute bus ride to work or while on their lunch break. In fact, if they see giant blocks of text, they tend to go looking for another story because they think they won't have time to finish it.

So, the writing style of webfiction is built around actions and descriptions of action, using short prose with a focus on dialog and few long descriptions. Filled with tight prose, punchy sparse adjectives and active verbs, it's designed to convey the story in an efficient way for a writer who has to crank out a chapter or two a day in addition to doing another job to pay the bills.

Characters speak in lots of clear, direct dialog and actions are described in straightforward and simple ways. Since dialog reads faster than exposition, webfiction writers will usually have characters express important information instead of saying it directly to the audience, using head-hopping to give different perspectives and points of view. It's a very cinematic style of writing which is more focused on what happens than how characters feel about it.

Here's two brief examples to give you a sense of how they compare. In this scene from a horror-thriller, a group of young hikers in the mountains are trying to escape from a crazed bigfoot that has been attacking their members.

Conventional Fiction Style:

The bridge was just up ahead of them, and the thundering creature was behind them. Andy kept yelling for the kids to move, staying at the back of the group to help any stragglers in case they tripped or risked falling behind. Every loud crash behind them the angry beast made sent his heart racing and fear rippled through his body, but he forced himself to stay at a slow pace and not to bolt ahead. He was responsible for these people, and that sense of duty kept him fixed where he was.

If it caught up, at least he could slow it down enough for the others to cross the rope bridge over the chasm and escape. But, being a hero was a lot harder than it looked, and he resisted the urge to yell and scream for the group to move faster- panic being the last thing the group needed more of.

Finally, Tina, who was at the lead, reached the edge of the bridge and began ushering the kids onto it, telling them to hold the ropes and not run. It was a forty-meter drop, and the more the kids ran the shakier the bridge would become. The

shaking bridge would make it harder for the rest to cross, slowing the group down, to say nothing of the chance of someone slipping and falling.

The bridge was old, having been built in the 1940s, and the weathered planks that spanned it looked about that old too. The ropes that held it together didn't look much newer, and their thick sun-bleached cords had more than a few frayed strings sticking out at odd angles. If there was any choice, they wouldn't have come this way, but the creature left them only one option, and as the kids trundled across Andy could only pray that their grandfather's work was as solid as the men who built it.

As the last of the kids started across the bridge, Andy caught up with Tina. Filled with nervousness, he was just about to tell her to cross when they heard a scream. Looking over, they saw one of the kids, Louis, was hanging from the bottom of the bridge, held up by the hands of two of his campmates, Terry and Lin. Andy guessed a board had broken under the boy's feet.

It was a delay they didn't need, and then things got worse.

Behind them, the creature broke through the trees onto the path, a quarter ton of black hairy muscle charging at them like a freight train...

The Webfiction version:

"Move it! Move it!" Andy screamed at the kids, urging them on.

He could see the bridge over the chasm just ahead. It made him feel like there was a chance.

Somewhere behind them, the creature smashed through the forest in pursuit. It made Andy's heart race, but he hung back to catch any stragglers. He was the group leader, and no kid was going to get left behind on his watch.

In his head, he searched for ways to slow the creature down if it caught up. The kids needed time to cross, and he would have to give it to them somehow.

Tina was at the front of the group, so she reached the end of the bridge first.

"Miss Tan, is it safe?" Leo asked from beside her, pointing out over the aging rope bridge's thirty-meter span.

Tina glanced down at the straight forty meter drop next to her and forced a smile. "Sure it is, Leo. You just have to make sure you hold on to the ropes tight, okay? And don't walk too fast. If you run, the others will run too, and the whole bridge will shake a lot and make it harder to cross."

The boy nodded, and grabbed the guide ropes, starting across. As each board creaked under his feet, Tina winced, but all she could do was usher more children onto the decaying bridge and try not to think about what might happen if something broke.

Andy was beside Tina as the last of the kids stepped onto the bridge and their eyes met.

"You go," Andy said. "I'll wait until you're..."

He was cut off by a scream

Spinning around, they saw one of the kids, Louis, was being held in the air by the hands of his campmates Terry and Lin. Louis had fallen through a broken board and was now dangling under the bridge while the other two tried desperately to pull him up.

It was a delay they didn't need.

Then things got worse.

Behind them, the hairy creature exploded onto the path, charging at them like an angry black freight train...

As you can see, the conventional fiction version is all about the details, with long paragraphs and no dialog as the story is presented to the audience in a tense and dramatic way. The audience learns how the characters feel, the details behind the situation they're in, and the perilous nature of the rope bridge. The webfiction version, on the other hand, is a collection of short paragraphs focused on the simple play of events with dialog and different points of view used to fill in the information needed while keeping the story flowing. It also makes heavy use of white-space to make the story look simple and easy to read, making it appealing to time-pressed audiences.

The goal is to make the audience experience the events of the story in a fast-moving, easy to read style that mimics comics and film more than it does conventional novels. Like Japanese manga, it's meant to be a cinematic play of the events as they happen without a lot of deeper detail and leaving the rest to the imaginations of the audience.

And it isn't just about the writing style, the story itself is structured in a way which is meant to keep the action flowing. There are never any boring bits because boring bits equal lost readership in a highly competitive market where another writer's story is only a click away. Successful webfiction writers always give their readers a reason to keep reading, filling their works with dramatic hooks and dramatic questions that the reader is always reading to find the answers to. And, the moment one dramatic question is answered, the then the story immediately jumps to another one which was already being set up while the first one was playing out.

For example, while the main character was fixing things after a misunderstanding with their lover, the audience saw their business rival was planning a big move to steal a major contract from the lead's business. Then, when the relationship issues are done, the lead suddenly gets a panicked text from their manager that they've just lost that major contract. But, while they're in the process of getting the contract back, more trouble is brewing with their father's health, which leads to them having to rush to the hospital after the rival's threat is defeated.... And, so on.

There is always more trouble lurking in the background, and B-plots which set up events that will happen in the future and create questions in the reader's heads about how things will all turn out.

Also, to keep readers coming back to read the next installment, webfiction chapters almost never end without some form of cliff-hanger. It doesn't always have to be life or death, but they need to end on some dramatic question which makes the audience need to read the next chapter to find the answer to. Then, once they've started the next chapter, that chapter will pull them in and keep reading until the next dramatic cliff-hanger, which makes them read the next chapter, and so forth. (More on this conveyor-belt system in the chapter on Writing Your Stories.)

However, avoiding boring parts does not mean avoiding slow parts. Slow parts and parts not about combat are perfectly fine, but they must have some dramatic hook to them to keep readers engaged and reading. Powerful action scenes often require lots of setup to make them work, and good webfiction is balanced at creating sine-wave type patterns of slow and fast moments to give readers a break between the dramatic tension.

The power of quiet character moments to connect with readers should never be underestimated, or their importance in building stories. So, good webfiction writers always remember to let their audience breathe and relax in between the dramatic highs.

CONFLICT-DRIVEN

Webfiction is driven by primal conflicts.

Characters fight over power, status, honor, resources, love, romantic partners, family, friends, revenge, and a whole lot of other basic human needs. High minded concepts like justice, ideology, philosophy and nobility have no place in a webfiction story- these aren't stories about the human condition or the questions of why people exist. These are stories driven by characters who want something, and that puts them in natural conflict with others who want the same thing - because if there's something you want, someone else probably wants it too.

Since the stories are often about characters battling against systems of power, most of the opponents who appear will be characters who are exploiting the system (often undeservedly) and benefitting from it in bad ways. This makes them naturally fearful of the main character and want to put them in their place, as any character who is a disruptor affects the status quo, and people who benefit from the current system won't want the character to win- putting them in direct natural conflict with each other.

One of the strongest human impulses is for people to hold on to what they have. And whether it's a palace romance, where the king's new favorite is stealing away time from his older flames, a corporate story where the talented rookie is threatening the jobs of his superiors, or a fantasy story where a powerful new warrior is challenging the champions of the battle guilds- people in power don't like the idea of losing that power. Thus, those in power will always be looking to deal with rivals before they become a threat.

This creates an endless series of natural opponents, and the settings of webnovels are usually like a jungle floor- lethal places where only the strong survive and the weak die. They operate on a single principle – the strong rule the weak – and if you're strong you're able to do whatever you want to those who are weaker than you. Characters in these settings need to be constantly watching their backs, and this brings a natural tension to the story, as the audience knows the main character will suffer if they make any serious mistakes.

But this also creates opportunities for the writer to really cut lose.

In modern American and European stories, the stories usually go out of their way to make sure that the characters are fighting defensive battles. In modern western thinking- aggression against others is bad. This is why characters in most American movies and books are often rebels or unwilling participants who are fighting because they're forced to fight, not because they want to. They might also fight because it's their duty, but in most cases, they will be fighting against enemies who "struck first," since after all nobody likes a bully.

This really limits American characters because they must always be fighting the "good fight," and aren't allowed to be aggressive except in rare cases where the character is an "anti-hero." But this approach really takes a lot of the fun and wish fulfilment out of the story because the writer can't let the character's more primal impulses run wild. People don't just want to read about nice guy heroes, they want to read about conquerors and characters who reach out and make their dreams into reality with their own two hands.

And, this is where the conflict-driven nature of webfiction stories becomes a big advantage.

If the setting is one where everyone is out for themselves, and the only law is the law of survival, then it's perfectly reasonable for characters to unleash their inner Machiavelli and do whatever it takes to win. Survival is the deepest and strongest human instinct of them all. Primal, conflict-driven settings become an excuse for a character to act in ways that might be looked down upon under other conditions or situations, thus allowing the wish-fulfilment aspects of the story to go crazy.

In webfiction stories, the main character will be taught the rules of the setting really early, usually in a harsh lesson that nearly crushes their soul. But they'll get back up from that blow having learned the lessons of power, then begin to fight so that they don't have to bow before anyone else. That will be the spark which sets them off on their journey, and it will only end when they sit at the top or die- there are no other choices.

It will be one glorious, conflict-filled ride, and the audience will be right there waiting for each new chapter of it.

ALWAYS RISING

Nobody likes losers, and nobody fantasizes about being a loser.

Webfiction main characters can start as a loser, but they need to become a winner really fast to keep the interest of the audience. The audience is here to escape from their daily troubles and enjoy watching a winner, win. Similarly, they don't like the feeling of losing themselves, or through the main character.

Thus, the main character should never really lose.

They might have setbacks, but these should be short-lived and lead to bigger victories later on. If they get beaten up, they should always be plotting revenge at the first available opportunity. If they lose, it should be because something was stacked against them, and it should be something they can correct fairly quickly and solve the problem. (i.e. Get revenge.)

They should never feel sorry for themselves, or mope, or get depressed, or go drinking (unless it leads to more conflict or victory later) because that would kill the fun of the story. The audience isn't there to read about their ups and downs, they're there to read about the main character's victories (and temporary setbacks) and share the wish-fulfilment glory with them.

Thus, while the threat of loss in a webfiction story should be constant, successful writers always make sure there is little or no actual serious loss faced by the main character. There should only be just enough to keep the tension high, but never really enough to make the audience depressed or down for any real length of time.

Of course, this just applies to the lead character, their friends, family and allies can lose a lot and usually do. They often suffer greatly at the hands of the main character's enemies, which then lets the lead show up and exact revenge in cool and interesting ways, thus restoring the balance while giving the audience an emotional high.

SIMPLE CHARACTERS

When it comes to how writers design main characters, for most webfiction the answer is simple- they look in the mirror.

The main character in most webfiction is a self-insert version of the writer, or at least a character who strongly resembles the writer in a large number of ways. This isn't a bug, it's a feature. There's nobody who knows the main character better than themselves, so naturally most beginning writers just write about a character who is basically an improved version of themselves under a new name.

Also, this lets the writer just jump into the story and let their fantasies run free- fantasies that their audience just might share. Other people who are like the writer and come from similar backgrounds will naturally connect with these main characters, and it isn't hard for them to imagine themselves in these situations either. So, as long as their fantasies run in parallel, the writer will have a ready-built audience who will keep coming back for more.

Again, webfiction stories are largely about wish-fulfillment, and as long as the author is getting their own fantasies served, the audience might just be enjoying the ride.

That said, most webfiction lead characters are pretty simple. They usually have the basic traits of most popular fictional characters- they're assertive, capable and attractive – but beyond that they're usually kept pretty generic. This is done to keep them relatable to the reader, since the more unique a character is, the harder they are to relate to for the audience, and the audience wants a character they can step into like a second self and imagine being. Thus, most webfiction lead characters only have a few small traits that make them special like ways of dressing, talking, or acting, but beyond that aren't really all that unique.

Another standard of webfiction is the love interest character, of which there will almost always be one. This character will be introduced early and be the writer's perfect dream partner that will be described in glowing tones. In fact, the love interest(s) are usually the only characters who actually do get an in-depth description in webfiction, with everyone else getting only simple sketches. This is done on purpose, of course, to emphasize how special and unique they are. Although this is usually just limited to their appearance, as their personality can often be pretty simple.

They exist to be the perfect counterpart to the lead character, so whatever would match the lead is what the love interest is like. If the lead is quiet, the love interest is cheerful. If the lead is active, the love interest is passive and supportive. If the lead is funny, the love interest will be serious. The goal is to have someone who balances the main character out so they naturally fit together.

And finally, villains in webfiction are usually as simple as they come.

Webfiction bad guys are often little more than cardboard cut-out villains who exist to cause problems for the hero and be smacked around and mowed down. They're evil characters who are driven by only the most primal and negative of desires- lust, status, greed, fear, pride, and revenge. Everything they do is about gaining or keeping those things, and they show these motivations right away to the audience when they're introduced. These are things that the audience automatically understands and looks down on, so they naturally dislike this character. The only exceptions should be characters who will reform (join the lead's team) and really major villains (sometimes).

This doesn't mean the villains can't have noble motivations as well, but they are tragically flawed by their major negative motivation. A greedy character can love his children, but if he's destroying the lives of other families to satisfy his greed, the audience won't feel too sorry for him.

Which is the goal.

Webfiction villains are written this way on purpose, and in fact adding depth to them is usually a bad idea. The audience is there to have the experience of watching this evil person who got in the main character's way get what they deserve, and they don't want to feel sorry for them because it kills the fun. If you add depth to villains, they become human, and the audience becomes conflicted over whether they deserve the punishment they receive. But the audience doesn't want to feel conflicted, they want to enjoy every second of the villain's punishment, and them being human would get in the way.

In the end, webfiction characters are almost always cliché stock characters because it saves the writer and the audience a lot of time. The writer can just focus on what makes this particular character special instead of worrying about how to put them together, and the audience can easily understand the stock characters because they know them already.

Like anything, it's not what webfiction characters are that's important, it's how they're used.

TROPE DRIVEN

Webfiction doesn't have a lot of time for new ideas or lots of detail. At heart, it's all about the action and getting the story moving and keeping it moving. Thus, webfiction writers rely strongly on tropes- things the audience already knows or is used to seeing in other stories.

Tropes act as a cheat for the author, allow them to jump right to the important parts of the story without having to spend a lot of time explaining things. For example, as mentioned above, they use a lot of stock characters- police officer, CEO, teacher, tiger mom, spunky younger sister, evil vampire, and so on. This is so the character can come in, do their story job, and leave without the writer having to worry about taking time to detail them or figure out anything about them.

They often don't even have names- because the truth is, they don't need them. Only important characters in a story should have names, and the rest are just parts of the setting that the character deals with as needed. There's no reason for the "handsome clerk" or "cute shop girl" to have a name if they're only in one scene and won't have any real important place in the story. If the audience cares, they can fill in the details themselves, if they don't, the story isn't slowed down by wasting time on some minor character.

Similarly, webfiction stories and plots are always very familiar. They're filled with rebellions, love triangles, lost relatives, plans to take over the world, and every other plot that your average twelve-year-old is already familiar with. Again, this is okay, as the audience already knows and likes (or doesn't like) many of these plots and situations, and it makes the story feel very comfortable for them. They don't have to think hard about what's happening, and can just sit back and enjoy the show. Tropes are tropes for a reason, after all- they work and people like them.

However, that doesn't mean the writer doesn't have to do a bit of work.

The audience doesn't want the same tropes they're used to done in the same ways- they want them presented in a way they haven't seen before. This is a skill that the best webfiction writers have mastered, and a lot of it is about playing with tropes- using them, subverting them, mixing them together, deconstructing them, and whatever else they need to do to generate surprise, anticipation, sympathy, and drama.

Often one of the better ways to play with tropes is to exaggerate them to make them greater or smaller than the audience might expect. For example, the character is a famous cowboy, but he's a terrible shot. In every other way he's a cowboy right from the audience's imaginations, but one part of his trope is changed to make him more unique. Or, if the trope is a demon hunter who needs to collect 100 souls to regain his own, then either he needs to collect 1 million souls, or he only needs to collect three. (But those three are really hard to get!)

By taking part of the trope and making it more extreme, it changes it just enough to surprise the audience and pique their curiosity.

However, a good webfiction writer is careful to never forget that the trope is still the core of the character or situation. It's a simple idea that the audience understands and has built their ideas around. If they play with it too much in an attempt to be "original" then it can lose focus and confuse the audience- something a writer must never do.

Thus, tropes with a little twist are almost always better than ones pushed too far.

LOOSELY STRUCTURED

Most popular webfiction stories are serials which are meant to run as long as the writer can keep them going. Sometimes this means dozens, hundreds, or even thousands of chapters- because often the more the writer writes, the more they get paid.

In addition, a really successful webnovel is a golden goose, and nobody kills a golden goose while it's making gold!

Thus, webfiction serials are usually planned on three levels:

1. An opening story arc which is usually well planned out.
2. Following story arcs which are loosely planned and will be written as the story progresses with modifications depending on what happens with each progressive arc.
3. An ending story arc which is very roughly planned and open to change.

This open form of planning keeps webfiction serials flexible, so once the story starts, they can adapt to the needs of the writer, the reactions of the audience, and the realities of webfiction publishing- all of which are important to think about.

First, the writer might come up with better ideas as they go along. Often webfiction writers are still new to writing, and they're becoming better writers with practice and experience. So, sticking to an outline they created when they were just starting out isn't always a good idea. Or, sometimes the writer gets bored with the story and decides to spice it up by taking it in a new and unplanned direction to keep themselves interested. In that case, the detailed outline ends up being a waste of time.

Next, webfiction stories are usually being written in close to real time, which is one of the great thrills of reading and writing webfiction. This allows the writer to actually see the reactions of the audience as they go along and change the story accordingly. If some character or situation is super popular, they can focus on that, or if the audience doesn't like something, they can try to wrap a plotline up early to replace it with something else. If there's a strict outline, that becomes a lot more difficult.

And lastly, webfiction publishing is a hard, grueling road where the writer needs to constantly be producing new chapters. It's a marathon, not a sprint, and some writers get burnt out or need to take breaks from time to time. Sometimes this means ending stories or even whole series earlier than planned, especially if the audience ratings drop. If the story requires a thousand chapters, but the writer gets burnt out at chapter 300, there's no way they can finish it properly, so having the flexibility to stop at chapter 320 if they wish could be a lifesaver.

However, all of this shouldn't be taken as an excuse not to plan at all!

It's better to have a plan you need to modify than a blank page you have to fill when you have a bad case of writer's block. Planning webnovels helps to fight writer's block, and the better they're planned, the smoother the process of writing them will go. They can be planned in as much or as little detail as you like, but there should at least be a few pages which outline the above three levels.

Individual arcs should be planned out before they are written, but it isn't a good idea to write them all in too much detail because those details will change as the story naturally evolves and the writer comes up with new ideas. Just a two- or three-page summary of each arc and where it will go is enough for most writers to have something to fall back on when the muse isn't singing and they need to get chapters out to meet their midnight deadline.

UNORIGINAL

The goal of writing successful webfiction isn't to give the readers something new- it's to give them more of what they already want.

Readers read genre fiction because it's giving them something light, fun, and comforting. They don't want challenging or hard to understand writing, and if you don't give them what they want, they'll go home unhappy. It's like a superhero movie without superheroes, or a romance story without a conflicted couple- it's missing the whole reason why audiences are there in the first place!

The world's biggest publishing market is romance, regardless of language or culture, and every single romance novel has the same plot - boy meets girl and they get together. It sells hundreds of millions of copies a year, and audiences can't get enough.

Therefore, if you want to write webfiction successfully, unoriginality isn't something to avoid, it's actually the goal! But, like tropes, to be successful at it, writers need to give them something familiar with a twist- a new coat of paint to make it just different enough that it feels like a new take on an old favorite.

How do they do it?

The most common way is writers pick their favorite stories (or parts of them), and modify them enough that the story has to play out differently than the original did. They need to take the key elements of the story they (and others like them) love, and then not just change the names, but the whole story enough that it becomes a different story with similar elements.

For example, let's look at the key elements of Harry Potter and the Philosopher's Stone by J.K. Rowling and see what could be changed to make a "new" story. In the original, an orphaned boy discovers he's a wizard, goes to a hidden magic school, makes friends, learns magic, uncovers a dark secret, and with his friends stops an ancient evil from being unleashed. Those are the key elements of the story, so how could they be changed?

- If he's no longer an orphan, he loses his background connection to the dark wizard who killed his parents. This changes both who he is, and the end of the story.
- If the magic school is public instead of hidden, then it's a world where magic is an everyday thing and we've changed the setting significantly.
- What if instead of making friends with a redhead and a know-it-all, he has no friends and was constantly bullied? Or maybe he falls in with the "bad" kids at the school. Would that change how he turns out? It definitely would.
- If the type of magic he's learned changes from typical European wizardry to elemental magic or cultivating spiritual growth, then that too will change the story.
- Does the school still have a dark secret? Or is the plot that there's a magic tournament coming up and he needs to help the school win? That will change the plot and the ending.
- Is there an ancient evil hiding in the depths of the school? Or is it just that one of the instructors is plotting to take over the school? A shift to politics from horror fantasy is a big one, and changes where the story goes.

As you can see, by changing the major story elements, it can become a "new" story which draws from the original, but now goes in a different direction. And, this is what most readers want- a different take on the things they already love. A new coat of paint, a few new parts, and it becomes interesting again.

This is also why it's so important to read extensively in your genre before you try writing stories. You need to know what angles have been done to death and what hasn't been done much, or at all. Unoriginality is fine, good even, but total unoriginality can mean nobody will be interested in reading it. (And it also becomes plagiarism and can get writers into a lot of trouble unless it's just used for fanfiction.)

To catch an audience, there needs to be some element of surprise or novelty which makes this story different from the others the audience has read. Just enough for something to feel familiar and different at the same time.

That's the key to building an audience and writing popular webfiction.

ASIAN WEBFICTION

Like many things in Asia, it all started with dragons.

The tabletop role-playing game *Dungeons and Dragons* (*D&D*) to be precise.

For those who might not know, *D&D* is a game where people pretend to be characters in another world and then tell a story together, a bit like a murder mystery dinner, except with chainmail and orcs. And, while it started in the United States in the 1970s, it didn't take long before it was translated and spread around the world.

In Japan in 1986, a young *D&D* gamer named Ryo Mizuno was having such a great time playing *D&D* with his friends, they decided to publish "replays" of their sessions in a Japanese computer magazine called *Comptiq*. Presented as enhanced transcripts which focused on dialog to keep things light and interesting, these replays were named after the setting, a fantasy world called Lodoss, and became known as *The Record of Lodoss War*.

This story of the teenaged boy named Parn, who was the son of a failed knight, and his companions as they fought to stop the evil Emperor Beld became extremely popular, and Mizuno later went on to publish novelizations of these stories in a series of books that were quickly turned into an anime.

Then, in 1990, a bulletin board operator named Keita Kamikita on the pre-internet Japanese chat service called *Niftyserve* was re-organizing their Science Fiction and Fantasy fan forums and ran into a problem. He was making smaller sub-forums for people to discuss different types of stories, and decided that youth-oriented fantasy stories like *Lodoss War* and another wildly popular title called *Slayers!* didn't belong with other more "mature" fantasy stories.

Thus, he created a new category called "light novels."

At first, this term was just one used by fans to describe these young-adult oriented fantasy novels which were mostly written in a dialog-focused style to encourage quick reading and enhanced with extra illustrations to give them a manga-like reading experience. However, after the magazine publisher *Takarajimasha* began publishing a series of guides to these books called *Kono Raito Nōberu ga Sugoi!* ("This Light Novel is Amazing!") in 2004, the term spread into popular use.

Of course, young adult novels had existed for over a hundred years even in Japan, but these new light novels with their anime-style stories and illustrations were marketed by major Japanese publishers as a fresh reading experience for a young audience that grew up on manga and began to not only take off, but earned their own space on the bookstore shelves. They came to cover many different genres, not just fantasy, and many would later be adapted into anime, manga, films, games and other properties.

But 2004 didn't just give the world the term "light novel," it also gave the world something else!

April 2, 2004 a new website launched in Japan called *Shōsetsuka ni Narō* ("Let's Become a Novelist!") which let users upload their own stories for free and share them with the world. *Narō* (as it's commonly shortened to), wasn't the first site to host online stories, but it quickly became the most popular Japanese site for online fiction.

How popular?

As of 2016, *Narō* hosted 400,000 stories, with over 800,000 registered users (you don't have to register to read stories), and ranked in the top 100 websites worldwide with over one billion pageviews a month. In addition, *Narō* became a greenhouse for publishers to find talented writers and stories they could publish and transform into media properties. Popular anime such as *Rising of the Shield Hero*, *Overlord*, *Konosuba*, *That Time I Got Reincarnated as a Slime*, and so many more are based on serialized stories that amateur writers posted on *Narō* in their spare time.

Those stories were picked up by publishers, re-edited and revised, and turned into light novels. In fact, if there's a popular light novel you're reading, the odds it or its writer started on *Narō*, and the relationship between light novels and online web fiction has reached the point where they're tightly connected with each other. Japanese online fiction is mostly written by young people for young people, and uses the styles and conventions developed by light novels which is what those young people are used to reading. Then, it gets turned into light novels, which are read by the next generation, who then use that style and thinking when writing their own stories online.

But Japan wasn't the only place where web fiction began to blossom in the early 2000s.

In fact, before *Narō* was launched in 2004, another site was launched in South Korea called *Joara* in 2000, a year when web fiction was starting to explode in Korea with online novels such as *My Sassy Girl* getting turned into movies. *Joara* would later go on to become Korea's biggest web fiction site, with 1.1 million members, 460,000 stories, and 16.2 Billion Korean Won in sales in 2016.

And it's the sales which are the important part.

Unlike *Narō*, which is a free place to read and write stories that mostly makes money from advertising, *Joara* found a way to make money for its writers by letting them sell their works on the site and taking a cut of the profits. This financial success propelled other sites to follow *Joara's* model such as *Naver Web Novels*, *Kakao Story*, and *Munpia*, who have also gone on to become sites with vast story libraries and millions of devoted users who buy credits with real money that they can use to purchase chapters or sets of whole web novels to read.

This system has let a reportedly 51% of Korean web novel writers to make money from their writing, and while they might not be living on their writing, it's still a profitable thing to do. On top of that, Korean webnovels have continued to be turned into manga, films, TV series, and mobile games at a fast pace, with a lot of modern Korean TV dramas like *Coffee Prince* being based on popular webnovels. On top of that, a Korean fantasy serial, *Legendary Moonlight Sculptor* helped to kick start the litRPG genre that would later sweep the world.

But the Koreans weren't the only ones to figure out that web fiction could be profitable. Chinese users were late to the game, but they more than made up for it with their intensity. *Qidian*, China's largest web fiction site was also born in the early 2000s, and with its sister sites *Hongxiu*, and *jjwxc.com*, exploded onto the Chinese internet to entertain China's growing internet using population. Each of these web fiction portals has tens of millions of readers and millions of user-written stories, with *Qidian* alone claiming to have over eight million stories available.

And, although using a slightly different model than the Koreans, the Chinese also found ways to make web fiction pay, and offer successful writers a path to fame and fortune. *Qidian* alone has produced a number of celebrity author millionaires just from the profits on the site, and these sites have turned into China's entertainment factories for TV, movies, and other merchandising efforts.

In fact, the webfiction coming out of China became so popular that it started a whole translation boom into English similar to the fan-translations of Japanese comics. Translators began to take stories like *I Shall Seal the Heavens*, *The King's Avatar*, *Tales of Demons and Gods*, and give them new life in the English-speaking world. English fans even started to sponsor (pay) translators to keep a steady stream of their favorite addictive Chinese web novels coming, and it reached the point where some fan translators were able to quit their jobs and make real profits translating the pirated web novels.

One group of these translators formed a site called *Wuxia World* in 2014, which attracted several million visits a day by readers and made enough money that it began to officially license the Chinese stories from the original Chinese publishers. *Wuxia World* became the hub for fans of Chinese fantasy novels, and was followed by *Gravity Tales* and *Volare Novels*, and a host of others who fell in love with Chinese web novels and couldn't get enough.

In fact, the English fan-translators were so successful that *Qidian* itself moved into the English market and opened *Webnovel.com* to provide official translations of some of their more popular works. Today, *Webnovel.com* has over six million users, and is a growing site where English writers are sharing their own original web fiction with the world. Webnovel has also imported the *Qidian* system of profit-sharing with successful authors, and as the site grows, so do the potential profits for those who write for it.

At the same time, Japanese light novels are starting to become a force of their own in English, having long lived in the shadow of the manga market. *J-Novel Club*, *Seven Seas* and *Yen Press* are bringing the best light novels over to capitalize on the explosion of light novel based anime, and light novels are becoming their own brand in English both in print and ebooks. Soon, we'll be seeing English publishers try to market original light novels for the English-speaking audience, so there's opportunity on the horizon there too.

And, that's where we are today.

Asian powerhouses producing web fiction, a multi-million-dollar translation market, and a new English market that is just starting to develop into something where writers might get paid for their skills. In fact, the major English web fiction sites like Wattpad are just starting to play catch-up as they realize the tide is coming and their writers don't just want to write for free anymore.

There's never been a better time to ride the dragon.

So, gear up, and let's see what you can do!

LIGHT NOVELS

The Japanese publishing format known as the light novel is a tricky beast. It isn't a genre, but it has its own special approach to telling stories. It isn't a writing style, but there is a writing style associated with it. It isn't for any particular audience, but it has a clear audience which reads it.

All of this, combined with the loose way in which publishers in Japan throw around the label "light novel," make it seem like, to quote light novel reviewer Justus R. Stone- "A light novel is whatever the publishers say it is."

But to say that ignores the fact that light novels do have a lot of special characteristics, and they are different from almost any other form of fiction being published today. So, with this in mind, let's look at what make light novels the unique creature they are.

AUDIENCE

While technically light novels aren't limited towards any audience like male or female, or young or old, the majority of light novels are clearly written with what would best be described as a young adult audience in mind. In fact, if there is an equivalent to the light novel market in English, it is the young adult book market where you find *Harry Potter*, *Twilight*, *The Hunger Games*, and other stories targeted at a teen audience.

In the case of light novels, this is specifically a Japanese teen and college age audience, so light novels tend to have anime and manga style covers and interior illustrations meant to enhance the storytelling and give them more appeal in a society of comic book readers. Often done by popular manga artists, these illustrations also let them tie the light novels into the huge anime/manga fan market, both at the start of the novel's publication and later when tie-in properties like comics, TV series and merchandise becomes part of the light novel's marketing profile.

LENGTH

By Western standards, light novels are actually pretty short. Most individual light novels clock in between 40,000 and 50,000 words, which puts them right on the line between Novellas (20,000-45,000 words) and Novels (50,000+ words) in standard publishing terms. Usually they have around six chapters in each volume, plus prologues, epilogues, notes, and artwork. It should be mentioned that each of these chapters is likely to be a bit longer than a North American chapter (6,000 words per chapter) and is usually broken down into many smaller scenes, but this still makes light novels fast reads, and your average light novel is intended to be read in about four to five hours' time by an average reader.

This short length makes light novels look less intimidating to young readers, especially ones who aren't the type to read long books. Seeing a thin illustrated volume with many pictures inside can make a light novel seem inviting and easy to read, making them more attractive to busy readers both young and old.

However, this is actually a marketing illusion.

Light novels are rarely stand-alone volumes, and each book is usually part of a longer series of books. What seems to be many short books is actually a single larger serial story broken down across many books for maximum profit on the part of publishers. Each volume (or two) is a story arc within a larger story, and tells a piece of the whole story readers must purchase if they want to enjoy the whole thing. So, the readers who wanted a simple short read and avoided the longer books actually end up reading something even longer than they would have if they'd tackled a single regular novel.

LIGHT NOVEL GENRES

When it comes to genre, light novels follow the trends which can be seen everywhere in webnovels and other types of young adult fiction. Fantasy and romance rule the light novel markets, with teen stories coming in close behind and others like comedy, horror, sci-fi and adventure following in somewhere in the distance.

For example, the magazine *Kono light novel ga Sugoi!* ("This light novel is Awesome!") which tracks light novels in Japan listed the Top 10 bestselling light novels of 2017 as follows:

01. *Sword Art Online* by Reki Kawahara (*Isekai, litRPG, High Fantasy, Harem*)

31

02. ***Konosuba –God's Blessing on this Wonderful World*** by Natsume Akatsuki (*Isekai, High Fantasy, Harem, NEET*)

03. ***Re:Zero –Starting Life in Another World*** by Tappei Nagatsuki (*Isekai, High Fantasy, Harem, NEET*)

04. ***The Irregular at Magic High School*** by Tsutomu Satou (*School Life, High Fantasy, NEET*)

05. ***Classroom of the Elite*** by Syohgo Kinugasa (*School Life, Science Fiction, Romance*)

06. ***Your Name*** Makoto Shinkai (*School Life, Romance*)

07. ***Eromanga Sensei*** by Tsukasa Fushimi (*School Life, Ecchi, Harem, NEET*)

08. ***Akashic Records of the Bastard Magical Instructor*** by Taro Hitsuji (*High Fantasy, School Life, Harem, NEET*)

09. ***Overlord*** by Kugane Maruyama (*High Fantasy, Isekai, Pseudo-litRPG*)

10. ***The Saga of Tanya the Evil*** by Carlo Zen (*Alternate World, High Fantasy, Isekai*)

Looking at the genre tags, this gives us:

- High Fantasy: 7
- Harem: 6
- Isekai: 5
- School Life: 5
- NEET: 5
- Romance: 2
- litRPG: 2

And, while some might debate a few of the genre tags, it still provides a very clear picture of what genres are most popular when it comes to light novels:

High Fantasy- A pseudo-medieval setting with lots of magic, usually one which resembles the setting of a typical roleplaying game of the *Dungeons and Dragons* lineage and almost always includes elves, animal-people (cat girls), and monsters. In fact, this genre is so standardized the author won't even bother to explain the setting except to tell how it is different from a typical fantasy setting, not from how it is different from our world. This can occasionally include modern or futuristic settings with magic as well, but settings that resemble a pseudo-medieval Europe are the gold standard.

Harem- A story where the focus is the main character gaining a group of attractive cuties who are in love with them and follow them around. (See below for more information.)

Isekai- This term, which literally means "Second World," refers to stories where the main character is a person from our world who ends up in another world, usually a high fantasy one. (See the chapter on Second Life stories for more details.)

School Life- A story set in or around the lives of a high school student.

NEET- A Japanese term meaning "Not Involved in Employment, Education or Training," these are shut-ins who hide from the world, often in their bedrooms, and spend most of their time on the hobbies and internet. Here, the genre tag refers to the main character in the story being a NEET who is forced out of their seclusion by circumstances. (And most often sent to a High Fantasy world, as NEETs and Isekai go together like bacon and eggs.)

Romance- A story which is primarily about a romantic relationship between two characters.

litRPG- Also called GameLIT, this is a subgenre where the majority of the story takes place inside a computer roleplaying game, or a high fantasy world which functions under the same laws as a computer RPG (in which case it's a pseudo-litRPG). (See the chapter on litRPGs for more details.)

And, there is an eighth "hidden" genre which also applies to every single title in that list, despite not having a tag or official label. You could label that tag "manga," or perhaps "anime," and it refers to the style and sensibility that light novel stories have based on their audience and authors. The audience is one which has grown up on anime and manga style storytelling and tropes, and as a result light novel stories reflect that. The characters, their reactions, their situations, and even the way the stories are presented, reflect an anime world view instead of a real one. (Often because the writers don't have a lot of personal life experience beyond reading manga.)

Just like Superman can put on a pair of glasses and become Clark Kent ("Hey, where's Superman, Clark?") and the audience just accepts it, anime and manga have hundreds of small hidden genre conventions and tropes that their audience just knows and accepts. These range from beautiful women falling over themselves to get together with passive men, to characters taking ridiculous amounts of damage in fights and still remaining standing. Some of these are exaggerations of Japanese culture, but many of them are simply ideas that have come to be part of the manga-driven popular culture and the audience just goes with for the sake of the story.

Anyone who wants to write light novel style stories (for a Japanese or Japanese-fan audience) had better be aware of these conventions, and know them off by heart, otherwise their stories will never feel "right" because they're missing the hidden genre assumptions that go with light novels. And, naturally, the only way to learn these conventions is to immerse yourself in Japanese popular culture, especially light novels, anime, and manga.

LIGHT NOVEL PLOTS

As you might guess from the genre tags above, there are a few plots which tend to rule the current light novel market- and these can be broken down into the isekai plot and the harem plot.

The isekai plot is covered in detail in its own chapter later on, but as mentioned above it's about a main character who typically ends up in a fantasy world and then flourishes there as a hero. They typically start out at the bottom of the pecking order and then use their cheat abilities to rise through the system to become a great hero. Along the way, they amass friends who become like a new family to them and change the world. (See the chapter on Rising Hero Stories)

The harem plot is a story where a young man (or woman) without really trying amasses a collection of cuties who are madly in love with them and follow them around. The story is about how each of the cuties enters their lives, and then becomes a part of their harem "family," often living together under one roof and enjoying each other's company. The passive main character naturally refuses to pick one of the harem members as a favorite (or is unable to), and thus the harem keeps growing as more cuties compete for the top spot.

These plots work across all genres, and are often combined into a single harem-isekai plot (see *Konosuba* and *RE: Zero*), but can also be used separately.

TONE

Japanese light novels are not meant to be heavy thought-provoking entertainment. They're meant to be light, fun reading experiences. Thus, the average light novel's tone is pretty light, positive and optimistic overall. And, even the darker light novels like *Ghost Hunt*, *Overlord* or *The Saga of Tanya the Evil* still ultimately have a fairly positive tone at heart where the protagonists win in the end, they just have to work more for their victory.

Settings in Japanese light novels tend to be fairly safe places where laws are followed and your average person is a good person. There are always bad apples, but those don't stay in power long or end up paying for their sins.

In fact, one could describe a typical light novel's journey as being like a trip through a theme park. There's fun, surprises, and maybe even a few scares, but in the end it's all pretty safe and you'll enjoy the experience. This is especially true in NEET-oriented novels, which are heavily just wish-fulfillment fantasies that don't let anything bad happen to the main characters or their companions because it's all happy fun.

WRITING STYLE

If there are two words that can be used to describe the writing style of light novels, those words are "efficient" and "fearless." They might not be the words most people would associate with light novels, but they do sum up the approach and philosophy most writers take when writing them.

To begin, light novels can be said to be "efficient" because all aspects of their presentation are based around a simple philosophy of "whatever works." This applies to not only their use of dialog and narration, but also extends to their approach to things like perspective, characters, and setting.

For example, as anyone who has read a light novel likely already knows, light novels can often be heavily dialog driven. While this is not always true, light novels are meant to be read fast, and dialog reads much faster than exposition does. As a result, it's not uncommon to find whole pages of light novels which are nothing but dialog and the most minimal character tags that the writer can get away with. Sometimes, the writers even skip the tags, and the reader is left to guess who is speaking based on style of speech and presentation.

Light novel writers also often use a style of exposition which is heavily based on directly telling the reader what's happening, as that too is more efficient than showing when it comes to speed. (Thus, breaking the first commandment of creative writing teachers everywhere- "Show, don't tell.") So, while a conventional English writer might give a paragraph describing how something looks or feels, a light novel writer will just say what a character thought of it in a single line and move on. Everything is filtered through character perceptions, but in a short, efficient way which is designed to keep the story moving.

It all depends on what the simplest, best and most lively way the writer thinks they can convey the story information is.

And this is also true of the characters and setting, who are largely described in only the briefest of details, with the focus being on the key facts the audience needs to know at the time without overloading them with needless extra information. Major characters will get at least a paragraph of description (if they're attractive and female), but that will depend heavily on the writer, as some only give a general character "hook" ("that's the sullen black-haired mage, and that's the talkative red-haired thief") and move along. Similarly, setting details can come in great depth if the author thinks they're cool or important to the story, but everything else is left to the reader's imagination.

One way to think of it is that English novel writers tend to focus on "what's different," while light novel writers tend to focus on "what's important". Owing to the Tolkien tradition, an English fantasy writer will go to great pains to detail their setting and hint at how it all works together, while a Japanese light novel writer considers the setting a backdrop for character interaction which is only important when it affects the story.

This may also be the reason why light novel writing can be described as "Fearless."

When the focus is on human interaction, and the background is merely a set for that universal human interaction, you can go nuts with trying different ideas, and light novel writers often do. While formal writers are often concerned with things like realism, consistency and accuracy, light novel writers jump right in and explore ideas without worrying about such things. If a story takes place in 16th Century France, then a formal writer will do research, but while they're doing that research, the light novel writer simply says "It's an alternate world setting like 16th Century France called Parisia" and does as much or little research as they want before publishing the book. (Usually at the point in time the formal writer is just starting their rough draft.)

Some of this may come from the fact that many light novels started as webnovels on sites like *Shōsetsuka ni Narō* where they were writing stories for fun and not getting paid for it except in the attention of readers. The freedom of not being paid lets them do whatever they want, and in terms of ideas and style lets them just have fun and experiment with whatever ideas they like. They don't have to worry about losing their contracts, and can just write whatever they feel like.

This open and fearless approach to writing can produce a lot of laziness and poor-quality stories and settings (something many have accused light novels of having), but it also encourages a more open and playful exploration of ideas. If the author wants to change the laws of physics, they just do it, or if they want to create a third or fourth sex, they do that too. Perhaps it's because nobody told them they can't do it, or maybe it's out of necessity as they try to stand out in a crowded story marketplace, but they have an open approach to ideas.

Combine this fearlessness with the anything goes focus on efficiency, and you get stories that are filled with experimentation. Where when an author says, "I wonder what would happen if a character from our world reincarnated into the body of a small spider in a high fantasy setting?" They just do it, and you get *So I'm a Spider? So What?* Or, they decide to have a world ruled by the God of Mischief and Chance, and you get a Ten Commandments that reads like the house rules at a gambling den. (*No Game, No Life.*) Or perhaps they're tired of heroic leads, and decide to make an evil skeletal lich king their main character instead (*Overlord*).

It's this fearless efficiency that creates unique stories that only light novels can offer, and that's something to be respected, if not admired.

That said, if you as a writer want to emulate the writing style of light novels, you're much better to pick the "fearless" part and try new and wild story ideas than you are to emulate some of the stylistic recklessness that light novels engage in. Normal English audiences have shown a willingness to accept stories that mix first person and third in recent years, but having more than one first person narrator can lead to confusion if used within the same chapter, and third person narrators are best used consistently. The more spartan, dialog-based writing can also be a matter of taste, although younger audiences seem to like it.

As always, balance the pros and cons of extreme stylistic choices- what some people call experimentation, others will consider bad writing and sloppy technique. You should know the rules and master them before you try to break them.

LIGHT NOVEL CHARACTERS

Light Novels have often been accused of overusing stock characters, and there's no doubt this is true. The casts of most light novels, especially the supporting casts, have a habit of looking so similar that even fans could be hard pressed to differentiate which cast comes from which story sometimes. It gets especially bad with female leads, who are so similar to each other they have stock names for each personality type. (*Tsundere, Yandere, Kuudere,* etc.)

Now, this isn't automatically a bad thing. The Ancient Greeks used stock characters in their plays to represent different parts of society and personalities. The Italians had their *Commedia Dell'arte*, which also drew entirely on stock characters and the Koreans had their *Talchum* (Mask-Dance theatre) where each wooden mask played the same role in every story. Every society has their social archetypes, and stock characters simply show which of those types the audience enjoys seeing again and again.

Like anything, it's not what you have, but how you use it that counts, and stock characters are no different. And, if there is any form which excels in playing with its stock characters, it's the light novel. Light novels are heavily character based, and literally live or die on their characters. A cast that connects with the target audience will mean life for a light novel series, while one that fails to hit the mark will quickly fall into obscurity and cancellation.

This is in no small part because many light novels aren't character-driven, but instead character-centered. In a character-driven story, the character and their desires ARE the plot of the story, and the story is about the lead character advancing on their goals through a series of challenges and obstacles. The story **is** the main character, so their success or failure is a part of everything that happens in the story and keeps the story on a steady course to the end.

In a character-centered story, however, the main character will have some form of loose goal, but the story really isn't so much about that goal as it is the characters and situations the main character interacts with along the way. The story is about the lives of those characters, and any goal which the main character has is at best a simple plot device to give the story some direction while those characters live their lives.

This is why thinking about the issue of passive leads versus active leads is so important when planning light novels. Active leads who chase their dreams tend to make the best lead characters for comic books, since they're easy to write and are inspiring for others with their go-getter attitudes. They make for natural heroes who the audience wants to root for and enjoy watching face challenge after challenge as they climb their way towards their goals. However, for some reason they're much less common in light novels.

But, light novels, unlike manga, seem to be a place where more passive leads flourish. With their slower pace, and more character-centered approach to story, light novels allow passive leads the chance to be themselves. Not only that, they're often preferred by audiences because passive leads tend to be somewhat blank slates that are easier for the audience to project themselves into. While Naruto might inspire people to try their best, it's hard for most people to imagine themselves as Naruto, whereas a more passive and introverted character like Bell Cranel from *Is it Wrong to Try to Pick up Girls in a Dungeon?* is more relatable and makes for a better reader surrogate.

Also, in many light novels which have a harem theme, the point of the lead character is to act as a reader insert character anyways, as they interact with the story's assortment of beauties and learn the key to opening each of their hearts. Having a more passive lead character allows the reader to project more of themselves into the character while at the same time giving the writer an excuse to not have the lead character actually pick a favorite from the growing harem. After all, when the lead character picks a favorite, the story is over, so the indecision must continue as long as possible, something it's harder to believe an active lead would do.

And, the choice of an active lead or passive lead will also determine a lot about the story and supporting cast as well. If the story has an active lead, then the supporting cast will usually be a little more passive as they are usually people who are brought together and given focus by the energy of the active main character. The main character will be the leader, or at least the one providing direction to the story, and so the other supporting characters are there to show how cool and interesting the main character is by being reflections of them. Since the main character is so active, those supporting characters need to be more passive to achieve balance and provide a little drama.

On the other hand, passive leads need the energy of others to get them moving, so they will be surrounded by much more active characters that all have goals and directions. Again, they are reflections of the main character, but in this case they're reflections of what the main character could be if the lead only got off their butt and actually applied themselves. The supporting cast might include people who give the main character orders, threaten them, entice them, or inspire them, but it will always be filled with people who exist to make the otherwise boring life of the passive lead interesting. The story in a character-centered light novel with a passive lead comes from the interactions the character has with those more-active people around them.

Keep in mind, that when talking about a passive lead character here, this is not necessarily talking about someone who refuses to do anything or is actively trying to avoid doing anything (although you will find both of these types of passive leads in light novels), but just about someone who has no particular long-term goals or direction. They might be very active in their short-term thinking (like a NEET who ends up in another world and now needs to survive or die), but they don't have any grand plan they're working on or thinking about as they do what they do. Also, passive leads may naturally morph into being more active leads as the story goes on and they're given goals by the circumstances and supporting cast. (Again, though, their goals aren't coming from within so much as coming from outside of themselves as they work to meet basic human needs.)

Light Novel Opponents

Opponents are another area where light novels diverge from shonen manga, and in fact from a lot of fiction in general. While in a conventional story a lead character will often have a clear main opponent, like a villain, whom they are working to overcome or defeat, in a light novel typically there is only a vague threat on the horizon that's like a distant storm that may or may not show up someday.

Typically, light novels prefer story arc opponents who will menace the character for a volume or two and are around just long enough to fit nicely into printed collections (to keep the volumes semi-self-contained). Really major opponents, like the lieutenants of the main villain of the story or the big bad themselves, will only appear when the author feels the story needs a dramatic boost or the light novel serial is starting to get close to the end. In both of these cases, the author is dangling the prospect of major story developments and a possible ending in front of the readers the way a carrot is hung in front of a horse to keep it moving.

One final thought about light novel opponents is that the Japanese love bittersweet stories, and nothing is more bittersweet than a main villain who is noble but tragically flawed. There will still be negative traits that make the character a clear villain, but often they will be characters with good intentions who have gone down the wrong path and are too far to turn back. This adds a nice pathos to the story that the Japanese often can't get enough of.

Light Novel Supporting Characters

Supporting casts in light novels tend to either run anime/manga standard (the best friend, the girl/love interest, the mentor, the cool ace, etc.) or they tend to be harem focused. In the case of harems, they've become so standardized that each of the personality types of the harem members has a special name and traits that go with it. Most of these have the suffix "-dere" at the end, which comes from the Japanese slang "Deredere" (pronounced "day-ray-day-ray"), which means "lovestruck" in English. Thus, most harems will consist of some (or all) of the following stock characters:

Bokkuko – This is a tomboy, a girl who dresses and acts like a boy, usually a tough one. In Japanese she uses the male version of "I" to refer to herself (which is "boku") and speaks like a man. In most stories, she is often very strong, a tiny bit shy, and doesn't know how to express her emotions. Quote: "Hey. Uh. You wanna play some ball?"

Dandere – This is the cute, shy girl with glasses who is unsure of herself and is typically a bookworm. She tends to get embarrassed easily, and super-talkative when she feels emotionally safe or is asked about her area of expertise. Quote: "I...Ah...I think....Maybe....Ahh.....Oh...Never mind."

Deredere – The cheerful, loving girl who tries to smother the target of her affections with love, warmth and caring. Sometimes motherly, sometimes playful, she tries hard to show the target of her affections she can be the perfect partner in a caring, open-hearted way. She can be so sweet that diabetics need insulin shots after just being near her for more than ten minutes. Quote: "Oh darling, let me feed you. Open wide! Here comes the airplane into the airport...Zoom! Zoom!"

Himedere – "Hime" is Japanese for princess, and that's exactly what this character acts like. Sometimes they're an actual princess, and sometimes they were just raised like one, but either way they show proper manners and decorum befitting a princess at all times (except when they get flustered). They often dress in regal clothes and almost always have long straight hair as well. Quote: "Oh my! A real LGV bag for only $15,000? I'll take five. Wrap them for me in the lilac perfumed paper and send them to the address on this card."

Kuudere – "Kuu" in this case comes from the English world "cool," as in cold. This is the cold, logical girl that doesn't speak much, and when she does is direct, blunt and rational. Despite this Vulcan-like attitude, she does actually have feelings and can warm to people she feels emotionally safe with. Quote: "He doesn't like you because you are loud, have poor hygiene, and you hit him a great deal."

Loli – This is a character who is either a precocious young girl, or has the appearance of one. She is usually very cute, and often has the personality of the *Kuudere*, *Dandere* or *Deredere*. She may literally be the younger sister of the main character, or just act like she is. Quote: "Big brother...When are you taking me out for ice cream?"

Mayadere – This is a beautiful enemy lieutenant who falls in love with the main character and crosses over to join his harem/team in hopes of getting together with him. She is usually a badass (and may also be a *Sukeban*), and still sometimes slips back into her villainous ways. Quote: "You dare to touch my... my.... Friend! I will show you new dimensions of pain!"

Sadodere – "Sado" here comes from "sadomasochist," so if you guessed this girl likes torturing and playing with others emotionally, you'd be right. This type of girl enjoys playing with the targets of her affection and messing with them, making sure that she is always the one in control of the relationship and situation. (Usually to hide her own insecurity.) Quote: "If you want something from me, you'll have to play by my rules."

Sukeban – This is the gangster girl, who usually comes from a rough background and is the toughest, meanest, b*tch you're going to meet. That doesn't mean she's a bad person, and she is usually very passionate and fiercely protective of her subordinates and friends, but she hides it all beneath a tough "take no prisoners" attitude. In Japanese stories, she wears a customized school uniform and usually has some hidden (or not so hidden) weapons. Quote: "Yo! You picking on my friend here?"

The Genki Girl – A happy, upbeat, energetic normal girl who is positive and supportive. She is usually sporty and fearless. Quote: "You can do it! Go for it!"

Tsundere – This is a girl who runs "hot and cold," which means while she likes someone, she doesn't want to actually admit it and is usually pretty standoffish towards those she likes romantically (but warm and friendly toward everyone else). She gets embarrassed at showing her feelings, and occasionally violent. Quote: "Idiot! It's not because I like you or anything!"

Yandere – This is the girl who seems all nice and normal on the surface, but who turns into a jealous stalker out to eliminate the competition once she falls in love. She's not a bad person, but she's fiercely protective of her "territory" once she's claimed it, overly so. Quote: "Why were you talking to him? What's your relationship! Tell me! Tell me!"

Yangire – This is a *Yandere* who is actually crazy, like serial killer level crazy. Real Yanderes are mostly harmless, but the *Yangire* is a psycho stalker from a horror movie. Quote: "I hope you like the hamburger, it's 100% real...That girl who talked to you on the bus yesterday!"

Generally speaking, most female leads in Harem stories are either *Tsunderes* or *Derederes*. The *Tsundere* takes a long time to warm up and become emotionally vulnerable, so she's perfect if the main character is chasing her. On the other hand, if the female lead is the one doing the chasing, then the *Deredere* is perfect- she's trying hard to be a perfect girlfriend to the lead but all these other women keep getting in the way.

A basic Harem usually consists of a *Tsundere* (or *Deredere*), a *Yandere*, a *Dandere*, a *Loli* and a *Bokkuko*. The main character will be emotionally involved with the *Tsundere* (or *Deredere*), the *Yandere* will be the one trying to break them up (for comic relief), the *Dandere* will be the calm rational one, the *Loli* will be there to be cute, and the *Bokkuko* will be there to steal the sympathy of the audience as she loves the main character but knows she'll never be with him, no matter how close they get. (Poor Mako-chan... Sniff!) Other types of girls may or may not join up as needed.

LIGHT NOVEL SPECIAL FEATURES

There are a few story elements which while not unique to light novels, tend to be much more common in light novels as opposed to other kinds of webfiction. Two of these are the NEET Hero and the Harem Plot, which deserve special attention.

The NEET Hero

As mentioned above, a NEET (aka Shut-in, Drop Out, That Guy Who Won't Get Out of His Mother's Basement, etc.) is a member of society who has chosen to shut themselves off and live a closeted existence. The term actually originated in the United Kingdom as a clinical way to describe young people dropping out of society to live in their own little bubbles, but has since become popularized around the world, especially in Asia. There are many theories for this phenomenon, but these are often creative and highly sensitive young people who find the real modern world overwhelming and so they retreat into their own small worlds where they feel some sense of control. At the most extreme, there are stories from Japan of NEETs whose families moved away or died without them noticing until strangers turned up to evict them.

There is some confusion between NEETs and *otaku* among Japanese culture fans outside of Japan, and what the difference between the terms mean. Since they are often quite intelligent, NEETs very often fill their lives with hobbies which fill the void left by real human interaction, and these hobbies can include collecting, researching, playing games, building things or any other task which they find gives their lives meaning, just like otaku. However, the best way to understand the difference is that while many NEETs are otaku, not all otaku are NEETS. People who are otaku often have jobs and participate in society; they just live their lives to a large degree around their hobbies. NEETs, on the other hand, have no life except for their hobbies, and have as little to do with society as they can get away with, preferring to reject the real world.

Most NEETs are also extremely active online, where their virtual lives replace their real lives, and they live in online communities dedicated to their own personal niches. It should be no surprise then, that some of the most popular online places where NEETs gather are the online writing communities like *Shōsetsuka ni Narō!*, which offer an endless source of free entertainment (NEETS are often low on funds) and a place to express their creativity with others who have the same interests.

As a result, NEETs are an active voice within the Japanese webfiction community, not only as readers and reviewers, but also writers. In recent years, this has resulted in more and more webfiction which is written by NEETS, and since like most webfiction writers, NEETs write stories which feature versions of themselves as the hero, we've seen the rise of the NEET Hero in Japanese webfiction and light novels.

See if you know this story...

A socially awkward young person is thrust into another world where the talents and hobbies that make them an outcaste in our world turn them into a powerful hero who is able to easily crush their enemies and gather a harem of attractive cuties who follow the hero around. Slowly, the young person builds a life for themselves in the new world and becomes a powerful and respected member of society. The End.

If this plot doesn't sound familiar, you haven't read a light novel published in the last few years, or watched much anime, or read much manga. While rising young heroes have always been a staple of young adult fiction, the rise of NEETs in the Japanese webfiction world have made this particular plot the gold standard, and the story of the NEET Hero has been shown to have widespread appeal.

And why wouldn't it?

Everyone feels awkward, especially as a teen, and wishes that their particular talents or interests would be appreciated more by the world around them. The NEET writers, by expressing their purest wish-fulfillment fantasies in their writing, have tapped into that, and while they're really writing for themselves and each other, its managed to strike a chord with the very Japanese society the NEETs have rejected. Not that NEETs will complain if publishers want to turn their webfiction into light novel franchises and give them money and respect for doing what they love. (Ironically, making their dreams come true, in a way.)

The problem comes that some of these really are the purest of wish fulfillment fantasies, to the point where it's very easy for them to become a form of mental masturbation. NEET Heroes are often so overpowered that they rarely face actual challenges, skipping rising up through the ranks in favor of becoming instantly awesome and beloved by all. Reading some of their stories is like watching a perfect playthrough of a video game on YouTube. While this might feel good for the writer, it takes a lot of the fun out of the story by removing any real tension, and can result in a story which is so bland and inoffensive as to be like the story version of baby food.

Not only that, NEETs are people who have shut themselves away from the real world, so the thing they're most lacking is actual real-world life experience. Their entire concept of stories and characters is based not around their own lives, but the stories and characters from their favorite media. So, their work is usually entirely based on the work of other writers, who based their work on the works of other writers, who based their work on the works of other writers. This produces a huge amount of creative inbreeding and sharpening, where the characters and situations don't even resemble anything in the real world anymore because they're copies of copies.

This can make them pretty extreme and bizarre sometimes, where the story is so influenced by the writer's anime skewed view of the world, membership in internet subcultures, and odd ideas about sex and human relationships that it becomes hard for regular people to relate to it. A factor that has probably been one of the reasons why so few NEET Hero webnovels actually become light novels and the ones that do succeed are heavily edited from their original versions.

In any case, should you wish to write a NEET Hero story, the formula above is pretty straightforward. Take a Passive NEET type hero, force them out into a world which seems harsh but is really a place where they can shine, and let them be awesome. Even something as simple as being really good at researching (*Trapped In Another World With My Smartphone.*) can be turned into a NEET Hero plot by making that the solution to the world's problems. And, the story doesn't have to be set in a Fantasy world either, any situation where the hero must leave their cave to interact with real people who turn out to appreciate and admire their talents can be a NEET Hero story.

The Harem Plot

If there is any element which divides light novel fans, it's the medium's overuse of the harem plot. At its simplest, a harem plot is a story where every attractive girl (or boy) the main character meets falls in love with them and begins pursuing them romantically. This plot, which is the result of a mix of publisher marketing (sex sells) and fandom demand, has been around for a long time, and is not unique to light novels, but light novels have taken it and made it an art form of its own.

Once upon a time, heroes would have to defeat opponents and the love interests they gained were the prize for being heroic. However, the modern light novel harem plot has done away with that approach and simplified it down to get rid of any extra characters. So, instead the modern light novel hero usually starts with one or more girls handed to them at the start of the story, and then each story after that becomes about how the hero either defeats or helps the next member of their harem. In other words, the harem, and how it's acquired, **is** the plot of many modern light novel stories, no longer a separate sub-plot or side plot.

In this pure modern version, the main character is most often a passive lead who just by being himself draws the harem to him like bees to honey. Once they enter his life, they just stay there generating comedy, fan service, and drama, while the lead is struck with paralysis at the thought of choosing any one over the others, and just continues to collect/attract more and more of them until the story collapses under the weight of the cast size. (The problem with the pure harem plot is eventually, you end up with so many girls you can't add any more and it stalls out.)

The controversy among fans comes from the problem that many light novel writers marry a harem plot with what might otherwise be a decent story idea for a non-harem story at the beginning, and then over time focus on the harem to the frustration of some fans. So, for example, say the story was set up as a magical tournament duel story at the beginning, which brings in the fans of fantasy dueling, but as the main character defeats female combatants they begin joining his group as his harem. Before long, the growing harem, and showcasing it, becomes most of the story and the magical dueling takes a back seat. Some magical dueling fans feel like they were bait and switched so they leave, while the harem fans are happy so they stay, making the writer focus even more on the harem to keep the harem fans from leaving, making even more of the magical dueling fans unhappy, so they leave and... the downward spiral continues until what started as one story has transformed into another.

Another common problem that those who don't like harems complain of is that the harem members often don't add a lot to the story. They're there to be cute and add fan service, but after their initial introduction story often don't really contribute to the plot (if there is one), but mostly serve to hang around and steal story time. After all, each new story arc is about a new character joining up, but the writer has to come up with something for the old characters to do to keep their fans happy and remind the fans they exist. As the old cast grows larger and larger, this gets harder and harder to do well within the limited space of each light novel volume.

There are a few solutions to this, however.

First, is to keep the main character the focus, not the harem. This can be trickier than it sounds, because there will often be a strong demand to showcase the harem as much as possible, and that becomes easier if the harem members become the focus of the story. However, if you keep the main character and their story the focus, it will keep the core readership there to follow the main character's journey and the harem readers will still be there waiting for the return of their beloved to the spotlight. All this requires is coming up with reasons to rotate the harem members in and out of the story, either because the lead character is moving around or the harem members are busy/elsewhere and rarely all together. Oddly enough, this is also easier if the harem members are actual useful members of the cast instead of just there to look nice.

Thus, the other solution is to make sure that each new member of the harem is actually adding to not just the immediate plot, but the overall long-term story. For example, each one has skills that are needed for the main character to complete their final mission, or gives the main character access to new resources. This gives them a reason to come back and be developed as characters, and makes it much easier to write storylines for them as they're an actual part of the main cast.

In either case, don't waste time on harem members who don't contribute to the story, or be afraid to get rid of ones which don't develop. Harem cast bloat is the greatest disease of the genre, and should be avoided at all cost to make the story successful and long running.

CHINESE WEBNOVELS

Imagine one day someone comes to you and offers you money to walk on a treadmill. You'll get 100 dollars for every kilometre you walk, but there're three catches:

1. You will be one of tens of thousands of people on treadmills walking.

2. You only get paid if you're in the top 5% of everyone, the ones who walked the farthest each day.

3. If you miss a day, you're out of the program.

Would you do it? Knowing that every day you have to run farther and faster than your competition, or you'll get left behind. Knowing that taking a break costs you money, and that no matter what you feel like that day, energetic or sick as a dog, you have to keep walking or else lose your spot.

This is the life of a Chinese webnovel writer, who on sites like *Qidian.com*, is expected to churn out 60,000-120,000 words a month (2000-4000 words a day) of story while fending off the competition so their story stays up in the rankings. All this, while maintaining a personal life, family, work/school (it doesn't pay enough unless you're really popular, so you usually need another job), and knowing that every hour you're not writing, you're losing money. (And, did I mention if your rankings drop too low you get kicked out of the profit-sharing program?)

Sounds like writer's hell, doesn't it? (Or, as some prolific indie writers call it, Tuesday...)

So, why do they keep doing it?

Well, for the same reasons writers always have, first, writing is their passion and they enjoy writing. Second, money. The top 1% of Chinese webnovel writers can make millions of (American) dollars, and that's a pretty good incentive to not only write, but keep writing as if your life depended on it. (Because in a hyper competitive society like China, it just might.)

As a result, since Chinese writers are a clever bunch, they fairly quickly figured out the best way to game this system to get maximum results for the minimum amounts of effort they could put in. The result is the Chinese webnovel- serialized fiction written in a quick and dirty manner around popular genres and utilizing the simplest of styles, plots and characters to crank out chapters as fast as is humanly possible.

It's a very practical way of writing stories based on the fundamental principles covered in the chapter on What Popular Webfiction Stories Have in Common, but it works, and works well.

Let's take a closer look.

AUDIENCE

Chinese webnovel audiences are fairly broad, since they can be accessed by anyone with a mobile phone connection and an app, and are a pretty cheap form of entertainment. However, the majority of webnovel readers seem to be teens and college students, who have extra time to read (and write) webfiction. Most popular stories are ones which strongly appeal to youthful audiences, and are about young characters rising up and taking their place in the world.

This isn't to say there aren't housewives, grandfathers, and business professionals who don't relax with a few chapters of a webnovel during their breaks, but most stories are by and for younger audiences. A look at the *Qidian* genre rankings below shows a strong lean towards youth-oriented fiction and away from stories that older audiences enjoy.

LENGTH

Qidian, which is the largest webnovel site in China, has a system where the writers of webnovels can get paid only after they've written their first hundred chapters. Chapter 101 is the first paid chapter, and everything before that is free to the public-which means *Qidian* makes advertising money from the first hundred, but the author doesn't get any money until after they write over 200,000 words.

As you might suspect, this strongly encourages Chinese writers to write long epic stories, with the first hundred chapters being an introductory hook to a main story that can literally last thousands of chapters. After all, the longer the story keeps going, the longer the story will stay in the upper ranks and the more chapters the writer has to earn money from.

So, while shorter stories do exist, the most popular Chinese webnovels are usually really long. At minimum, they're usually a few hundred chapters which are written as serial adventures and soap operas to keep the audience and story going for as long as possible. A winning story is a golden goose, and Chinese authors are encouraged to keep it producing gold as long as it still can.

CHINESE WEBNOVEL GENRES

Webnovels are first and foremost genre fiction, written using popular tropes and made to appeal to the largest possible audiences. Since for these authors, more readers means more money, it's a simple and logical choice, and just like everywhere else, genre fiction is what sells.

Here's the top 10 genres on *Qidian* based on the 2.9 million stories on the site in 2019:

1. Girl's Fiction/Romance (27%)
2. Eastern Fantasy (*Xuanhuan*) (25%)
3. Urban (Modern Setting Stories) (13%)
4. Cultivation Fantasy (*Xianxia*) (8%)
5. Western Fantasy (*Xihuan*) (5%)
6. Science Fiction (5%)
7. Light Novels (4%)
8. Games (4%)
9. Historical (3%)
10. Suspense (2%)

So, you can see the webnovel genres that sell best, are (of course) fantasy and romance, which also dominate everywhere else in webfiction. However, the Chinese have their own spin on the genre, and the most popular fantasy genre isn't what they call "western fantasy" (Tolkien/D&D fantasy), but their own eastern fantasy genre of *xuanhuan*. *Xuanhuan* being fantasy with Chinese characteristics, set in places that vaguely resemble old China as seen through the eyes of video game makers and novelists. (In other words, "fun fantasy" versions of old China without any connections to the real world to make things messy.)

Romance stories also have their own Chinese spin on things, and will be mostly based around characters dealing with personal and social barriers which keep the couple apart. The Chinese also adore period romances, maybe even more than western audiences do, but instead of setting them in real old China, these will usually be set in a xuanhuan version of it that sidesteps historical detail for a vague setting that lets drama play out using historical tropes. Modern Romances are mostly about spunky girls from poorer backgrounds making it in the big city (and marrying high powered men) or high school girls balancing love and dreams.

Urban stories are stories set in the modern world, but can range from teen school life and ambitious businessmen to urban fantasy and general dramas. It's a bit of a catch-all category for anything set in the modern world. Cultivation (xianxia) stories are about characters levelling up in fantasy settings, and while these might be the most popular outside of China, inside China they're just considered a smaller part of eastern fantasy stories. Science fiction stories aren't as popular in China as they are in the western world, and like in English, game stories (litRPGs mostly) are also niche.

Light novels are webnovels written specifically in a manga/anime style incorporating the common elements of Japanese light novels. Manga and anime are popular in China, so it's no surprise that some fans want to write those kinds of stories. Historical stories are "real" period stories set in the past, and since those tend to require a lot of research they aren't quite as popular for writers. And finally, suspense is their crime fiction category, which is mostly mysteries and thrillers. Suspense is a genre that tends to be enjoyed by older readers more, which is likely why it's so low in the *Qidian* rankings compared with how popular the genre is in English bookstores.

WEBNOVEL PLOTS

There are two plots which tend to pop up in Chinese webnovels- the rising hero and the avenging hero.

In the rising hero plot, the main character is a young person who is thrust into a difficult situation where they must fight to survive while mastering the ways of a new "world." They might be a new intern at a hospital, a survivor of a remote plane crash, or a character thrust into a fantasy world of magic and monsters, but they will find themselves in a dangerous situation and have to learn to grow and thrive in that situation. The key is they start at the bottom of some system or order, and they begin working their way to the top while fending off rivals and enemies.

A good example of this type of character is Xiao Yan from the webnovel *Battle Through the Heavens* (*Dòupò Cāngqióng*), who starts the story as a young man living in a remote village and at the bottom of his clan's power structure. However, thanks to a ring containing the spirit of an ancient ghost master, he's able to unlock his potential and start quickly working his way up to taking on the world. (Literally.)

Unlike the rising hero plot, where the character starts off weak (but with some cheat to help them grow quickly), the lead character in an avenging hero plot is usually strong right from the start (or near the start) of the story. They need this strength because the story is about them avenging some past wrong and using their power to bring justice. This is usually a wrong done to them, their family members, their friends, or their loved ones, but this central goal of getting revenge will drive them to quickly rise and conquer their enemies.

A good example of this is the character of Nie Li, from the webnovel *Tales of Demons and Gods*, who survives the death of his whole clan, family, and friends to become a powerful warrior, only to be killed and defeated by his greatest enemy. After his death, he wakes up in the body of his 16-year-old self before all the bad things happen, and sets out to use his vast knowledge to change the future (and get a whole lot of revenge in the process).

There are other plots, but stories about rising heroes and avenging heroes seem to be standards among Chinese audiences.

TONE

If Japanese light novels can be described as a trip through a theme park, then Chinese webnovels are like being dumped in the middle of a jungle thousands of miles from civilization and told to survive or die. They often have a very brutal tone where everything is black or white and the character lives in a chaotic world where it's pure survival of the fittest.

Nobody is safe, not even the main character, and they must continually fight to keep themselves and their loved ones from danger. They are usually surrounded by enemies and people who will betray them for power or status, and must always be on guard against everyone except their closest friends. Everyone pretends to be a good person, but how good they really are will be revealed by their actions.

Some of this reflects Chinese society, where the writer is one of 1.4 billion people who is trying to survive and make a living in a highly competitive world. And, some of it is just to push up the levels of drama and suspense, since a character being in such a harsh situation is an instant drama creator that hooks audiences and keeps them reading to find out if the main character survives.

Either way, while Chinese webnovels often do have tender moments, times of playful fun, and even flashes of child-like surprise and wonder, underneath there is almost always a tension there because the worlds the characters live in are unstable, and happiness is often all too fleeting until you reach the top.

WRITING STYLE

China has few creative writing schools, and almost all webnovel writers are self-taught. They base their work and way of writing on the other stories they've read, and like most young writers they mimic their favorites as they dive into bringing their fantasies to life. Those favorites tend to be other webnovel writers, so as a result each new generation of writers is participating in the creation of a new style of writing optimized for webnovel production.

The style, as it currently sits, is best described as third-person omniscient, and is heavily based around breaking the golden writer's rule of "show, don't tell." Chinese writers will "tell" constantly, preferring to use a distant storyteller's type of voice when writing their stories, one that dips in and out of different character perspectives and moves around as needed. They also narrate away events, and aren't as concerned with a cinematic style as English writers often are.

Some of this is probably coming from the Chinese tradition of storytelling, since China has an ancient writing tradition dating back hundreds of years. Also, this is the style of the Chinese classics like *Romance of the Three Kingdoms*, *The Water Margin*, *Journey to the West* and the other books which all young Chinese are expected to read, so it's a foundation that they know they can build upon.

However, even more than that, the style in which webnovels are written can probably be blamed on the youth and inexperience of its writers. These authors don't have much life experience they can use to describe the world the characters live in beyond what they've seen and read in other stories, so they can't fill in those details without research. However, since they're writing under the pressure to publish quickly, they don't have time to do research- thus they use a distant style that is light on the details and heavy on the drama in order to cover this flaw.

As a result, Chinese webnovels look a lot like typical light novels but unlike the Japanese, they tend to use first person narrators less and put more emphasis on exposition over dialog. At least, exposition which describes fictional subjects and events that the writer can make up as they go and base on other fictional worlds they like, not which requires time consuming research.

CHARACTERS

At first blush, typical webnovel lead characters aren't much different than the leads from any other kind of fiction. However, as usual, the Chinese have put their own spins on things.

First, when it comes to male leads, the thing to remember is that they're power fantasy characters, which means that they're ultimately more clever, strong, handsome and charismatic than everyone else in the story. Sure, they might start at a disadvantage (usually due to some tragic family event), but once their potential is unleashed, they transform into a levelling-up superman who spends most of their time cleaning the floor with ever-bigger opponents.

The female leads, on the other hand, will vary by genre. In romance stories, they'll be clever girls, since clever is easier to relate to than smart. But, in other genres, the female lead will sometimes be intelligent in a sharp or calculating way- a female version of the male power fantasy character who outthinks her opponents as she works towards her goals.

The next thing to understand is that, at least in *xuanhuan* stories, Chinese lead characters are usually pretty ruthless. Unlike leads in English stories where the main characters will generally avoid killing other people except when necessary, Chinese lead characters in webfiction tend to kill at the drop of a hat. A lot of this is practicality, since because of the concepts of face and duty, if they don't kill their opponents, they'll be forever looking over their shoulders or have greater problems later.

Or, as a *xuanhuan* lead character might put it- "Being merciful to others is being merciless to myself."

However, there is also that power fantasy element- these stories are written by people without power for people without power to imagine what being powerful is like. To them, power means the strong rule the weak, even killing them like insects, and this survival of the fittest thinking is a big part of xianxia fiction.

Lastly, webnovel leads tend to be fairly simply sketched characters- blank templates upon which the reader can project themselves. This is done on purpose, as the author wants as many readers as possible to connect with these characters and making them too distinct will turn off some readers.

Also, there usually isn't a lot of personal character progression in webnovel leads- they tend to get more powerful as the story goes, and more confident, but that's usually about it. (For male leads anyway.) These unchanging characters will usually stay pretty much the same character from beginning to end, with only their statistics growing and confidence level developing, not their personality or worldview.

Opponents

In Chinese webnovels, the focus is on lead characters delivering face-slapping justice to their enemies. And, the more evil the enemy and the more the audience hates them, the more enjoyable it is to watch the main character take them down. Thus, bad guys in Chinese webnovels tend to not just be a little selfish or greedy, but loathsome people who are often driven by the worst human desires.

The bad guys in webnovels are ruthless characters who will do whatever it takes to gain power or to keep the power they have. They also love to abuse their power, and often inflict abuse on those weaker than they are for their amusement. Would-be rapists are common as flies in webnovels, and many of them have plans to assault the female lead(s) the first chance they get.

Occasionally, there will be opponents who are actually noble or righteous, and oppose the main character due to trickery or misunderstandings. However, the situation will almost always be worked out eventually before it turns into a real blood feud or characters die.

In either case, webnovels usually don't have a main opponent, or at least one isn't introduced until near the end of the story when it's time to wrap things up. The enemies in webnovels are more like "level bosses" who are defeated at the end of story arcs to show the main character has grown more powerful and capable. Since webnovels are unlimited stories, introducing a final boss is usually avoided at all cost until the end really is in sight.

Supporting Characters

In most Chinese webfiction, the main character will have a best friend/close ally character they have a strong connection with, and a love interest character they're pursuing. The friend is needed to give the character someone to talk to and give the character someone they need to rescue or help from time to time, and is usually a likeable and funny character.

The love interest will be a "fairy" or "angel" who is introduced fairly early on in the story, and often separated from the main character by circumstances so that they can spend the rest of the story trying to get together. This gives the main character both a motivation to act, and lets the love interest serve as a prize for the character to "win" when they've reached their goals at the end of the story.

Beyond these two, there will usually be a collection of allies, innocents the main character needs to help, a few jealous rivals, and a mentor/master or two who helps the character along the way.

SPECIAL FEATURES

Xuanhuan

Chinese fantasy, also called *xuanhuan*, refers to the particular form of fantasy popular in China and other parts of East Asia. This style of fantasy is characterized by stories set in Chinese (or Asian) pseudo-historical settings and layered with Chinese ideas of culture, religion, mysticism, and other traits unique to China and its neighbors. This distinguishes it from *xihuan* (Western, Pseudo-European fantasy) and is the type of fantasy setting that Chinese audiences strongly prefer.

Xuanhuan has many fathers, ranging from the Chinese classics like *The Journey to the West* (aka *The Monkey King*) and *The Romance of the Three Kingdoms*, to the pulp *wuxia* adventure serials of the mid-twentieth century by Jin Yong and Gu Long, to Hong Kong martial arts cinema of the late 20th century, to popular online comics and video games. All of these influences have combined to form a mythical China that never was, but which lets audiences escape into a place which feels both familiar and wonderous at the same time.

This fantasy China lets readers and writers escape from the constraints of the competitive modern Chinese world and China's modern political and social realities, and go to a place where their imaginations can play freely. Where clever peasant girls can win the hearts of kings and become a new empress, where determined martial artists can evolve spiritually into gods, and where brave hearted adventurers can build kingdoms and empires with their own sweat.

It is a place of play and freedom, a China that never was, and where any kind of story can be set a writer desires. This, of course, makes it perfect for webfiction writers, whose whole understanding of China's history mostly comes from webfiction, TV shows, movies, games, and other pop culture entertainment. They don't have to worry about historical accuracy, and can really let their imaginations cut loose. They can alter reality, re-arrange society, introduce ideas from video games and other pop culture, and pretty much do anything they want.

However, that doesn't mean these settings aren't linked to real Chinese culture, since they very much are, and the writers know that the more wildly they change things from what their audience is willing to accept, the smaller their audience will be. Thus, most Chinese fantasy stories still follow a basic set of conventions that have become generally accepted by audiences. Just like Middle Earth and Westeros still resemble medieval Europe, certain elements of China are always there in xuanhuan, and these concepts are the key to understanding it.

Wuxia and Xianxia

Two of the most common types of xuanhuan stories (in English, at least) are wuxia stories and xianxia stories, which are both action genres about martial arts practitioners who spend most of their time proving their fighting abilities. In endless duels and adventures, the heroes of these types of stories alternate between improving their skills and using them to defeat a series of tougher foes until they're accepted as being the best fighters alive.

Understanding how these two are different, however, requires a little bit of background.

The original wuxia story (or rather, story collection) is considered to be *The Water Margin* by Shi Nian during the Ming Dynasty, and is the story of a collection of various martial artists and members of the underworld who live in the edges of polite society called "the water margins" in Chinese. Also known as the *Outlaws of the Marsh*, *All Men Are Brothers*, or *The Marshes of Mount Liang*, this book set the tone for the adventures which were to come with incredible martial arts feats, secret societies, and wild characters who wandered from place to place.

By the early 20th century, what came to be called wuxia ("warrior hero") stories became a popular staple of Chinese culture, especially in early pulp magazines. They basically held the same cultural place as Westerns or stories about heroic knights in American and British culture, and were filled with wandering swordsmen who travelled around in old China righting wrongs and getting into trouble for the sake of beautiful ladies and justice.

Eventually, a writer named Louis Cha (pen name Jin Yong) appeared in Hong Kong in the late 1950s and transformed everything. Much like Stan Lee would revolutionize American superheroes in the 1960s, Cha took the standard wuxia story and with influence from western writers like Alexandre Dumas and Robert Louis Stephenson, began to transform the tired old wuxia stories of wandering fighters into something fresh and different.

Over the course of fifteen serialized novels and short stories between 1955 and 1972, Cha brought the idea of the rising hero story into wuxia with stories about young heroes who started at the bottom and through learning and effort became great adult heroes. He also pioneered the "harem" story where a young male protagonist has multiple young women who follow him around, but is too innocent or focused to pick any one of the beauties until the end. And, he took martial arts abilities that were slightly magical and turned them into full-on martial arts superpowers with characters flying around and using magical qi abilities to perform incredible feats.

Unlike Stan Lee, who made gods into men, Cha took realistic martial arts heroes and made them into gods, or at least demi-gods. However, where he and Lee did have something in common was that both grounded their stories in the real world, and Cha was a devoted historian who set his stories in real historical periods with great detail and accuracy. This may be why his works are beloved parts of Chinese culture until this day, and have been translated into so many languages. He set a new standard, and wuxia would follow that standard for many years.

Cha's heyday also coincided with the rise of Hong Kong cinema, and so it was natural that movie makers would start to adapt his popular stories to film. These too were popular, and it popularized Cha's work into common culture all around Asia, and even into closed-off mainland China where bootleg copies were eagerly watched by young Chinese. And, when Cha and the great age of wuxia writing slowly faded into history by the 1980s, wuxia continued on through movies and television programs, and slowly transformed into a visual genre from a literary one.

By the dawn of the twenty-first century, wuxia had so merged into general Chinese culture, it really wasn't even distinct anymore. Most period dramas had some wuxia elements in them, any historical video game was wuxia based, and people everywhere used phrases and ideas from Cha's books as common idioms and sayings. Of course people with martial arts could fly. Of course a tiny teen girl with a sword could beat a huge armored warrior with ease. Of course you healed people by channeling your qi into their body. These weren't even special anymore- they were just common (pop culture) sense.

And then, in 2007, a webfiction writer who went by I Eat Tomatoes started an online serial called *Stellar Transformations* on *Qidian.com*. Taking elements from popular video games, he fused them with the Taoist concept of spiritual evolution through development of the soul and turned it into the story of a young man named Qin Yu becoming a god. Thanks to a mysterious and mystical artifact called the Meteoric Tear, Qin Yu is able to go from a common peasant to a warrior god through a long series of duels and adventures.

Stellar Transformations became the first modern xianxia ("immortal hero") novel, and was a smash hit right when the whole webnovel industry was just starting to take off. It took the general pseudo-historical wuxia setting as a base, but then brought in high powered magic and elements from games like *League of Legends* that modern audiences could relate to. Characters now went up through levels like video games, and whole societies were built around "cultivators"- people who sought immortality by finding mystical spells, items, and knowledge.

As a result, for almost a decade xianxia-style stories became the new standard in webfiction, and I Eat Tomatoes went on to become a very rich and successful author with a very silly online name. Countless imitators copied him, and the xuanhuan genre was flooded with xianxia stories for a time like *I Shall Seal the Heavens*, *Martial World*, *Against the Gods*, and *Battle Through the Heavens*, before xianxia too began to fade in popularity.

Today, only a quarter of xuanhuan Chinese fantasy stories on *Qidian* are xianxia stories, but the influence the genre had on the audience is still huge. Video game elements in xuanhuan stories are now as normal as flying martial artists, with most stories measuring things in points and levels, and rising heroes who usually start out at first level and climb to the top of the system they live under. The idea of "cheats" from video games is also a legacy of xianxia, and it's also rare to find stories where the hero doesn't have some sort of cheating ability that helps them get through the story at a nice pace.

Wuxia evolved into xianxia, and xianxia has now evolved into the new standard. Where Chinese fantasy will go from here is anyone's guess, but the next story to spark a revolution could be written anytime- maybe even by you, as these genres have gone international.

Classic Wuxia Tropes

The following is a list of conventions, tropes, and quirks that you'll find in most traditional wuxia adventure stories. These are drawn from classic Jin Yong and Gu Long type stories, but a lot of them are still common in modern serials because they're so linked with Chinese adventure fiction and xianxia as well. They come from a time when wuxia stories were more swashbuckling and playful- when a hero was a gentlemanly figure who was expected to uphold most of society's virtues.

"Kick butt first, ask questions later."

Wuxia stories seem to be filled with hot tempered people who will fight at the drop of a hat or the slightest provocation. Often a xia (a wuxia hero) will dive into fights without even bothering to figure out who is wrong or right, for as simple as the leader of the losing side is wearing their favorite flower, or a member of one side reminds them of the guy who stole their ex-girlfriend away from them!

"I will channel my qi into my meridians and expel the poison!"

Drawing from traditional beliefs in Taoism and martial arts, in wuxia stories all living things are connected by life energy called "qi" that a xia can learn to harness and channel in many different ways. The most basic way is to enhance their physical abilities to make themselves stronger, faster, tougher, or able to leap huge distances. However, advanced practitioners can use it to attack by channeling it into their weapons to improve damage or accuracy, or even their own blows to bypass armor and inflicts extra internal damage. And, in some of the wilder wuxia stories qi was used as an explanation for outright superpowers like flight, fireballs, stealing life-force, and magic spells.

On the other hand, qi is linked to the Chinese belief in meridians- lines of life energy that run through the human body. Acupuncturists in the real world are trying to manipulate those meridians through needles and other techniques, but in wuxia stories people can just use fingers to affect the flow of energy in the body. By sealing or opening key points on their own body or others, xia can affect how inner power (*nei gong*) flows and heal, paralyze, expel poison, and perform other amazing feats. It's use it only limited by the creativity of writers and the credibility of audiences.

"Wait a moment, if you're her, then who are YOU?!?"

Wuxia stories thrive on mistaken identities, and they are also another source of regular conflict. Often heroes will mistake a maid for a princess, or a thief for a noble, almost any kind of mistaken identity is possible. This is an age where the only pictures are hand drawings, which often aren't very accurate. What happens when you look like someone's long lost cousin who is the only other person who can claim the family fortune? Or worse, when you look like the rival martial artist's brother who a group of thugs have been sent to kidnap? The possibilities are endless.

"Honorary Brother, I will not let you down!"

Heroes in wuxia stories form semi-familial relationships at the drop of a hat, any hat. Remember that to the wuxia, "brotherhood" (or "sisterhood") is everything in a world where you can only rely on your friends. So, you form as many contacts as you possibly can, and the ones with whom you bond are people you may regard as close as members of your own family.

Of course, with all these relations comes obligations and networks of favors owed by various people to each other. When someone kills the master of your honorary brother in a duel, it is your obligation to offer your sword in avenging him if the duel was an unfair one. When your friend needs to pay back a debt, he may ask your help, especially if the task will be difficult or expensive.

"She is the most deadly fighter I have ever seen! I wonder if she is married yet?"

In Chinese culture the most central and important unit is the family, and it is the duty of every member of that family to ensure the success of the family line. Part of that means bringing the best possible people of blood, skill and fortune into the family to improve the family's lot. Unmarried women are always looking for the chance to marry a successful man, and unmarried (and married! Men can have multiple wives!) men are always looking for impressive women, especially in wuxia stories.

It's no exaggeration to say that wuxia epics are filled with weddings and funerals, and marriage is both a source of peace and trouble. (Can you say "Romeo and Juliet"? Or should I say..."Hui and Ming Ming"?) Marriages are often also arranged, which means people can't always pick their partners, and with marriage comes obligations.

Of course, not everyone will always agree with an arranged marriage, especially the real lovers of people betrothed to someone else....

"I am Wu of the Condor Clan of the Five Sword Clans of Mount Hua!"

If you are a xia and know martial arts, someone had to teach them to you. That means you not only have obligations to your master, honorary brothers and sisters, and anyone else associated with the clan, but you will also have associations, rivalries, and even blood feuds with other clans! When the master calls back his students in times of need, where will **you** be?

"Heavens Above! He knows the Double Tailed Snake Sword Technique*!!!"*

With martial arts training will also come a fighting style, and probably a bunch of special techniques which are associated with that style. There are, of course, a number of catches:

1. Obviously, the special techniques are only taught to those who are worthy and advanced enough to learn them, or those who can steal the notes of a master. (Who always seem to write them down in places where they can be stolen...)

2. Martial Arts styles are systems of attack and defense, and like any system they will have holes and predictable responses to one who knows them or how to counter them. Often a xia can find his prized sword technique is suddenly useless against an opponent skilled in a counter-style, or who has studied his moves. Suddenly, in order to defeat his nemesis, a swordsman will have to learn a new sword style, or technique which will require a great quest or training mission to learn....

3. Often special techniques (which can be anything from simple tricks to army crushing maneuvers) will require great efforts to learn, and can only be learned at great risk to the student. ("You must meditate for five days on your head, then rest for five days to let your chi properly settle. If you try to use your chi and fight during that time, your muscles will explode and you may die.") To learn almost any special technique requires the development of the user's "chi" life energy and pathways, and this can be said to cause any number of side effects or conditions which will (temporarily?) afflict the user if done improperly. Usually the more powerful the technique, the more dangerous it is to learn it, and more conditions come with it. Of course, once your DO master it, you will often gain serious power to be reckoned with!

4. Special techniques can often have counter-techniques which can be learned to neutralize them, of course the counters are often as hard to learn as the original techniques and require special help of some kind to learn. The

student may even need the co-operation of multiple masters to develop a counter technique, or to convince the originator of the original technique to develop a counter for him before the next big showdown.

"He has the Thunder Sword of Mount Zou! The greatest of all weapons!"

In wuxia fiction, the usual focus is on the skills and abilities of the xia, not their weapons, and as a result magical weapons are often actually quite rare. When they do appear, they are almost always extremely powerful or significant, and desired by almost everyone you can name. The problem with being a xia with a magical weapon is that you need to be powerful enough to hold onto it because everyone and their brothers who know you have it are going to be trying to take it away from you!

Weapons are often not significant just for their high quality or magical properties in wuxia fiction, they are also very often pieces of greater puzzles or sources of legends. For example, two fine daggers each carved with half the map to a legendary gold mine, or two swords which legends say the master of both will be the rightful emperor of the next dynasty. Neither set of weapons is necessarily magic per-se, but they are likely to be both high quality, and sought after by more parties than you can name.

"Scholar Zu! It's the lost city of the Valley of Five Rubies!"

China is a **big** place with over 10,000 years of history, and has at various times been filled with hundreds of small kingdoms. As a result, there are a whole lot of "lost" places in wuxia stories waiting for the heroes to discover. From secret tombs where the ancient princes were buried, to bandit hideaways, and even ancient lost cities buried inside mountain cave complexes- it's amazing what a traveler can stumble across. Of course, these will often be filled with traps and guardians, but no place is perfect.

"Wait...I remember you...You're Hou's Cousin Wan Po!"

Wuxia stories are absolutely packed with co-incidences, and sometimes it seems like the incredibly huge empire is a small town with twenty families. Everybody always seems to be connected with someone you might know, or has heard of someone you probably do know! To top it all off, if your father had a dishonored brother who became a monk and you go to a monastery, there is absolutely no question who is going to be running the show when you desperately need the monks help! Nobody who isn't really dead ever seems to go away, they always seem like they are waiting their turn in the wings to make an appearance! You never know when you will run into someone you know, and they have a habit of showing up at the damndest times, both good and bad!

"I am Chairman Feng of the Five Lilies Society! And you, are about to face justice!"

Chinese culture has spent most of its history filled with "societies," formalized networks of social contacts and loyalties which act much like extended family units. "Secret societies" in wuxia stories can be anything from a small group of friends to a massive network with members numbering in the hundreds of thousands. They will normally have a nominal stated purpose (i.e. restoring the rightful emperor, avenging a wronged man, bringing justice to a corrupt city, worshiping some god, or just bringing the members money or power), a slogan ("Death to the Ming Family!", "Justice before Money!") and some form of power structure (usually a chairman, a council of elder members, and various ranks beneath).

You never know who might be a member of such and such a society, and just like belonging to any family there are rights, obligations, dues, responsibilities and perks involved. They can be extremely useful for travelers, providing lodging, food, and other needs for members, or equally detrimental if the wrong person turns out to be a member of a rival society and they discover your loyalties.

"...The most insidious poison developed, there is only one cure!"

In wuxia stories, people love poisons and alchemical mixtures, and are constantly using them for various effects. Of course, nobody ever develops a poison without developing a cure in case they get exposed to it, but getting that cure from them is often extremely hard if they wish to see you dead. And if you can't get it from them, you can get it from someone else, you just have to find the right person, or the right mixture of ingredients.

Poisons don't always kill either, sometimes they will cripple, impair, render unconscious, or do any other number of other nasty things. And of course, there are the other alchemical mixtures people use, for example, aphrodisiacs are extremely common, and can serve many purposes if slipped into the right person's food, and then there are booster mixtures which can enhance certain abilities or qualities temporarily.

"Fine Wine! Fine Women! What more could a living man ask for?!?"

Wuxia are warriors who risk their lives for many causes, and before (and sometimes after) they settle down, they enjoy a pretty wild and boisterous life. The Chinese are a "drinking culture," and they have a strong love of drinking games, and enjoying the good life when they can. Of course, drinking, gambling and womanizing costs money, and often gets you into trouble with a wide variety of people....

"After you!....No, after you!"

When dealing with opponents they consider honorable wuxia will almost always fight honorably as well, and treat the fight as more of a contest of skill than an actual duel unless circumstances dictate otherwise. Opponents are rarely killed unless necessary, and fights are to prove and test one's skills, not to cause serious harm to an opponent unless something happens in the heat of battle by accident or purpose.

Sparring is a common way to settle disputes, especially between rival societies, clans or other martial groups. How serious it is depends on the situation and how far the opponent takes it- if the fight starts with hand to hand combat, then it stays there unless someone escalates the fight. Killing an unarmed or lesser skilled opponent in a duel with a weapon is a good way to get a bad reputation and can produce results far worse than losing the fight in the first place!

"You're Lu Xiao Bei, I've heard of you!"

In the wuxia "underworld" reputations are everything and easy to come by if you have any talent or deeds of note. Anything you do can get you a reputation and that reputation can follow you around for a very long time, regardless of whether it's good or bad. People love to gossip and tell stories, and in a world where one's skill and accomplishments can mean everything, this can be a real mixed blessing. If you have a great reputation people expect great things from you (perhaps more than you are capable of), and many will seek you out for a variety of reasons, from wanting to learn from you to wanting to challenge you to a duel! A bad reputation can get you expelled from membership in societies, shunned by people who know you and even result in consequences for anyone associated with you.

"I must kill any man who sees my face....or marry him."

Wuxia are constantly making and living under oaths to their friends, families, and teachers. If a wuxia makes an oath, they have to stick with it, and will stick with it often until death because their own personal honor and face is at stake. While it depends on the personality of the person who makes the oath, characters in wuxia stories take oaths extremely seriously, and will literally make life-changing (or death dealing) decisions based on them. Common reasons for oaths include revenge, displays of loyalty, familial obligations, or because they must do it in order for their master to teach them special techniques.

Of course, what the master may make them swear to do is not always the most rational thing in the world, and is often from personal and selfish motives. For example...

- Teach my art only to your second son

- Marry my daughter and continue the school
- You must never drink alcohol or eat meat
- You must name your born first son after me
- You can only fight when you are attacked first.
- Never marry unless that man/woman can defeat you in mortal combat
- When I die, you must come and clean my grave once a year, and dump a bottle of the best wine on it.
- You must kill all members of another martial order
- You must never wear armor; it shows you are weak and cowardly and disgraces my name.
- You can only use this technique if you are defending another's life.
- You must build a school made of jade atop Mount Flying Deer.
- You must marry five wives, one from each of the major holy martial schools.
- You must travel to each of the four borders of the Empire, and teach my arts to one person there.

"I challenge you....to a contest of Calligraphy....on that cliffside!"

Wuxia are all about skill and personal achievement, they get much of their immense egos and pride from their abilities, and that doesn't just extend to martial arts, although that is the most common focus. It also needs to be understood that xia are all about proving who is the better man (or woman), and they don't just mean in a fight, often they are trying to show who is closer to the Confucian ideal which runs so strongly in their society.

Anything artistic can be used as the basis of a duel, as can any form of physical contest, and in wuxia stories these are often combined into some pretty wild contests mixing both! If both men are xia and poets, why not have a contest that shows both skill in swordsmanship, carving, and poetry at the same time? If both women are equally skilled painters, why not see if they can paint a giant mural on the castle wall before sunset? (Who needs scaffolding when they can run up the wall-side?) Chinese wuxia duels can take almost unlimited forms, but they will often involve some of the following arts:

Calligraphy Contests: Calligraphy is an art that any great learned gentleman should have. The Chinese respect for scholars and wisdom knows no bounds, and as a result anything related to writing and reading is held in high esteem. One of those things is calligraphy, which has been a high art in China for literally millennia, there are many ways and styles to write Chinese characters, and a man can literally make a living painting characters if he is skilled enough and has a unique style.

Poetry Contests: Often, these will be combined with the calligraphy contests, turning it into a contest of both style and wit. The Chinese have a great love of poetry, and their language contains poetic levels that cannot be expressed or explained in English terms because the very characters the poems are written in can have multiple meanings and histories that extend far beyond the surface reading. Of course, the poems need not always be deep and meaningful, they use poems to tell dirty jokes, and political satire, and for many other uses. Most of the "artistic" poems, however, like those of English will be ones about longing for home, a missed love one, a family or perhaps childhood. (Note: These are also used as passwords by secret societies, sometimes the society will have a special poem written by its founder...only a member can recite this poem, or finish it if presented with the first half.)

Jokes: Believe it or not, the Chinese love to tell jokes as much as any westerner does, and these jokes can be as clean or as dirty as anything you can hear. (Although of course a proper gentleman will never tell "yellow" (dirty) jokes, especially not in the company of others he respects or wishes to keep the respect of.) It's perfectly common for xia to have contests to see who can tell the best joke.

Singing Contests: Especially popular for women, but men pride themselves on their singing too, in some parts of Southern China couples will literally sing to each other as they try to win the heart of the one they love, and the object of their affection will sing their feelings back in a song that will flow back and forth as the two negotiate a relationship.

Storytelling Contests: You have five minutes to tell a tale that will make the hardest warrior's heart weep...GO!

Riddles: Mental puzzles are extremely popular, especially in wuxia stories. These riddles test the brain, and often they will be used as a secret password by secret societies. (Only a member will know the real hidden answer to the riddle.)

"Your Ma-po Tofu is nothing compared with my Sichuan Style Dumplings!"

In China, there is a saying, "Europeans are obsessed with sex, Chinese are obsessed with food," and it's not far from true. Cooking and food are an extremely important part of Chinese culture, and recipes can literally be secrets guarded with one's life in a wuxia story. There were periods in China when great chefs held social power greater than many lords because they were so prized, and people would literally travel across the empire to eat just once at a famous restaurant. Chefs would wander the countryside seeking masters just as wuxia do, and sometimes a xia will be a master of multiple arts. Cooking can be the source of contests, medicine, health, wealth, power, and social status, and should not be taken or done lightly.

Xianxia Tropes

As noted above, modern Chinese fantasy incorporates a lot of the above as a default setting, but then pushes it to other extremes by adding more fantastic elements. A lot of these are drawn from video games, but they can come from superhero movies, western fantasy, collectable card games, mobile apps, and more.

Here are a few common "tropes" or standards that seem to pop up over and over in the majority of xianxia stories:

- It takes place in a pseudo-historical Fantasy world often based on old China and filled with wuxia story elements and conventions.

- The main character is (almost) always a weak young man of low birth.

- Despite being of low birth, the lead has some weird cheat advantage over others in becoming a Cultivator which kicks in around the time the story starts. (Common ones are they are reincarnated from another time and place, they have been transported to a fantasy world from our world, they have some unique skills from a strange background, or they have some magic item that activates around the time the story starts.) The cheat lets them whiz through the story at a brisk pace, avoiding the boring bits and keeping the action flowing.

- There is a system of rankings which all Cultivated beings in the setting will follow. (This usually involves a combination of Numbers and something else. So, the character might be a "Bronze Rank 3 Fighter" or be working up from "Level One White Mage" to "Level 99 Black Mage", with the colors designating approximate level of spiritual development.)

- All cultivated beings have some pool of Qi Points (Magic Points) which they use to enhance their physical abilities and cast magical spells. These points are linked to the spiritual development of the character and their level/rank.

- Magic and magic items are plentiful in the setting, but are pretty much only used for fighting, healing and levelling up. (Other uses of magic like growing crops or cooking aren't even on the radar- it's all battle, all the time.)

- The setting will be filled with wandering monsters of varying ranks (which corresponds to the ranks of character development as well) and these monsters will produce gemstones when killed that can be used in various ways. (Commonly, to be absorbed by the lead to help further their Leveling.)

- Often the main character will get one of these monsters as a pet early in the story, which will be his companion and level up with him.

- The main character usually has a mentor, but the mentor will be pretty unreliable and tends to disappear for long periods of time. (Only to show up to help the lead get over critical challenges and occasionally as a Deux ex Machina.)

- There are clans/sects/guilds that the character will have to become involved with to get the things they need to level up, but by allying with one group, you gain the enmity of their enemies. (Thus, perpetual conflict.)

- Each of the above groups has their own power levels in their society, and there are always top ones which dislike the main character for some reason. (Thus, being the high-powered opposition that the main character will need to face toward the end of the story and often they hunt the lead at some point.

- There are two kinds of clans/guilds/sects- noble and corrupt. The noble ones are trying to achieve some greater goal and generally make the world a better place and follow strict codes of conduct. The corrupt ones exist to just benefit the leadership and the members are just pawns in the games of the leadership. The corrupt ones are much more common than the noble ones, and it's hard to tell the difference sometimes because the corrupt ones all pretend to be noble until their show their true colours.

- There are a handful of "Immortals" who have reached top rank in the setting, and the world tends to revolve around them. Some are friendly toward our hero, while some will want him dead. The most dangerous of these will be the "final boss" the hero will need to face to finish his quest.

- There was once a great lost civilization in the setting who littered the setting with lost tombs and hidden places filled with cool magical items and books.

- There will be some variant of a Magic Satchel (usually a bag or ring) which is easy to carry but which allows the lead to store massive amounts of stuff they find with almost no weight.

- There will be "healing pills" which restore health, and "power-up pills" which help in the character's levelling. (Sometimes the latter are the gems that monsters leave behind when killed.)

- The character will gain some bizarre magical superpowers during their journey that seem weak at first, but level up into something massive over time.

- There is a main female love interest character who is introduced early on, but something always keeps them apart. (Usually she is the daughter of one of the clan/sect/guild heads, and will be described as "a fairy" or as the most beautiful woman in the world.)

- In the meantime, the lead will be pursued by a host of other young cuties who will tempt him and keep the drama flowing and try to seduce him at various points in the story.

- The female lead will have some ability that enhances or is complimentary to the male lead.

- Every young man wants to be a warrior/fighter- it's their dream to fight for their clans.

There are other standards, but these tend to be the big ones and the most common ones. Each author will put his own spin on a number of these elements, and sometimes come up with some interesting twists on them, but most of them will be there in some form. (Which will then result in others copying that twist, and innovating it in other directions, keeping the genre evolving.)

The only way to understand xianxia (and wuxia for that matter) is to read it, and a whole lot of it. Read it until it's coming out your ears, and then read some more- only in this way can you understand the dao of xuanhuan.

KOREAN WEBNOVELS

The South Korean webnovel market is one of the oldest and most developed in the world, having been already established in 2000 and being one of the only markets where the (bare) majority of webfiction writers can actually get paid for their content. This has produced a system where writers are encouraged to produce the best quality work they can, and has let Korean webfiction develop at its own style and pace.

AUDIENCE

As with China and Japan, the Korean webfiction market is primarily driven by a youthful audience. Older people tend to be too busy with their lives to spend time reading or writing webfiction, so young people are the ones who devour it the most. This may change as a generation which grew up on webnovels ages and continues to enjoy them, but most of the content is still targeted at youth.

LENGTH

Unlike Chinese webnovels, which tend to be long-running epics that go into the thousands of chapters, Korean webnovels are usually shorter, running just a few hundred chapters at most. Since Korean authors can be paid for shorter works as well, there is less incentive for them to produce giant sprawling epics to keep the story going as there is in China.

Also, as Korean readers pay by the chapter if they feel a writer is padding things out or playing them along, they will be more likely to drop the title. That means that each chapter of a Korean webnovel must provide a fulfilling and interesting reading experience on its own, and decreases the incentive to pad out works like what often happens in Chinese webnovels. Korean audiences want to feel the story is moving and they're getting their money's worth.

Finally, since Korean webnovels often get turned into dramas and comics, making them too long can actually work against a writer's chances of getting picked up. The average Korean TV drama is no more than 20 episodes, and if the story runs too long it might be hard to compress it down into the story for a TV series. Shorter and tighter series are also less risks for comics adaptations.

KOREAN WEBNOVEL GENRES

The Korean webnovel industry is fairly well developed, and thus has a bit more variety than you'll see in the Chinese market, being more like the Japanese manga market.

For example, looking at the top 198,000 stories on Korea's webnovel site *Joara's* stories by the main 10 genres on the site we get:

1. Fantasy (25%)
2. Parody (20%)
3. Fusion (9%)
4. Boys Love (8%)
5. Romance (8%)
6. Game (6%)
7. General Fiction (Unclassified) (6%)
8. Romance Fantasy (4%)
9. Literary Works (4%)
10. Light Novels (3%)

Looking at the list, it comes as no surprise that "Fantasy" is the top genre, since that's the genre with the greatest appeal to most youth. Inside this fantasy genre will be a mix of Korean-style fantasy and western-style fantasy, and the site doesn't differentiate one from the other. However, most of this fantasy will be heavily influenced by games, and much of it will have a role-playing game system element in it somewhere.

What the site called "Parody" is basically humorous fanfiction, with serious fanfiction having its own separate category later on. "Fusion" is a mixed genre category which includes a lot of stories that mix science fiction and fantasy with other genres like litRPGs. "Boys Love," are romance stories about two young men falling in love, which are as popular in Korea as they are in Japan, and it is tied with general male-female "Romance" for popularity.

If it surprises you that romance is so low on the list, being such a popular genre, it's because they're splitting the three main types of romance (romance, boys love, romance fantasy) into three different categories. Together, they're 20% of the site's stories, which makes them the second or third most popular.

"Game" fiction is mostly e-Sports stories about people playing virtual reality MMO games or competitive gaming. "General Fiction" will include dramas and anything unclassified, while "Romance Fantasy" is exactly what it sounds like – romance stories set in pseudo-historical fantasy worlds. "Literary Works" are attempts at more complex fiction styles and themes, while "Light Novels" are Japanese anime/manga style works.

What's interesting about the above list is that there's no science fiction genre category on *Joara*, and in fact there isn't one on *Naver* either. Only *Munpia* has a science fiction category tag, and it's only at 2% of the stories on the site. Despite being one of the more technologically developed countries on Earth, Koreans show relatively little interest in science fiction, with most science fiction stories being science-fantasy (fusion) stories or hidden among other categories.

PLOTS

A typical Korean webnovel is about a young person in a very difficult situation trying to solve their problems through some opportunity which has come their way. This "opportunity" is usually a cheat (see the chapter on "What Popular Webfiction Stories Have in Common") that is allowing them to game an existing system for their benefit.

Koreans love underdog characters a lot, so most Korean webfiction leads tend to start their stories in a really, really bad position. If the main character's life doesn't suck at the start of a story, you're probably not reading Korean webfiction. When the story begins, one parent will be dead or missing, the other will be dying of cancer, there will be four younger siblings all relying on the main character, the main character will have just lost their job, and they will also be in debt to gangsters for a pile of money the dead/missing parent owed- and that's just if they're lucky!

Okay, that might be a bit of an exaggeration, but the Korean webnovel fans who just read that list were smiling and nodding along, because it isn't far from the truth. Korean webfiction tends to go for the most straightforward and quick ways to grab the sympathy of the audience and keep it- most of which are based around family. Koreans are a very family-oriented culture, so giving the main character a tragic family situation is instant sympathy to them.

Also, in most stories, the story will start with the character gaining some controllable cheat that they then slowly figure out how to use their best advantage while beating up evil and selfish people who stand in their way. This lets the audience dream "if I had that ability, what would I do?" and then enjoy the ride as they watch the main character use that ability in creative and fun ways. Interestingly enough, Koreans seem to prefer controllable cheats with growth potential over characters having uncontrollable cheats, since they prefer the idea that the character's destiny is in their own hands.

Since Koreans have a great passion for games, stories with RPG gaming elements are especially popular, and most stories for boys (and sometimes girls) will have some gaming element built into the story. If the story involves a fantasy world, then that world runs in the rules of a typical fantasy Massively Multiplayer Online video game with levels, character classes, magic points, and so on. If the story is a modern action story, then the setting runs on ideas and rules similar to fighting games or first-person shooters. And, even if the story is a romance, it might run like a dating sim, where there are "affection points" that only the main character can see and use to know how others feel about him or her.

How important the game elements are in the story will depend on the writer or audience. They may be game elements that everyone in the setting has access to, or they might be part of the main character's cheat abilities, but they will almost always be there somewhere.

As usual, the exception is romance stories targeted at girls, which tend to be more realistic romantic dramas or straight-up pseudo-historical romantic fantasy stories without the gaming elements.

TONE

The tone of Korean webnovels is generally optimistic, but much more realistically so than in Japanese light novels. While the world in Korean webfiction isn't the dog-eat-dog fight for survival that you find in Chinese webnovels, it still has an edge to it where the strong clearly rule the weak and everything is about your rank in society. The only difference is that Korean society in webnovels usually has a sense of order to it instead of the lawlessness common Chinese webnovels.

The strong rule the weak, but the strong are still controlled by society in Korean webnovels, and the average person can still live a decent life if they are willing to play by the rules.

If a Japanese light novel hero can be said to be walking through a fun theme park, a Korean light novel hero can be said to be going on a wilderness hike. There's some danger and unexpected challenges, but overall, it's still something they can handle with a bit of thought and effort. Heroes in Korean webnovels usually have a very rough time because Koreans like their heroes to suffer for their victories, but they do still win in the end.

WRITING STYLE

Webfiction writers in Korea follow the trend of writing light action-oriented prose. Stylistically, they write similarly to the Chinese, with third-person stories that use lots of short one-two sentence paragraphs and a heavy focus on dialog and telling the story as opposed to showing the story.

Sometimes they will also use First-Person, especially for romance stories or thrillers, and in that case, they will go into much more details about the characters, their thoughts, and their surroundings. A few stories like *Dungeon Defense* are very detailed to the point of being more like literary fiction and less like normal light fiction.

Unlike Chinese and Japanese writers, however, Korean storytellers are more stylistically consistent. If they pick a perspective like third person limited, they will stick with that perspective. They're much less likely to mix third person and first person in the same story, or go "head hopping" and offer multiple perspectives in the same scene. If they want to change perspective, they will have a scene break and then jump to a new perspective to indicate the change in viewpoint like most English writers do.

CHARACTERS

Most main characters in Korean webnovels are clever, decent, hard-working types who care about their friends and families, but who usually have bad luck to be saddled with debts or a poor social situation. Their poor starting situation gives them both motivation and desire to change their lives when opportunity comes along, and it usually happens at the start of the story.

They are everymen (or everywomen) who are just trying to get by in the world even though life has dealt them a bad hand. (At first.) And thus, they tend to be a little generic and are meant to be audience insert characters who are just different enough that they have a personality, but not so different than the audience can't relate to them.

Opponents

As per usual in webfiction, Korean opponents are usually pretty clear villains. While things aren't as black and white as they often are in Chinese stories, Korean opponents are usually selfish, arrogant and powerful people who treat those under them like crap. Usually they're people who benefit from the current system and use it to abuse others, and the system-wrecking lead character then enters the story and wrecks them as well when they get in his way.

The difference is that Korean villains are often smarter about it all than Chinese villains are. A Korean villain is usually willing to stand down against a stronger opponent rather than face them and get killed, and might even be willing to work for the main character. Or, if they can't get at the main character directly, they'll look for weak points and use the main character's family and friends against them in their efforts to get revenge.

Supporting Characters

Korean culture is very family-oriented, and family is still at the heart of most Korean society. Thus, a Korean character will almost always have some sort of family connections in the story which make them part of society. For example, many webnovel characters have single parents who are struggling to feed their families, or younger siblings who need to be taken care of by the lead. These connections ground them in Korean culture, and motivate the character to act to protect and support their family members in the story.

Even a character who doesn't have a family because they've gotten dumped in a fantasy world will often make a new family out of the friends they meet, and their relationships will become more like family than friendships. The desire for that family-like connection, especially among young people who might not have it in real life, is a strong part of Korean culture and so they want to feel it through the relationships of the characters in their stories.

Naturally, they also prize friendships, and Korean characters are also usually looking for kindred spirits who they can trust and work with to rise up in their situation. A true friend is worth their weight in gold, and in fact Koreans say, "There is nothing on this earth more to be prized than true friendship." Which, of course, is something the readers long for as well, so they feel happy when the character finds true friends.

SPECIAL FEATURES

Korean Fantasy

Korean fantasy stories tend to have a pretty good mix of Asian-influenced and western-influenced settings. Koreans have their own historical periods they can draw on to write Korean fantasy settings as well. Often these stories will be set in non-specific historical Korea but with martial arts magic elements akin to Chinese wuxia stories, which is a genre that Koreans called "murim." Like Chinese wuxia, murim stories are basically about martial artists and martial arts societies at war with each other and follow pretty much all the same rules.

On the other hand, since they play a lot of video games with a western fantasy bent, and loved *Game of Thrones* as much as anyone else, a lot of Korean fantasy stories will be set in European-style fantasy settings that look like typical *D&D* worlds. They will have their own Korean spin on these settings, but again, most of those settings still stick close to the generic game fantasy model, and may in fact be a game setting...

The (Gaming) System

Finding a culture that is more obsessed with games than Korea would be difficult. Koreans are obsessed with games to the point where they have news programs entirely dedicated to gaming airing on their regular television stations. Being a professional gamer in Korea is also a realistic option, with tournaments offering huge amounts of money and teams recruiting the best of the best to play for them in paid positions.

So, it's no surprise that most Korean webfiction stories targeted towards a male audience are connected with gaming in some fashion. Fantasy settings in Korean webfiction are more often western fantasy than they are set in actual Korean-inspired settings. And, those stories will often be either litRPGs where characters are adventuring inside games, or pseudo-litRPGs where the world is real, but the reality of the setting functions just like a game with levels and statistics. Game-isms like levels and monsters dropping treasure, even in non-litRPG stories where they use "magic" to explain it, are everywhere.

WEBFICTION GENRES

If you were to browse your local bookstore, or ask the clerks there, you would find that fiction book sales are generally dominated by four categories: romance, general fiction, mystery/suspense/thriller, and fantasy/science fiction. This is a trend which has been pretty consistent across time, and their popularity generally goes in that order as well.

On the other hand, if you were to look at webfiction publishing statistics based on genres and what people are reading and writing, you would find the big three are romance, fantasy (without the sci-fi), and teen fiction. This is true regardless of culture, and while the popularity of the big three will shift depending on the target audience of the site (male/female), those big three will always be there at the top of any large general audience webfiction site.

The reasons for this difference are pretty simple.

Fantasy, romance, and teen fiction are all genres that appeal greatly to young audiences, and it is young audiences that are reading (and writing) most of the webfiction out there. Yes, there are many older readers, and some older writers, but webfiction is the playground of the young, and the young are filled with dreams and idealism that reflect in their reading and writing tastes.

However, even inside those big three webfiction genres, there's a lot of room for different types of stories, and many, many sub-genres have popped up over the years as people have learned what audiences like and what they don't. This book couldn't possibly cover all of them, but it's worth taking an in-depth look at a few of the biggest sub-genres and what makes each of them special.

- **Rising Hero Stories** - the most common heroic serial story of them all
- **Fantasy Stories** – stories set in fantasy world or fantastic situations
- **Second Life Stories** (Isekai) – characters from our world travelling to other places and times
- **litRPGs** – characters playing video games or entering virtual worlds
- **Task Stories** – characters trying to create, manage, restore, learn, or teach
- **Conquest Stories** – characters trying to wage war or advance within an organization
- **Romance** – characters trying to make relationships work

- **Slice of Life** – interesting people doing normal things, or normal people doing interesting things.

Each of these are types of stories that can be used with any of the big three webfiction genres, and you will see that many webnovels and light novels will fall under one or more of these webfiction sub-genres. As you go through each chapter, pay close attention to what makes those stories special, and what makes them appeal to different audiences. Also, try to find the one which resonates with you the most, because that will be the one you should probably be writing in.

RISING HERO STORIES

If there is a type of story with universal appeal, it's the Rising Hero story - a story where a young person rises up and changes their world. These are stories that transcend genre, culture, and time, from Charles Dickens, to Horatio Alger, to J.K. Rowling.

They can be a story about a kid becoming class president, a newly reborn vampire learning the ropes of their undead existence, a young recruit beginning their career at a big company, a new concubine rising up in the royal harem, a youth venturing out into a post-apocalyptic world, or a peasant child becoming a sorcerer-god. Any and all of these can be a Rising Hero story because they meet one simple criteria- a young person faces a new and challenging system and grows as they find their place in it.

It's no surprise then, that these stories are also the most popular kinds of webfiction stories, and a quick glance at the stories sitting at the top of the Chinese, Japanese, Korean, or English webfiction charts will reveal that most of the non-romance stories there are Rising Hero stories of some kind. So, if you want to write successful non-romance webfiction, you're probably writing Rising Hero stories.

This chapter will cover exactly what Rising Hero stories are and how you can write them in detail, with a focus on planning your stories so that the writing goes as smoothly as possible. You just need to remember that Rising Hero stories aren't a genre, they're a type of story, so they can be any genre and cover almost any subject matter. So, you can combine it with any other kind of story to produce something new and yet with universal appeal.

Let's begin.

RISING HERO STORIES VS. COMING OF AGE STORIES

Usually, stories about young people becoming adults are called Coming of Age stories, since they're about young people finding their place in the adult world. So, you might wonder what the difference is between a Coming of Age story and a Rising Hero story, and if they're really that different from each other.

The short answer is that while many Rising Hero stories are Coming of Age stories, not all Coming of Age stories are Rising Hero stories. A Coming of Age story is about a young person learning what it is to be an adult, but that can cover a lot of territory. Stories about a young person getting their first job, or having to deal with new bodily functions like shaving or menstruation, dealing with their grandparents dying, learning how to get along with siblings, dealing with parental divorce, or the many other things that mark the difficult teen years, are all Coming of Age stories.

However, they are not Rising Hero stories.

A Rising Hero story is specifically about a person entering a "new world" (to them), and then learning to not just survive, but thrive and conquer that new world. They are rags-to-riches stories about starting out at or close to the bottom and rising up to the top, and what it takes to be a success. They are usually about young characters growing, which is where the overlap with Coming of Age stories comes in, but that doesn't mean they're about the small life changes people go through on the road to adulthood.

Instead, while Coming of Age stories are often about facing the small challenges of growing up, Rising Hero stories are about facing the big challenges- making life changing and critical decisions that will determine the rest of the character's life. They're not about what to do when you get your first pimple, they're about what schools you need to go to if you want to work at a world-class hospital after you finish your medical degree.

If the story isn't built around a big challenge, it's not a Rising Hero story.

With rising heroes, it's always "go big or go home."

RISING HERO AUDIENCES

The target audience for Rising Hero stories is young people who are still finding their place in the world. Anyone else can read them, and many will enjoy them, but these are youthful fantasies of power and control that appeal especially to a younger audience who don't have those things in their lives.

Rising Hero stories appeal to this audience because they offer a few things:

- A story of how someone won at life
- Wish fulfillment power fantasies
- Knowledge of how the world works

- A roadmap for how to deal with other people
- New ways of looking at the world

These are all things that young audiences are looking for, and while older audiences might enjoy the nostalgic feeling of them, young people crave these things. Teenagers especially have just realized how big and complex the world is, and so are trying to find as many possible roads to success as they can to help them navigate an increasingly scary future.

Accordingly, these stories exist to give them information about how others manage to succeed while at the same time reassuring them that it will all be okay. Just like the characters in the stories, they will find their places it the world and be able to make their mark on it. This is reassurance that readers of these stories desperately want on a subconscious level, and the more popular Rising Hero stories are ready to step in and give it to them.

RISING HERO THEMES

You might think that the themes behind rising hero stories are pretty obvious, especially since the characters often say them out loud during these kinds of stories.

- The value of hard work
- The power of teamwork
- The power of friendship
- Finding your place in society will bring out the best in you
- Don't give up on your dreams
- Be true to yourself
- Nothing worth having comes easily
- People respect those who give it their all
- And other ideas about how the world rewards those who follow their passions

Which makes sense, because these stories are meant to be about encouraging young people to try their best and become productive members of society. However, while on the surface Rising Hero stories often focus on these ideas, the truth is that the messages successful rising hero stories are really sending can actually be very different.

In reality, a modern successful Rising Hero story isn't there to support and encourage (although it does that too), it's there to confirm the beliefs the audience already has about themselves.

- You are special.
- You can change the world.
- There is a place out there for you, no matter who you are, and you just need to find it.
- Someday you will rise to the top and make people respect you.
- As long as you just try, your special talents will come out and make you a hero.

These are things the audience wants to be true, and successful Rising Hero stories do everything to encourage these beliefs. Their main characters are misfits and outcastes who are declared special one day and then given a series of lucky breaks that let them quickly rise to the top and gain the adoration and respect of those around them without too much of that hard work stuff.

Look at any Rising Hero story at the top of the charts, and you will find it quietly supports all of these beliefs while pretending to declare the virtues of hard work, community, and fighting for what you believe in. They succeed because they know what their audience really wants- an ego massage, not a lecture on the value of labor.

THE RISING HERO PLOT

Pretty much all rising hero stories have the same plot. They differ in the presentation and specific events, but in the end they're pretty much all the following:

A sympathetic character enters a new world where they find allies and learn to grow and thrive in that world's system while facing many challenges until they eventually reach the top and change that new world.

It's a pretty straightforward story, and one that you have probably already seen dozens or maybe hundreds of times in your life. However, just because it's straightforward doesn't mean there isn't depth there, so let's break it down to look at some of the parts in more detail.

A Sympathetic Character...

As with most stories, the audience needs to find the lead in Rising Hero stories sympathetic in some way. This is one of the reasons why Rising Hero characters almost always have difficult lives at the start of the story, but try to stay positive and help others when they can.

If you look at any Rising Hero story, you'll see the lead will usually have a terrible life when the story starts. Usually they're someone who is just managing to keep their head above water, has a challenging home life, and is often the target of bullying. Orphan lead characters were already a rising hero standard in Charles Dickens' day, and are still almost the standard today. Another popular one is the main character having lost only a single parent, but now being in charge of the remaining family members in a struggling family. And finally, there's the bullied outcaste who everyone looks down upon because they're different or weird. Any or all of these will make for a sympathetic lead that the audience relates to and wants to see succeed.

But the main character can't take their poor situation as an excuse to sit and cry-they have to be making the best of that situation. They need to be someone who has a strong spirit that won't let them give up or pass their misery on to others. Despite it all, and maybe even though they act like a jerk sometimes, they at least try to be a good person and show through how they behave that they're someone worth supporting and who others can rely on. This too makes the audience want to see them succeed in their lives.

And finally, they should be shown doing something good for other people-preferably something that brings them no benefit and might even cause them trouble. Maybe they give someone else their lunch money, they rescue a cat from a tree, or they stand up for someone being bullied. By doing things like this, they'll show that they are good members of the community they live in, and people that the audience can like and respect. The audience likes to think they're the kinds of people who would also do these things, and seeing the lead character do it will make the audience like and respect them.

Thus, the ideal main character lives a difficult life, but is trying to make the best of it while still helping other people. This is someone the audience will almost always find sympathetic and thus be ready to cheer on as they go forward into their new life.

...Enters a New World...

Obviously, the main character's life is about to change, usually for the better, and this change in situation is called the "new world" the character enters. It can literally be a new world, if it's a fantasy story where they travel to another reality, but it doesn't have to be. Leaving the village where they grew up to move to the big city is entering a new world, as is joining a new company, entering a new school, or going on a long journey. Learning a new skill, sport, or hobby can also be entering a new world, because there are usually whole subcultures that go with those activities that the character will now become a part of. And lastly, a major change in situation like joining a club, trying to run for office, moving into a new community, or taking on new responsibilities can also be new worlds to a character who hasn't dealt with them before.

The key here is that the character leaves the comfortable and familiar world they knew before (even if it kinda sucked), and are now in a strange and challenging place which will force them to change.

...Where They Find Allies...

Even the lead character can't do it alone, and even if they can, they still need someone to talk to. Characters learn and grow through their interactions with other people, and they'll need allies to keep them going forward on the right track. The rest of the cast is there to motivate the lead character and teach them the things they need to know to succeed.

Most supporting characters in Rising Hero stories fall into one (or both) of two categories– motivators and resources.

Motivators are people who give the lead a reason to do what they do. They can be people who order the main characters to take action, or people who the main character needs to help in order to accomplish their goals. They also include love interests, who are the prize(s) the main character gets if they finish their journey and represent the end of the story. Most stories are built around a collection of motivators who exist to get them moving and keep them moving even when the character would rather be settling down and resting.

Resources, on the other hand, are there because the main character can't go it alone. They need mentors to teach them the skills they need, knowledgeable people to give them the information they need, good listeners to provide them with emotional support, and a host of other people they can't accomplish their goals without. They might need a vehicle or dragon to reach a place on time, a clue to help them put a puzzle together, or a dealer who can offer them the latest weapons or magic spells. But all of these come from other characters, and are the result of a support network the lead character is going to need to have and maintain to reach their goals.

Sometimes characters act as both resources and motivators, and that's good to have too, but they're people too, and they won't help the main character unless they want to. Part of learning to be a rising hero is learning to navigate and negotiate through the challenges of dealing with others and finding ways to make the right friends and connections.

Also, the most fun and entertaining parts of the story will often come from the main character dealing with other people. So, make sure your supporting cast are a collection of lively, interesting and likeable people!

...And Learn to Grow and Thrive...

While there might be a steep learning curve at first, the lead characters in Rising Hero stories don't take long to figure out what they need to do and start doing it. Often, they are thrown into sink or swim situations, and they not only learn how to swim, but how to swim faster and better than the people around them.

This is typically due to a combination of determination, quick thinking, bravery, talent, and a whole lot of lucky breaks. In fact, in order to keep the story moving at a fast pace, typically rising heroes are incredibly lucky, and are almost always at the right place, at the right time, with the right knowledge to get the job done. However, if the writer just gives the character the things they need "for free," the audience won't feel very satisfied or happy, so there must always be something the character has to do to earn their good fortune. They will need to use their determination, quick thinking, bravery or talents to seize the prize, often going to incredible lengths to do so, but it will be their luck that gets them to the right spot first.

Also, no matter how mismatched they seem on the surface to the new world they're entering, it will always turn out that they and the new world are a natural fit for each other. They will always have some talent (and usually a cheat), which gives them a huge advantage over everyone else in this new world, and thus they'll be able to quickly rise and prosper in this new environment like it was made for them. (Because it was.) They just have to still put in the required amount of work to find what their advantage is and figure out how to use it properly to make this new world theirs.

...In That World's System...

As was covered in the chapter Things Successful Webfiction Stories Have in Common, there will almost always be a system that the character is a part of. This is especially needed in Rising Hero stories for a few reasons.

First, it's required because it gives the audience a simple map of the character's position in the grand scheme of things. A Rising Hero needs to rise, and the audience needs to feel them rising and understand what they're rising through- that's the system the world they're entering lives under. It's a simplified version of the type of systems that exist in our everyday world- social, financial, economic, educational, and more. But, in a Rising Hero story we pick a specific system and say "the hero is rising up through the ranks of [system X]" and then show them doing it.

Examples include:
- The lead is rising up through the ranks of student government.
- The lead is rising up through the ranks of alchemists.
- The lead is rising up through the ranks of cupcake decorators.
- The lead is rising up through the ranks of collectable card game players.

Whatever the world the character is entering, that world will be structured around a system or hierarchy which keeps it clearly organized and lets the audience easily see the character's position in it at any given time. This keeps the story simple and focused on what the character needs to do to improve their situation and position in the world.

Also, the audience being able to see where the character is located in the system makes it possible to give them a thrill as they watch the character quickly move through that system. Each goal post or accomplishment that lets them rise up brings with it new challenges and opportunities that will excite the audience with the possibilities. They wonder "what can this new ability do?" or "how will they defeat this new opponent?" and try to guess what will come, exciting themselves even more with their own ideas.

Not only that, systems also make it easier for the writer to organize the story and structure it in a simple way that also keeps the story on track. If there's a clear roadmap, then the writer can more easily plan where the character needs to go and figure out the most interesting paths to getting there. Characters rarely travel in a straight line because that would bore the audience, so instead the writer needs to come up with a way to get them to their destination while not looking like the character is just going from A to Z. This is much easier if the writer can see the overall situation and plan accordingly.

And last, of course, if the character is going to have a cheat, they need a system to cheat!

Whether they can control their cheat or not, their big advantage requires a system that it exploits in order to help the character. This was already covered in a previous chapter, but the right cheat needs to be matched with the right system in order to work. A genius talent for finances won't help the character trying to climb a social hierarchy inside a swimming club, but a talent for reading body language could make all the difference in the world.

...While Facing Many Challenges...

Obviously, if the lead character can just walk right to their goals, there isn't going to be much of a story, and there won't be any reason for the character to grow, adapt, improve, and learn. Humans learn through success and failure and this requires conflict to create situations where they have to push themselves and try new things.

Nothing good should come too easily for the main character, who should always have to be figuring out the best way to reach their goals. They might lack information, ability, resources, opportunities, or a host of other things that they'll need to acquire in order to keep moving forward on their path, and none of these comes without a cost of some kind.

At the same time, there are others on the same path as them, and those others think they're the main characters in this story and that the real main character is standing in their way. They have worked hard to get where they are (or at least feel they did), and have no intention of giving the lead their spots or letting themselves be passed by. They will work against the lead character and do their best to stop them and slow them down because they don't like being beaten any more than anyone else does.

And finally, there are still other characters who like the way things are right now and don't like the wave of change that the lead character is bringing with them. Loss aversion is an incredibly strong instinct in humans- we don't like to lose things we think are ours – and even characters who are fundamentally good people will react badly to others who want to take away what's theirs. Of course, the audience isn't there to see "good" people fight each other, so mostly it will be evil selfish characters who deserve to get stomped by the lead character that stand in their way.

Whatever the challenge, whenever the main character needs to move to the next phase of their journey, there should be a "level boss" (to borrow a video game phrase) or equivalent challenge they need to grow and overcome in order to move on to the next level.

...Until They Eventually Reach the Top...

The whole point of a rising hero story is for the main character to get to the top, so don't even think about any other result except the character winning in the end. The audience knows and expects this, and if you don't give it to them, they're going to be pretty angry. A Rising Hero story without the character reaching the top is like a romance story without a happily ever after ending, or a mystery story without the crime being solved- it defeats the whole purpose of the story and the reason the audience is reading it.

However, the end goal of the character winning isn't the interesting part of the story, the interesting part is what happens along the way. How the character reaches that goal is the thing that the audience reads the story to find out, and how all the dramatic questions and plotlines that pop up in the story get resolved. The audience also knows the hero is going to win, but they don't know the fates of the side characters they fall in love with along the way, and often that becomes just as important to them as the fate of the main character.

...And Change That New World.

Stories are about change, and that can be character change or setting change, but in Rising Hero stories while real character change is optional, there always needs to be setting change. The audience for Rising Hero stories is young people who want to feel they can change the world, and they want the lead characters in their stories to change the world as well.

Even if the main character never really changes except to get more powerful, or maybe matures a bit, there needs to be a sense that they are having a strong and clear effect on the world. This might be through changing the views of characters around them, overturning existing power structures, re-writing or destroying the dominant system in the story, adding new life and innovation to dying systems, or even just offering a new path forward for others, but there will always be some major change that will happen by the end of a Rising Hero story.

If the main character doesn't bring revolution with them, then the audience will feel cheated and unhappy. They want to see actions producing results, and the power that someone with the freedom to do anything has to re-shape the world. This is a dream, a fantasy that the audience has, and their fantasy needs not only a happy ending, but a meaningful one that shows that no matter who you are, you can remake the world in your own image.

THE RISING HERO OVERALL STORY STRUCTURE

You might think that to plan a rising hero story you just need to make a rough outline of the system that the character will be navigating and then use that to plan out your story. That would work fine, and if you want to do that you can. However, there are five basic steps of growth that most rising heroes go through on their journey to the top. These can be considered the five basic arcs that these types of stories go through, and together form a type of five-act structure that gives these epic stories shape.

- Arc One - Settling In
- Arc Two - Gathering Resources
- Arc Three – Growing Stronger
- Arc Four – Worldly Distractions
- Arc Five – Reaching the Top

Each of these steps represents a major phase in a rising hero's ascension, and organizing them like this gives you the minimum number of story arcs to consider when planning your own story. They are infinitely flexible in length (especially Arc Three and Arc Four, which are often broken down into many smaller story arcs), but knowing what goes where can only help your story planning and writing.

Let's look at each in more detail...

Story Arc One: Settling In

The character is forced out of their old world and into the new one. This will rarely be a choice the character themselves would have made because it involves a lot of big, scary change and a leap into the unknown. This sudden change is usually at or near the start of the story because it makes a strong dramatic hook to get the attention of the audience, and make them want to read on to see what's coming. In many serial webfiction stories, this shift into the new world often happens at the end of chapter one, after the character's old life was established.

Once they're forced out into that new world, the story shifts into the main character trying to get their bearings and settling into their new situation or environment. They usually encounter their very first ally, who will generally go on to become their guide and sidekick for the story, and may even be their long-term love interest. They will also encounter their first big challenge of the new world, which they will end up overcoming after a few difficult moments and will help them to gain confidence about their ability to succeed in this new world and/or accomplish their goals.

Story Arc Two: Gathering Resources

Now that they've gotten their bearings, the main character will start to work towards their main goal, and to do this they will need resources. They already have their guide character, but that won't be the only ally they'll need to accomplish their goals. So, they'll need to start connecting with more people who can help them to reach their goals. This is the point in the story where the writer introduces the larger world to the audience through the characters that the lead meets, and often shows just how big and challenging the whole situation is.

Some characters they meet won't become allies right away, and some might even be rivals or enemies at first, but later become allies. Either way, the character is introduced to the larger culture and society they are now a part of.

The main character will also need other resources- money, equipment, knowledge, connections, status, or anything else their goal requires, and they will spend this arc getting the minimum of those resources in place. Money is going to be essential, since food and shelter doesn't come cheap, but even if they have that covered, there will always be other things they'll need to even have a chance at reaching their goals.

This is also the arc where they will meet their first major challenge. The previous arc's final challenge was just a preview, but this arc's final challenge will be something that will take everything they've got to just barely beat. This will show the character (and audience) just how far the main character still has to go to really reach their goals, because there are even bigger challenges ahead and they barely beat this one.

Arc Three – Growing Stronger

With a new sense of purpose and their resources in place, the lead character will begin battling their way towards the top. The character is now actively involved in the competition and culture that surrounds their activity and this phase is about them meeting new allies and enemies and growing stronger in the process.

While this can be a single story arc, it is often actually a series of story arcs, with each phase representing something they have to go through to grow and move closer to their goal. How many arcs is up to the writer and the audience, and this is the phase that serial writers usually spend the most time on as this is where a lot of the "fun" parts of the story actually happen. If the audience is enjoying themselves, there isn't really a reason to move on from this phase until the audience starts to get restless or the writer themselves feels they want to move on.

Typically, this phase will end when the main character takes on a challenge which is so great that defeating it proves they're ready to start playing for the top spot in their system. Something that is so impressive that even the "gods" of this system have to start paying attention to them and considering whether the main character is a threat to their positions.

Arc Four – Worldly Distractions

The main character has now reached the upper levels of their system and has some fame among the people and cultures involved in it. If this was a sport, they've gone from the minor leagues to the major one, and are now playing at the highest professional level for their sport. They're at the bottom of the top, but they're still in the top ranks, and have earned the respect of the people above them for their accomplishments.

However, with the big leagues comes bigger problems, so they won't be in a position to relax and enjoy their new status. There are people below them who want their spot, there are people at the same level who don't want to be passed by, and there are people above them who might be starting to consider the main character a threat.

Also, since they've reached the higher ranks, they now have a greater responsibility to take care of their friends and allies. The people who supported them along the way also need their support, and the lead probably owes a whole lot of favors for help they got along the way that they now need to pay off since they're able. Mistakes they've made will also come back to haunt them, and they'll have some of their darkest personal days during this phase as they have to pay a price for their sins.

And, on top of all that, they have entered a new society, and will find it filled with traps and unseen dangers as they need to deal with the people who are already at the top. These people will try to get the main character to join their teams and offer the lead big rewards and opportunities in trade for becoming their followers. Often at the moment the character is their weakest, these people will offer their helping hand and say they can make all the trouble go away if the main character just "slows down" and stops where they are "for now."

Of course, accepting these offers will end the main character's journey to the top, and these are actually bribes to eliminate the main character from the competition. If they accept them, the story is effectively over, or at least they will quickly learn it was a mistake and now have to fight to break free of the trap they've put themselves in. Either way, this is their last temptation to give up, and a test of their will and spirit they must pass in order to move on to the final phase.

Like the strengthening phase, this phase is actually often many smaller arcs which happen after the main character shows they deserve a higher position. How long the writer wants to spend in this phase is up to them, and it can run as long as the writer and audience are both interested in exploring the highest levels of the story's central activity. However, try not to stay in this phase too long, because the audience can see the end in sight, and will feel they're being played if you delay the final conflict too much.

Arc Five – Reaching the Top

With their will forged in the hottest fires of the worldly distractions phase, the main character moves into the final conflict stage. This is where they face the enemy at the top of the food chain in a battle which only one of them can survive. They are no longer the person they were when they started out, and the world is no longer the place it was either, having changed with their rise.

Now, they face the one who most wants to keep the old world from changing and to maintain things the way they were. This character is usually a darker version of the hero themselves, a twisted mirror image of the lead who followed a similar path, but chose to do it the wrong way. They committed some sin along the way that the main character avoided thanks to their allies or willpower, and this sin twisted their character and has left them flawed. They are now ruled by a lust for power, greed, or revenge, and this makes them and their position unstable.

Of course, facing this final opponent won't be easy. The main character's mistakes will still cause them problems, and it will take all the skills, allies and resources they gained along the way to help them finally overcome their last opponent. They will have to prove they deserve to be the new king in a real display of their ability, and give everything they've got to win their final challenge.

Allies will die, tragedies may happen, and promises may be broken, but in the end, they will be victorious and be able to claim their prize. Often this includes the main love interest (or interests, depending on the story and setting) and a clear sense that the world is now a different place with them in charge. They have the respect, admiration, and power they always dreamed of, and the world is a better place for it.

As a writer, just remember to tie in the hero's end accomplishments with things they did along the way, so it feels like they came full circle and earned their spot at the top. It's also better to have a brief epilogue after the final victory to answer any remaining major story questions and then end the story fairly quickly. The audience wants a sense that everything is going to go well for the future and that a new balanced order has been restored, so give it to them and move on to your next story.

OTHER APPROACHES TO PLANNING RISING HERO STORIES

Another way a writer can plan out their Overall Story for a Rising Hero plot is to simply look at the procedural steps involved in whatever goal the character is trying to achieve and use those as a guide (whether the story itself is a Rising Hero story or not). This is useful for any kind of story, and can be broken down into five basic approaches: the step approach, the level approach, the status approach, the cluster approach, and the acquisition approach.

The Step Approach

In most stories, the main character is almost always working towards a relatable goal that has a series of steps involved with accomplishing it. This is a great advantage for the writer, since that means there is already a pre-defined set of steps to learning that skill or gaining that knowledge out there, and the writer can use those as a guide. It doesn't matter whether the topic is playing Poker or becoming a Politician, there are guidebooks and videos out there to teach you the steps you need to know to master any activity. The writer just needs to break those steps down into story arcs (or chapters), and use those as a guide for what happens in each of those parts of the story.

In Rising Hero stories which are set in fantasy situations, you're doing much the same thing, but since the story often isn't rooted as deeply in the real-world the writer is free to come up with their own steps instead of using pre-existing ones. That said, there are great advantages to using real-world steps for somewhat related fictional subjects, including that it makes the character's journey much more realistic and relatable for the reader. Not only that, it makes the writer's job easier as well, since they're not forced to re-invent the wheel.

So, for example, if you're writing about a character learning magical combat spells, you could base their learning steps off the steps involved in learning martial arts moves, or maybe coding computers, or perhaps in learning to play an instrument. Each of these has clear steps, and while you might need to add a few more to include magical training or modify the steps, the point is that it makes your progression more natural and adds depth to your story.

The Level Approach

Since the modern world is inundated with video games of all kinds, readers are naturally familiar with the concept of characters having a ranked level at an activity, and this goes back to roleplaying games like *Dungeons and Dragons*, where the characters had numbered levels to represent their advancement in the game world, and it spread from there to computer games and fighting games. Therefore, it's a natural transition for characters in fantasy Rising Hero stories to have levels as well, and you can use these to help rank your characters in their world.

Of course, numbers (or other ranking systems like colors, crystals, metals, etc.) don't actually mean much to you or the reader unless you sit down and quantify them. What can a Rank 5 Magical Fighter do that a Rank 1 Magical Fighter can't? You're best to decide what the range of ranks is (say 1-50, or 1-500) and then decide what the top rank can do and the bottom rank can do, and figure out the steps in between. You don't have to quantify all the steps, but make notes about what happens on the major ones ("When they reach Level 14, they can learn a second magical element.") and what ones will result in the character's change of social status as well. (Rank 1-5 is newbie, rank 6-10 is Learner, rank 11-15 is Journeyman, etc.) Also, think about the difficulty and requirements to advance between levels as well because some level based systems become progressively harder to advance in the higher you go (often requiring more time/experience to move up to the next level), and there may be special things the character must do to move between rank categories (You must make your own magical staff to progress from Newbie to Learner, for example.)

Levels in Rising Hero story also serve another purpose- they're instant drama creators. When the audience can clearly see the level difference between a character and their opponent, it's a fast way to create tension. Maybe the main character can overcome a five-level gap, but could they overcome a 10-level gap or a 50-level gap? No way! In those situations, the main character and the audience knows that combat just isn't an option, and it creates instant tension. Just be careful not to overuse this trick too much, or the audience will get tired of it.

Obviously, you might think that the level approach doesn't apply to more realistic stories, after all, we don't have ranked levels in real life activities, right? However, this isn't entirely true. In the ancient board game of Go, players have roughly 39 ranked levels (30 learner levels and 9 master ones), and this learner/master level system is also used in East Asian martial arts as well. (They got it from Go.) Likewise, there are some other activities out there where players or participants have ranked levels, including games, in education, and some organizations. So, using levels to measure a character's progress in a story is completely do-able even in some real-life situations.

However, outside of those fairly specific situations, level systems don't work well for realistic stories overall, and aren't a good way to structure progression. So, most writers aren't advised to use this type of system unless it really fits.

The Status Approach

A third way to structure a character's progression is based on the character's status within the society or culture that surrounds their activity. In this approach, the character must meet certain requirements to move on to the next status rank, which will have a name instead of a number like in the level system. These requirements often come in the form of skills, experience, time, social/political favor, or accomplishments, and as a result sometimes combine with the Step Approach.

For example, maybe the character needs to learn a certain ten skills to go from Dishwasher to Assistant Cook, and so a whole story arc could be constructed around the learning of some of those skills. Or perhaps a character needs to log a certain amount of time on the job to go from Trainee to Rookie, and one or more arcs can be about the character's "Trainee" phase, and then the following one(s) will be about their "Rookie" phase, and so on. A political character might need to win a certain number of elections, or a certain size of constituency to move up in rank, and that would be the structure for their arcs.

And so on.

As you can see, this is often the real-world equivalent of the Level Approach, but tends to work better for realistic stories because it also includes natural requirements to move between levels. The only downside is that you have to teach the audience what those ranks mean and the requirements that go with them, and then a use a system that the audience will remember. But, in a realistic story teaching about real-world things is often half the point, so that usually isn't an issue.

Where things get trickier is with Rising Hero stories, but even there you can use real-world models to help guide your progressions. For example, you could use an Apprentice> Craftsman> Master progression like the trades of Bakers, Carpenters and Masons traditionally used, but expand it out to include steps like Apprentice> Novice> Learner> High Learner> Journeyman> Master> Grand Master. Or, not expand it at all, and just have the character spend a certain phase of their story as an Apprentice then move to Craftsman at the halfway point, and then become a Master at the end.

The only issue here is that audiences like to see progression, and if you use large steps or have long periods with no progression, the audience may feel like the story isn't advancing, which isn't good for a Rising Hero story. Also, if you choose not to use a real-world model, and to create your own terms for the different status ranks, you need to make sure they're ones the reader can easily follow and understand without constantly checking a chart. (One of the advantages of numbered ranks.) One tip here is to use a ranking system that the reader knows and modify it a bit into a status system. For example, audiences know the relative ranked values of common metals (Copper> Silver> Gold> Platinum) and those could be worked into the names. (So, a Copper Apprentice ranks lower than a Silver Apprentice, and that's obvious to almost all readers.)

(See Conquest Stories for more details about the Status Approach)

The Cluster Approach

The second last method for structuring a story around progression is one where the author clusters skills or attributes to be learned based on the needs of the story at that point rather than any real-world progression system. For example, the character is going through a social arc, so they must learn social skills, or a wilderness arc needs survival skills. These may or may not be building toward a greater test of ability at the end of the arcs, but it does allow a grouping of the types of skills needed based on story needs.

Also, the writer can base these clusters of skills off abstract things like stages of life or spiritual enlightenment, or use them to reflect the story's Thematic Statement by working through examples or counter-examples of the greater point they're trying to make. If you're arguing that characters should have self-confidence to be successful in life, for example, you could structure your story arcs around what you think are the steps the character needs to go through to find that self-confidence. (Which may or may not involve some research into human psychology.)

Of course, this method has the dis-advantage that you can't really use it well to rank the character among their peers, or to show clear progression in a quantified way. The audience might vaguely understand the progression, but it likely won't be as exciting or visceral as you might want a Rising Hero story to actually be unless you combine it with one of the other methods in some way.

The Acquisition Approach

This is about a story where the main character's goal is to collect objects, people, titles, or anything else that involves a clear progression towards having a complete set. The key here is that the main character's final goal can only be completed if they have a total set of something, and the progression is represented by completeness of that set. This approach is especially good for Rising Hero stories where the main character is not changing much beyond getting more skilled or powerful, so making the focus on some other exterior kind of progression keeps it simple. In addition, this also naturally creates plots as different things being assembled will have different circumstances that go with each of them.

One issue with Acquisition stories that writers should be aware of, though, is that you need to establish the goal right from the start, and if you have too many things you need to assemble the story might end up being too long and run out of energy. Or, on the other hand, if you have too few things to assemble the story might be over faster than you'd like because the audience wants progression, and if you slow down the progression too much it might result in audience frustration.

A simple way to fix this, however, is to combine the Acquisition approach with one of the others, so that the character(s) are progressing in different ways and the audience feels both moving forward. This can allow the audience to accept slower progress on the acquisitions front while enjoying the lead characters gaining strength or ranks. But, as the writer, you will still need to decide which one you're actually structuring the story around from the start, with the other being more there for flavor and audience fun.

In the end, the key to using progression as a guide for story structure is to just remember everything learned in life involves beginner, intermediate, veteran and mastery phases. The types of stories you'll find using a Rising Hero plot are no different, and these make for great guides when planning and plotting your long-term stories.

RISING HERO SETTINGS

These stories can be set anywhere there's a system in place. From stories set in fantasy kingdoms with their nobility systems and magic systems, to modern schools with their social pecking orders and academic rankings. As long as there's a hierarchy-based system with a bottom and top for the main character to climb, and a culture which has built up around it, then it can be used as the core of a rising hero story.

And, the culture part is important.

Human beings naturally create communities with others who they share common interests with, and once you have a focus that creates both a common interest you will quickly get a subculture growing around that common interest. For example, let's say you decide to start playing chess, and after a few rounds on the computer, you want to try it live against other people, so you put up an ad at your local library. A couple people answer your ad, so you meet up at the library and play, and the group of you have a good time. Soon, you're meeting to play chess on a regular basis.

Bang! You are now part of a local community of chess players, whether you're officially organized or not.

Also, as you play and get to know each other, you will develop relationships with those people, and slowly a connection will form between you. Chess is the thing that brought you together, but that common connection has now created a shared subculture with you and the other members of the chess group.

But chess is also a competitive game with winners and losers and different rankings of skill and ability, and given the competitive nature of people, it's only natural to want to know who is better at the game your group loves, so you begin tracking your games and assigning wins and losses.

Now you have a group with a ranked hierarchy, from best player to worst player.

So, you can see that if there is an activity which involves a ranking system of some kind, then there will be a culture or subculture which has formed around it. The size of the community can be a few people, or millions, but whenever you have an activity that people focus their lives on, and which acts as part of their identity, there will be a subculture that exists between those people.

And, the bigger and more attention that subculture gets, the more it will become tied to the identity of the people involved with it. A few friends who play chess at the local library won't tie their whole personal identities to being chess players, but someone who is dedicated enough to be involved with national or internationally ranked chess competitions might. Especially once people start making money from something, it no longer becomes a hobby, and starts to become their passion, their identity, or even their career.

Also, if an activity is popular enough, and starts to generate enough money and interest, then it won't just have a subculture of people who are directly involved in that activity, but also a subculture of people who are fans of that activity. There will be the inner circle of the participants, and the outer circles of the audience- fandom, merchandisers, related businesses, media coverage.

Thus, when a character in a Rising Hero story joins an activity, they're not just joining a sport, or hobby, or school, or business, or martial arts tradition, they're joining a whole subculture of players and fans which exists around that activity. If you want to really bring your stories to life, take some time to think about not just the culture that the main characters are involved in, but the other cultures of the setting which might be connected to it as well.

RISING HERO FINAL THOUGHTS

Rising Hero stories are a core part of young adult fiction, and something that naturally connects well with young people, thus isn't no surprise that they're a staple of webfiction as well. They also come in many forms, and the next few chapters are mostly other story types that combine with the Rising Hero plot to create different stories.

However, at its core, a Rising Hero story is always about one thing- rising through the ranks. It's about how one young person navigated dangerous waters to find their perfect future, and the things it took for them to get there. It's a story of connection, where their efforts brought them friends and allies, and a story of growth, where they grew in confidence and ability as they worked hard to achieve their dreams.

And, even though they might have a few shortcuts or tricks that help them get where they're going, watching them go from the bottom to the top is a thrilling ride that keeps the audience coming back for more again and again.

As you go through this book, and plan your own stories, always keep the Rising Hero story in mind, and how you can mix it with your own creativity to produce your own rising hero story- one where a writer rises to the top of their field.

Good luck!

FANTASY WEBFICTION

If there is a genre which is hard to nail down, it's fantasy.

On the surface, it seems very simple. Fantasy is any story with magic in it, right?

However, that definition fails to cover a lot of types of non-magical stories which are still very much fantasy. And, it has the added wrinkle that you also need to define what magic is to make that concept of fantasy work, and not everyone agrees what magic is.

For some other people, and perhaps the general public, the definition of fantasy is even simpler- it's *Dungeons and Dragons*, not as experienced through playing that tabletop roleplaying game, but through its novel, video game, and television descendants. *The Wheel of Time, World of Warcraft, Game of Thrones,* and countless other popular fantasy stories which built on the *Lord of the Rings/Dungeons and Dragons* setting and ideas have become a natural part of popular culture to the point where that pseudo-medieval-with-magic-and-monsters setting is now the default setting in people's minds when they picture fantasy stories.

But, of course, that definition is even worse, as it overlooks everything from *Alice in Wonderland*, to *Harry Potter*, to Chinese *xianxia* stories set in a China that never was. Therefore, it limits what fantasy is more than helps us to understand it.

So, in the interest of trying to be inclusive rather than exclusive, and cover the many possible types of fantasy which exist in a broad blanket definition, here's how this book is going to define it:

Fantasy is any story which includes unreal characters, unreal situations, unreal settings, or any combination of those three elements.

So...

If a minotaur becomes a Wall Street Banker in our very real world, it's fantasy.

If two senior citizens switch bodies for a day, it's fantasy.

If a schoolgirl finds herself on the Islands of Venus fighting to save the Cloud People, it's fantasy.

The world "unreal" in this case refers to something which can't (or shouldn't) happen in our reality as we understand it, and the above is a pretty wide definition, but using it allows for a lot more creativity. Magic (which would come under "unreal situations") becomes optional, and the focus of the story can be on alternative characters or settings. Be they a setting like *Harry Potter* (which includes all three, but not in the standard *D&D* sort of way), or alternate dimensions/realities where everything is the same world we know but the people are different, or even characters going on road trips to Heaven or Hell.

Using this approach allows us to divide up the most important elements of fantasy without limiting them to any particular setting or style, and to think about fantasy in different ways. For example, how "unreal" that element is can also vary by the story. An "unreal" setting can range from one which is a historically accurate version of ancient Sumaria, but which changes the political system or culture in some small way, to dreamlike settings where even the laws of nature no longer apply. Unreal characters can range from a girl with cat ears to Godzilla-like dragons, and such beings may be regarded as normal everyday things to see, or as horrific natural disasters in their appearance. Unreal situations might range from a painting which cries blood to a battle between wizard armies casting thousands of spells per second at each other.

It's all fantasy, but by playing with what elements are unreal, and how unreal they are, you can come up with different combinations and not be limited to the traditional *D&D* type of fantasy. Although, it should be noted that *D&D* style fantasy itself also plays with those elements, creating things like high fantasy (where there is lots of magic/unreal situations) or low fantasy (where magic is rare or unknown) and settings where non-human races are the norm or where humans are the only sentients in the place. It's all up to the writer to decide what unreal story elements they want to push and which ones they'd rather leave alone.

And this, leads to perhaps the most important thing for writers to remember when they're writing any kind of fantastic fiction (or science fiction)...

THE BIG IDEA PRINCIPAL

There is an old writer's truism that says, "Each story can only have one big idea."

What this means is that a general audience will accept one really big change from what they're used to, and the things that spin off from that big change, but anything more than that will push the audience's suspension of disbelief and risks leaving them unsettled or confused. So, while the audience might accept superpowers in a modern-day setting, they'll have a harder time accepting superpowers and magic together. Magic is fine in a fantasy setting, but magic and aliens is a harder sell for a general audience.

And that's the key, a general audience.

Because the Big Idea Principle isn't based off reality, it's based off what the audience is used to.

So, if the audience isn't used to superpowers, then having a character with the powers and abilities of a spider is a pretty big idea and the writer should probably stop with having people with strange and amazing abilities. BUT, if the audience has already seen many movies about superpowered characters, then that becomes normal to them, and the author is free to try adding another big idea like aliens or magic to the mix without it confusing or upsetting the audience.

It's all about what's familiar to the audience.

To apply this to fantasy, since the general audience already knows the basic concepts of what a fantasy setting is like from popular culture (*D&D*), then that frees up writers to try new ideas like having a main character who is a monster, or having a setting where the rules work like a video game, or having characters able to grow in spiritual strength and power. These can work because the writer's big idea isn't a fantasy setting or magic, but how that fantasy setting is different from the standard one.

But, if the writer were to try to do that with a unique fantasy setting the audience isn't familiar with already, then those same creative and original big ideas might be too much for some audience members to accept or get into. So, while you could do a story in a setting where the laws of physics worked differently in a "generic" fantasy setting without much trouble, if you tried to do the same story in a setting based on African mythology that's completely new to most of the audience, then it might not work so well.

The simple truth is people are lazy thinkers, especially when it comes to stories they're reading for fun, and the more you ask them to think about and the more mental work you ask them to do, the less they're going to enjoy it. So, a single "big idea" is fine and fun and interesting, but two big ideas becomes work, and three big ideas becomes more trouble than it's worth for a lot of the audience. This is one of the reasons why fantasy as a genre is stuck in *D&D* type settings- the audience is happy there and doesn't want to leave because it's familiar to them. It's also why the original fantasy settings that many authors spend years crafting will go largely ignored or be outright shunned by the general reading audience- unless the writer can give the audience a really compelling reason why learning about all this setting stuff is worth it, then they're not interested.

Now, before those of you who are world-builders despair completely, there are three ways you can get an audience to accept new and unfamiliar sets of big ideas (like you can find in an original setting): visuals, acclimatization, and grounding the focus.

First, if a story is presented visually (like a video, comic book, or illustrated story) then you can get the audience to accept a lot more than you can if they're reading plain text. This is because (hopefully) the visuals are doing a lot of the work of explaining the big ideas in a clear and simple way, and this overcomes a lot of the resistance on the part of readers. For example, Japanese manga are often filled with strange new settings and weird ideas, but non-Japanese audiences still adore them because the best Japanese manga creators present their ideas in a simple visual way designed to make the audience understand them clearly.

Of course, those same manga creators also make great use of acclimatization- getting the audience used to something before introducing something else. They don't hit their audiences with ten different big ideas at once and instead introduce the big ideas as slowly as possible to let the audience get used to each one before adding anything else. For example, if the story is about time-travelling superpowered ninjas from space who fight aliens and demons, they'd start with superpowered ninjas (since the Japanese audience is already familiar with ninjas they don't count as a big idea, but superpowered ones might), then they'd introduce that they're fighting demons. Then, it would be revealed that the ninja clans actually descended from aliens who came to protect the Earth. And finally, the demons would be revealed to be time- travelling aliens, which the ninja might have to travel through time to stop.

It's still quite a bit to swallow, even presented that way, but before you scoff too much at those wacky Japanese, all of those elements (except ninjas) have been introduced into the Marvel Cinematic Universe over a period of more than twenty films, and you probably didn't bat an eye when the Marvel movies did it. Why? Because they did it slowly and let you get acclimatized as they went.

But the Marvel movie gurus also did one more thing- in each movie they grounded their focus.

Every Marvel film's hero starts with the character in the "real" world and then slowly takes them out of that world and into the more fantastic one. Tony Stark is a regular businessman who invents incredible powered armor. Peter Parker is a typical high school nerd who gets bit by a radioactive spider. Even Thor starts as a young man kicked out of his family home by his father and sent to live in a small typical midwestern town. These are "real" people with real people's problems and situations that slowly become extraordinary as the films progress, which is something Marvel Comics always credited their success as a company to.

By grounding the story in our world at the beginning and then slowly expanding out to something incredible, they allowed the audience to get used to the amazing things they were going to experience, and kept the story about a relatable character the audience could empathize with. By doing it visually in comics and movies, they were also able to take advantage of the power of visual mediums to give the audience something new with as little effort required as possible. And obviously, it worked pretty well for them!

So, when you're planning your stories, always remember the Big Idea Principal-the more you're going to deviate from what the audience accepts, the harder it's going to be to get them to accept it, and each big idea you add makes this twice as hard to write well.

DIFFERENT CULTURAL VIEWS OF FANTASY

Without a doubt, fantasy is the single most popular genre of webfiction there is globally. Only Romance can compete with it, and even then, fantasy tends to get the edge in some markets. Given the genre's universal and historical appeal, this is hardly surprising. Fantasy stories appeal to men and women, young and old, and people of every background. For modern people especially, there is a dreamlike desire to imagine a simpler world that never was, and how our lives might be better or easier when magic can solve so many of life's problems.

However, while the appeal of fantasy might be universal, different cultures have their own spin on not just what fantasy is, but also what they like to get from their fantasy stories. Americans, Europeans, Japanese and Chinese all have different takes on the fantasy genre, and while there is a lot of common ideas and crossover, it's important to understand what makes each tick.

American Fantasy

The American fantasy genre as it exists today is a hybrid of the works of J.R.R. Tolkien combined with the Western genre, as represented by the tabletop roleplaying game *Dungeons and Dragons*, and the many video games that followed and popularized *D&Ds* approach. It is built around stories set in a pseudo-middle ages/renaissance European-ish world filled with magic and mystical creatures. Unlike real Europe, however, the land in American fantasy is not settled and organized, but a dangerous place filled with hostile creatures and untrustworthy rival races. The land is ancient but empty, the previous inhabitants having fallen from grace, and now it is up to the adventurers to help change that. American fantasy is about Man vs. Nature, and the setting is a dangerous place to be conquered and wrestled into obedience with bravery and determination.

American fantasy is about living the American Dream- using your guts, skill and determination to carve your place out of the world and make yourself into a success. American fantasy heroes tend to be the best at what they do, being combinations of fighting skill and brains, and their stories are epic ones where they use those talents to bring order to a chaotic land. Destiny is on their side, and the world is theirs to be taken if only they have the guts to do it.

European Fantasy

The European fantasy genre varies a lot by country, and like the American one shares a huge amount of influence from Tolkien. However, unlike the American one which is focused on a hero who conquers the land, European fantasy is more social and historical. The Europeans have an actual time when their countries resembled the modern fantasy setting, and can look back at how their cultures were in real history. But, more importantly, unlike the Terra Nova of America, Europe has been filled with people for thousands of years, all of them packed together and interacting with each other. European society has classes, prejudices, traditions, and other social forces which affect them and make them part of a social network that isn't easy to break out of.

Thus, European fantasy is about Man vs. Man, and Man vs. Society, where the individual must navigate inside a world that already exists, and advance inside the existing power structures. There are few monsters, and those that exist are special cases or come from the outside, because the real enemy is almost always other people. This isn't to say they don't have magic, ancient civilizations, and lots of adventure, they do, but it's always rooted in a world that has already got someone living there and is about navigating existing structures instead of finding new ones.

This tends to give European fantasy a much more realistic and grittier feel than Americans are used to. Europeans draw from their own history and cultures, and not some idealized versions of what they might be like, and they understand how much a role society and social connections play in our lives. In European fantasy, actions have social consequences, and the main character is rarely the epic hero but just a slightly above average character using luck and brains to get ahead.

Japanese Fantasy

An interesting part about Japanese fantasy stories is that they don't usually take place in old Japan. Maybe this is because of the true escapist nature of Japanese fantasy, but more likely it's because the Japanese know their own history so well it doesn't leave a lot of room to fantasize it. (And makes telling stories set in old Japan a lot of hard research work.) Also, most of their ideas about fantasy come from video games like *Dragon Quest* and the early *Final Fantasy* titles, which are based on *Dungeons and Dragons*. So, as a result, they mainly write stories set in alternate worlds, usually the standard pseudo-European one, with the occasional Japanese-style fantasy setting thrown in.

Like Europeans, however, the Japanese idea of fantasy is still a social one. Their fantasy worlds are populated places, and the stories usually revolve around characters in conflict with other characters as opposed to monsters or the land. Unlike Europeans, Japanese fantasy tends to be very light and escapist, with a strong "video game" version of reality that isn't realistic at all. There are exceptions, but in most Japanese fantasy stories, the setting is just a backdrop for the characters to have their dramas in front of, and has little influence on the characters and plot.

How do Japanese fantasy kingdoms work? The usual answer is "who cares, as long as it's interesting!" and the story goes on from there. The main character will also usually be extremely powerful, to the point of being overpowered, and always have some trick up their sleeve which gets them out of trouble and helps them win the day.

Chinese Fantasy

Chinese literature includes some of the oldest fantasy novels in the world- *Journey to the West* (aka *The Monkey King*), and *The Water Margin*. The first is an epic mythological tale about a priest and some gods on a quest who battle demon lords, and the second is a collection of rough and ready tales about rogues, pirates and warriors who live on society's fringes. In a lot of ways, these two books still continue to symbolize Chinese fantasy, although how they symbolize it has changed over time.

For most of the 20th century, *The Water Margin* would be the better example, as serialized Chinese wuxia adventure novels filled with wandering swordsmen, kung fu masters, and rogues dominated the culture. These apolitical heroes wandered the land, righted wrongs, protected Chinese culture from invaders, and navigated endless wars between different sects and secret societies. However, thanks in large part to video games and cheaper special effects, the epic mythological approach of *Journey to the West* has now become the norm, with godlike heroes who smash mountains and conquer multiple realities without a second thought.

Likely, this change also comes from the shift in Chinese culture as well. In the 20th century, China was undergoing many political and social upheavals, and the stories tended to be more low-key and adventurous. On the other hand, modern China is a social, economic, and cultural powerhouse, and Chinese society is bursting with energy and potential. Young Chinese dream of rising to the top and seizing power, and their heroes reflect that- an optimistic view that they can conquer the world and remake themselves into something greater.

As a result, Chinese love stories about rising heroes who conquer the world with their awesomeness, and while they might start small, they soon dwarf their Japanese counterparts in power. Unlike the Japanese, Chinese fantasy stories are usually set in fantastic versions of old China, and they only borrow from American fantasy without copying it wholesale. Like the Japanese, however, the settings in Chinese fantasy are still mostly backdrops and only play a minor role in the stories of conflicts between characters and groups. The characters are still part of social webs, and while they do transcend many of these limitations as they rise in power, they are still motivated by duty and personal ideas of honor.

So, as you can see, each culture has their own very different approaches to the fantasy genre. Naturally, there are exceptions, for example the Chinese do have a large number of stories set in *D&D* type settings as well, but they're dwarfed by pseudo-Chinese settings. Similarly, American fantasy has writers like George R.R. Martin who do more politically and socially-oriented fantasy, but even they lean heavily on the land as focus of the story.

Actually, if there is anything that perfectly epitomizes the cultural differences in fantasy, it is the humble universal fantasy creature called The Orc. This typical fantasy monster has a very different role in each of the cultures, which symbolizes their outlooks nicely. In American fantasy, the Orc represents the wild natives of the cowboy myth who raid civilization and stand in the way of civilizing the untamed land. In European fantasy, the Orc is the expression of loss of social control, a member of a savage horde from the East which threatens to crush civilization. In Japanese fantasy, the Orc is a target spontaneously generated by the environment which has 10 hit points and is there to help the character level up so they can defeat bigger foes and do greater deeds. Finally, in Chinese fantasy, there are no Orcs because they're not part of Chinese culture, but if there were, they'd make great servants for building the main character's new palace.

REALISM IN FANTASY WEBFICTION

To get it right out of the way, fantasy in webfiction is most often "fun fantasy," where the characters live in fantasy worlds that are really just peaceful modern societies with a fantasy overlay. Few starve in the streets (except where evil overlords rule) and most people live a happy semi-agrarian existence. For westerners, it's roughly medieval or renaissance Europe with lower population, a weaker church, less starving peasants, and magic. For those in the East, it's a version of China that never was, but is still for the most part a happy agrarian land where an Emperor rules instead of a bunch of kings.

There are a few reasons for this, the first (and most important) being that this is a commonly accepted version of fantasy settings that has become part of our global culture thanks to books, movies, television series, comic books, and (most importantly) video games. This is a setting that the audience knows, is familiar with, and accepts without question. It is also one the author probably knows as well, and so it requires minimal effort and research on the part of the writer. You don't have to explain what fantasy is, you just have to explain what makes this particular fantasy setting special.

Another reason why more realistic fantasy is rare in webfiction is that nobody wants to read about starving peasants or characters who bathe once a year while dying of the flu. Life for most of human history was short, nasty and brutish, and not fun to read about at all, so it doesn't make for good escapist reading. On top of that, it takes a lot of research to get realistic fantasy right, and few are willing to deal with the work involved (or the time it takes) to understand how people really lived in more primitive times.

And finally, most writers and audiences don't really care much about the setting anyways, except as a backdrop for cool characters to do cool things, and epic adventures to play out. If you don't agree, try starting your next epic fantasy story with five, ten or fifteen pages of setting material and see how well that works for you. If you have an editor, the first thing they'll do is rip all that out, because they know that audiences will drop that book by the second or third page and want a refund. Setting that enables interesting stories is okay, setting that gets in the way of character and story is deadly.

So, the issue is not how realistic to make your fantasy setting, but how gritty.

Grittiness means that it has elements of realism to it, usually harsh realism, but only pieces, not the whole thing. (Characters dying of cholera mid-story gets in the way.) Just like life in the modern first world has good places and bad, fantasy settings can have their dark and light sides, and grittiness represents which of those you intend to focus on.

How gritty or fun you want the setting to be is up to you, but a good rule of thumb is that audiences looking for some light fun don't like gritty very much, and that's most readers. You do get some exceptions, like *A Song of Ice and Fire* (*Game of Thrones*), but you might also notice that despite the success of that series, not a lot of other gritty fantasy is making the top ten bestseller lists. And even then, *Ice and Fire* is a deconstructionist fantasy story which purposely does the opposite of most other fantasy stories. It's like sushi – a nice change of pace, but it doesn't mean everyone wants a steady diet of it.

That said, if gritty fantasy is your thing, write away. You might be able to make it work when so many others have failed.

Levels of Fantasy

Fantasy stories are typically stories set in a pseudo-historical setting with magic, and the key isn't the fake historical setting, but the magic. Magic tends to dominate a fantasy story, and determines how different that setting is from our own history, so it's no surprise that fantasy stories are generally categorized into one of three levels based on how much magic is in them.

Low Fantasy – These are stories set in a more realistic setting where there is some magic, but not enough to keep the setting from resembling our own past. The magic in these worlds is usually invisible, subtle, and mysterious, and nobody is casting fireballs or flying. Instead, the magic here is often a dark power that is feared and not well understood, it is mostly used by villains and not for good purposes. These settings are best for dramas, romances, and swashbuckling stories where human skill and daring rules instead of magical power. Or alternately, they can be the settings of horror stories or darker stories, where mere mortals must face black sorcery with only their faith and wits to protect them.

High Fantasy – This is the level most people think of when they think of fantasy. This is where *The Lord of the Rings*, *Dungeons and Dragons*, and so many other stories and settings sit, where magic is an ever-present force in the world. This setting usually only superficially resembles our own, and magic has often replaced things like medicine and science to allow for a quality of life that is closer to our own than might otherwise be possible. Stories in these settings are epic by default, and usually involve the magical elements that make the world special.

Mythological – Mythological settings are where gods and men meet and sometimes humans can become gods themselves. There is so much magic it isn't special anymore, but a normal force in the world, and the world barely resembles our own because of how much magic has warped it. Often high-level characters travel through realms, worlds and dimensions with ease, and everything is so much bigger and more epic than normal. Flying whales the size of mountains ply the skies with cities on their backs, single fighters take on millions of enemy soldiers, and emperors rule thousands of years from their world-sized palaces. Ironically though, because everything is magic, and nothing is special, most of the stories are back to dramas and about the interactions of powerful individuals and families.

Generally speaking, Europeans tend to prefer low fantasy, Americans like high fantasy, the Japanese like high fantasy, and the Chinese like a mix of the two (wuxia tends to be at the lower end of high fantasy while xianxia cultivation stories tend to be at the lower end of Mythological.) These are just general preferences, of course, and you can find all kinds of fantasy in every market.

WRITING FANTASY MAGIC

If there is one single defining element of Fantasy as a genre, it is of course magic. But what IS magic? And how do you differentiate it from science?

Well, one way to look at magic comes from Don Chisholm, who defined it as a "force that people can control, but never totally understand." In other words, he sees magic as a power that characters in a story are able to use to one degree or another, but don't have a clear understanding of why it works or where it comes from. The characters might understand the principles behind it, methods of controlling it, or the source, but usually not all three- there is always something mysterious to the characters about it.

So, in most cases, a magic user might know how to cast a spell, and what the different parts of a spell incantation do, but they don't know exactly why it works or where the magic is coming from. Or, if they're a follower of a god who is merely borrowing their deity's power, they roughly know the source of the magic (the god), and the principles behind it (a higher being taking action), but they don't really have any more control over it than the god gives them. (Prayer.)

But what if the characters do completely understand all three parts- principles, control and source?

Then it really isn't "magic" anymore, it's an alternate form of technology.

With this in mind, one of the best views on how magic and story interact comes from fantasy writer Brandon Sanderson, who in a 2007 essay called "Sanderson's First Law" discussed how magic systems could be ranked on a spectrum between being "hard" and "soft." The whole essay is free online on his website (and is recommended reading), but to summarize, a hard magic system is one where there are clearly defined rules for how magic works which are consistent and understandable by the audience. Examples of these sorts of systems would be the magic found in the TV series *Avatar: The Last Airbender*, the anime *Full Metal Alchemist*, Sanderson's own books like *Mistborn*, and most *D&D* style fantasy RPG magic systems. In these stories, there are clear rules what magic (or at least the magic wielded by the individual characters) can and can't do, and at the far extreme it functions almost as a form of mystical science where consistent actions produce consistent results every time.

At the other end, we have soft magic systems, where magic is inconsistent, unreliable, and unknowable by the characters or audience. In these systems, there are no clear rules for why magic works or why it does what it does, and in theory it could do anything just so long as the plot requires it. Usually in these stories, it's wielded by support characters, or based around objects or rituals which seem to work but nobody understands why. The classic example of this are the wizards in *The Lord of the Rings* like Gandalf, who has magical powers that only he understands and which seem neither consistent or reliable. Magic in fairy tales and mythological stories also tends to be pretty soft, as there are no real rules to it for the audience to predict how it could be used.

So, in short, hard systems have clearly defined rules, while soft systems have no apparent rules at all. But it is a spectrum, so there are systems which have some consistent rules under some circumstances, but few to none under other circumstances (like *Harry Potter*) that fall in the middle, and other systems which are hard-ish (like *Naruto*), and soft-er (like *Discworld*). It all depends on how consistent and reliable the writer wants to be with magic in their setting.

And this consistency is important because of Sanderson's First Law:

"An author's ability to solve conflict with magic is DIRECTLY PROPORTIONAL to how well the reader understands said magic."

Or, in other words, if the reader understands the rules of the magic and when it can and can't be used, you can use it to solve story problems like any other tool. On the other hand, if magic can do anything, then using it to solve story problems becomes cheating and the writer waving away the problems by saying "and it's fixed!" So, if the reader understands when fire magic can be used and when it can't, then it's okay to have the fire mage use it to get out of problems because there are consistent rules to how it works. On the flipside, if the reader has no idea when magic can be used and when it can't, or how powerful it is, having the fire mage suddenly defeat an army by blowing them all up is impressive, but feels like a cheat. Why didn't he do that earlier when they were ambushed by goblins?

If the writer wants to write stories about dueling wizards with strategy and tension to the duel, then the audience needs to know what each side can and can't do, and the more they know, the more they can get into the fight. Think of it like watching a chess game or sports like football. The more you understand the rules, the more you appreciate the game you're watching. Magic is the same way. Understanding by the audience means more drama and tension, while lack of understand leads to confusion and disinterest.

Of course, this is only important if magic is a major story element, if it's something minor in the background then you can do whatever you want to do with it. In generic fantasy stories without lead characters using magic, then typically the magic using characters understand it and have some rough limitations, but other than that it's never very well defined. Mages can hurl fireballs, clerics can heal people, and necromancers can raise up undead, and how they do it and with what consistency is mostly up to the nature of the story and plot. Often there are simple limitations like needing wands, staffs, components, or casting time, but those will be waived when they get in the way or enforced as needed.

On the other hand, the more the magic is central to the plot and the main character, the better it should be understood. In Chinese xianxia stories where the character is rising through the warrior-mage ranks, the procedure for learning magic is often fairly well defined, and the audience knows the lead character's capabilities and weaknesses. This is important since the character is rising through the levels, and the audience needs to be able to see where they stand in comparison with the other characters. (At least until the higher levels, when the audience will know only their most powerful moves out of a vast library.)

A general rule is that the lower the level of magic, the softer it is, and the higher the level of magic in the story, the harder it is. In low fantasy magic is something done by elves, spirits and demons, and is unpredictable and dangerous, while in high fantasy magic becomes something that can be as codified as the laws of physics at the upper ends. Ironically enough, once you get to mythic levels, it starts to soften out again, because often the characters get so powerful, they can do almost anything, so limiting them is pretty pointless.

The other guideline to remember, which Sanderson notes, is that the softer the magic system, the more it should be used to get the characters into trouble, but the less it should be used to get them out of trouble. Soft magic shouldn't be their friend, unless they really work hard to earn its friendship and it's a special occasion.

FANTASY CHARACTERS

Fantasy covers a lot of territory, but generally speaking, there still tends to be a few commonalities.

First, the traditional *Dungeons and Dragons* character roles (admittedly loosely drawn from *The Lord of the Rings*), tend to still dominate the genre. These classes are the Fighter, Magic User, Rogue, Cleric and the Bard. Thanks to countless games (of the tabletop and digital variety), these character archetypes have become so baked into the DNA of "fantasy" that most stories feature some or all of them, and the lead character is usually clearly one of these five.

In short:

- The Fighter – A character who focuses on combat. They can be a Knight, Samurai, Archer, Martial Artist, Thug, Barbarian, Xia, Murim, Spearman, Ranger, or any other character whose main talent is their combat prowess.
- The Magic User – A character who has the ability to control magical forces. They might be called a Wizard, Witch, Warlock, Mage, Sorcerer, Cultivator, or other terms, but their talent is their ability to control and direct magical forces.
- The Rogue – A shadowy character who specializes in stealth and sneaking around. They might be called a Thief, Ninja, Spy, Scout or Assassin, but their talent lies in their ability to get in and out of places where they shouldn't be and interact with the darker side of society.
- The Cleric – A character who has the ability to channel or call upon other worldly forces. If they are part of an organized religion, they might also be called a Priest, Reverend, or Shrine Maiden, and if they're part of a less organized region a Shaman or Witch Doctor. Their talent is that their faith rewards them with gifts they can use to help (or hurt) others.
- The Bard – A character who uses their high social skills or talents for the arts to help themselves or others. Sometimes they're the more public face of the Rogue, and act as a Con Artist, other times they're a fiery Rebel Leader or Politician who incites crowds to action, and sometimes they're a wandering Actor or Singer. Regardless, they're someone who has a gift for dealing with others, and uses it well.

As you can see, these five roles cover a lot of territory, but what they all have in common is that they're all adventurers- types of people who live outside of normal society and are inclined to get involved with stories that your average person would stay away from if they could. They also existed in some form in real history (although in less simplified versions), and are social archetypes that audiences instinctively understand and relate to even today. (Fighter- strong person, Magic User- smart person, Rogue- sneaky/amoral person, Cleric- moral/philosophical person, Bard- funny/talkative person.)

Of course, these five also serve overlapping roles, which is why they've survived in gaming as long as they have as well. The fighter is usually a close-in combatant, the magic user is a ranged combatant, the rogue is needed for gathering information, the cleric is needed for healing and support, and the bard is there to gather the supplies the group needs and provide public relations.

So, it's no wonder that they pop up in roles in fantasy stories of all kinds, and that the lead characters in fantasy stories tend to be one of these types and are usually surrounded by the other archetypes in some form as well. Different writers relate to different members of this quintet and tend to write their stories based around whichever of the five they most connect with.

When writing about these roles, there are usually two approaches writers take-the Inward Approach and the Outward Approach.

The Inward Approach is where the writer takes the character role and explores the whole culture and society which exists around that role. For example, if the character is a rogue, then the story will be set in the world of backstabbing rogues and explore what it takes to live and survive in such a world. It might also explore the history and place of rogues in that setting and the setting itself will be viewed from the rogue perspective.

On the other hand, the Outward Approach is where the character is taken out of their natural environment and must use their talents and gifts to survive in the greater world. This is where the character joins together with other types of people (and character roles) and goes out to face the world and see what they can accomplish. By going out into the world, the audience learns about the character and their culture through contrast with other characters, and it is a story about the character finding their place in the greater world. (Or dying trying.) This is the adventuring party, or the character on a quest that requires them to leave their little world and become part of something bigger.

Both approaches, one which explore the smaller world of a church, dojo, or ninja village, and one which explores the clash of cultures and ideas in greater society, are equally good, but writers should think about which one they want their story to focus on.

Speaking of writers, the other major commonality among fantasy lead characters is that they're almost always gifted in some way. Fantasy lead characters are very rarely average people (at least, not in the fantasy world they're in), but are almost always exceptional. This exceptionality might come from being extremely smart, strong, or fast, or it might come in the form of a talent for some skill like magic, herbalism or archery. Or, most commonly in webfiction, it will come in the form of some magical gift/ability/cheat that gives them a big advantage over everyone else around them and lets them quickly advance through the levels of the setting.

Whatever form it comes in, the lead character's exceptionality makes them a wish-fulfillment character for both the author and the audience, who enjoy watching the character develop their gifts and use them to accomplish their goals. Nobody wants to read stories about a crippled pikeman who just struggles to survive (unless he's a very clever, mean and entertaining sort), but everyone enjoys stories about grand characters doing grand deeds. Even in low fantasy, the characters are still exceptional, just their talents and situations tend to be less epic or world saving.

THE DEFAULT WEBFICTION (WESTERN) FANTASY SETTING

Geography

The geography of the typical fantasy setting looks like Europe (or New Zealand), but with the human countries and settlements spread out like North America. Unlike real Europe, the people in fantasy settings tend to live in clusters to have protection against raids by non-humans and monster attacks, so what you have is a number of isolated cities/settlements. These cities are separated by very large stretches of wilderness, and there are trade-routes between those settlements, which have small villages along them to serve travelers, and might be patrolled by some form of guard or rangers. The only other way to get around is by ship, using rivers, lakes and oceans to avoid the dangerous wilderness, but requires dealing with sea monsters and other marine hazards.

This current civilization is built on the ruins of one or many great civilizations that came before it, and as a result there are abandoned cities and ruins scattered throughout the land, often filled with monsters of the humanoid and non-humanoid kinds. The farther you get away from "civilization" the more dangerous things become, and only the strongest and bravest live away from cities and trade routes.

Adventurers

In the real world, what we call adventurers in the fantasy sense were rare because they often didn't live very long, and being a homeless wanderer isn't all that fun. However, in this fantasy setting where there are always ruins to be explored, monsters to be driven off, and caravans to be guarded, there is a strong lure for those with a good sword arm or useful talents to leave home and try to make their fortune as adventurers. Most mistakenly believe a few good hauls and some luck is all it takes to make a poor farm girl into a rich woman, so naturally when their other option is subsistence level farming becoming an adventurer looks pretty good. The reality is that being an Adventurer is a hard life, and often a very short one, but for those who are blessed with skill or luck it can be a profitable and exciting one as well.

To service these adventurers, there will be various guilds formed by former adventurers looking to retire to help the new blood. Most commonly, there's a single Adventurer's Guild which has connections everywhere, and which exists to act as an intermediary between those needing to hire adventurers and those looking to be hired.

Think of it as a temporary employment agency for freelancers, and you'll have the right idea.

The Guild (as it's known), helps clients by holding onto the money (for a small fee) until the adventurers complete their jobs, and resolving any disputes impartially. It helps adventurers by making sure they'll get paid and with finding work that suits them, even going so far as to rank both adventurers and missions based on skills and difficulties. Commonly, missions are ranked based on either precious metals (copper being lowest, and platinum the highest), colors (white being easiest, and black being hardest), or even using plain old numbers or letters for ranking things. Similarly, adventurers are also ranked using the same system, with the idea being to match up the adventurers with the jobs that best suit their level.

The Guild will also usually be connected with the local governments in some way, and offer open jobs and bounties on things the local government wants dealt with. This can range from exchanging monster scalps or needed medicinal ingredients for coins, to putting together a posse to deal with raids by bandits and hostile non-humans. However, it is usually their policy to stay clear of offering jobs related to actual political struggles like police actions, wars, or in-fighting between nobles, as they want to stay strictly neutral in their politics.

Races

The typical webfiction fantasy setting has several different races sharing the land with humanity, sometimes peacefully, sometimes in competition. Generally speaking, humans are usually the dominant race because the readers are humans, and because most of the other races are either longer lived but have fewer children, or have shorter life spans. Humans are in that sweet spot of having a fairly long life span and being able to have many kids, so they've just won the demographics game over time.

The most common fantasy races besides humans are:

Elves- Very common, because everyone loves tall, fair haired and fair skinned near-immortal beauties with pointed ears. They are usually physically weaker than humans, but faster, smarter, and have a natural affinity to magic that makes up for it. They generally dislike other races who they view as being like children or animals, and only have a grudging respect for humans because humans are the new top of the food chain. (Often a spot the Elves occupied in the ancient past.) There may be other variant elven races which have different appearances, like Wood Elves or Night Elves, which are typically shorter lived and more (or less) human like than their higher cousins.

Dwarves- Short, stocky, bearded humanoids who prefer to live underground. Like Elves, they're long lived and have few children, so they've been crowded out by humans, but since humans don't live underground and they do, it's not as big a problem. They often seem grumpy to humans, but this is because as a long-lived race they like to do everything slowly and methodically, and the human tendency to just rush things gets on their nerves. Dwarves usually lack an affinity for magic, but they make up for it with their incredible talents for engineering. Also, because they're long lived, they are always looking for new sources of income, as the good life doesn't come cheap. Finally, while all Dwarves have beards, in some clans the males or females (or both) shave them off for cultural or personal reasons.

Demi-Humans- This isn't one race, but a catch-all term for races which are humans combined with other species. Likely the results of ancient civilizations experimenting to create servants with heightened abilities or pleasing appearances, cat-people, dog-people, dragon-men, mermaids, and other animal/human hybrids are a staple of fantasy. They can range in appearance from normal looking people with tails and ears in weird places, to what look like human-sized animals which have heightened intelligence and the ability to walk on their hind legs. It will all depend on the tastes and sensibilities of the writer, and how much like animals they want them to act. Some types of demi-humans may also have magical affinities which make them more adept than humans at spellcasting, or will be able to shift between animal and human form. Like most animals, demi-humans are often shorter lived than normal humans, and in many places, they're treated as subhuman and used as slaves.

Demons- This is another catch-all term, but it generally refers to beings from another dimension than the story setting which have horns, oddly colored skin, and an extremely high talent for controlling magic. They can be actual other-dimensional beings, or the children of other-dimensional beings which came and bred with humans. In either case, they're usually stronger and tougher than humans, live longer, and view other races as either potential slaves or a source of food and amusement. From their perspective this is reasonable, since they're superior, and see other races as more like talking animals than sentients. Depending on the setting, they may be minor warlords, invading armies, or even have their own kingdoms.

Goblins- These are short, skinny, green humanoids who live in clans and tribes in the wilderness and regularly come into conflict with humans. Goblins have short lifespans, breed like rabbits, and mature extremely quickly, which when connected with their aggressive nature, keeps them from advancing beyond the tribal level. Occasionally, Goblin Kings will appear and unite goblin tribes into organized kingdoms or even try to civilize them, but this rarely lasts past the death of the king.

Orcs- These are a particular pig-like type of demi-human which are very large and strong, but equally stupid. Their society is based on survival of the strongest, and they function very similar to the stereotypical Viking raiders, who survived by scavenging and raiding other settlements. They are quite bloodthirsty (literally), and will eat almost anything or anyone they can get their paws on. As a result, their clans are often nomadic, and move into an area to hunt before moving onto the next area when the local prey is exhausted. They are smart enough to be bargained with, however, and so some orcs have found work with humans or demons as soldiers or servants.

Politics

The standard fantasy setting has three political states in it: The Kingdom, The Empire, and The Theocracy. Occasionally, the Theocracy may be a powerful organization instead of a state.

The Kingdom is where the "good guys" live, and is a typical idealized version of what a medieval kingdom would look like without all the disease and absolute crushing poverty. The rulers can range from despotic (if they need to be overthrown as part of the story) to benevolent, but even if the ruler is fair and just there will still be a pack of scheming dukes and other nobles who are looking to oust them and take their place. The Kingdom usually just wants to be left in peace, but because of its neighbors is in a struggle to survive.

The Empire is where the "bad guys" live, and is a brutal expansionist state which has its eye on the neighboring lands, including The Kingdom. Typically ruled by a warlord Emperor (or Empress), the leader of the Empire is an ambitious figure who rules with an iron fist and has a legion of generals who carry out their orders. There is often a lot of political infighting going on in the Empire due to the "survival of the fittest" nature of its politics, and there may be an active rebellion happening as well (that the main characters can become allies with).

The Theocracy is a state ruled by a priest class who serve a high priest (or Pope) that is supposed to be the living incarnation of their god. Functionally, they are usually just like The Empire, but with a heavy dose of religion about everything and a belief that their leaders are chosen by their god, not political infighting (which is usually the reality of the situation). The Theocracy is filled with religious fanatics, who see it as their duty to carry out their god's will and bring "light" to the unbelievers. However, they usually lack the forces to do this militarily, so instead they try to convert the citizens and leaders of the other countries to their faith as a form of "soft invasion."

They may also be puppet masters, using their influence to direct the affairs of other countries, or control the balance of power.

Other Common Political States Include:

The Mercenary Kingdom which was founded by a mercenary warlord who took over one of his (or her) weaker clients, and now sends its soldiers to serve whoever will pay them. They are strictly neutral in their politics because they fight for all sides, although they often secretly back various players in the political struggles of the land. They may also act as information brokers, since they have spies and agents everywhere.

The Elven Kingdom which is where the last remnants of the elves live (since there are almost always elves), having been pushed out of their lands by the faster-breeding human population. Here, in these ancient lands, the elves go about their long lives and occasionally trade or do business with other races, but mostly keep to themselves and dislike the other races. The power structure is usually based along family lines, and overall the place is mostly like The Kingdom, just marinated in Elven culture.

The Merchant City which sits at the point where a great river meets an ocean, and is usually at the crossroads between at least two countries. This is a strictly neutral trade city ruled by a council formed of the leaders of the various merchant guilds or families, and is a dark and dangerous place where all manner of goods (from information to slaves) can be purchased for a price. It's place between two military powers and its usefulness keep it from being invaded, and it may contain the home offices of powerful merchant houses with ties throughout the world.

Magic

The default fantasy setting's magic level is medium-high, and is hard-ish. Typically, only one out of a hundred humans have the ability to use magic, which makes it uncommon, but not rare. However, magic is much like musical talent, where even among those who can learn it, not everyone has the same ability to use it, and it is a skill that must be mastered with long hours of practice and study. This means while everyone knows someone who can cast one or two simple spells, actual powerful magic casters are very uncommon to the point of being rare. (Maybe 1 in 10,000 or higher.)

Magic itself is fairly reliable (the right moves almost always produce the same result), and the principals for casting are well understood, but why magic works and the source of it may not be known. Casting time is usually based around the idea that the more powerful the spell, the longer and more difficult casting it will be. Casting magic drains the caster of energy, so there is a limited number of spells they can cast per day (the more powerful the spell, the more it tires the caster out), and magic casters often make use of crystals or other magical objects to enhance their casting endurance, speed, and ability.

Most often, magic also comes in different types, and each caster has an affinity for one or more of these types which allows them to cast those spells more easily (or only spells of that type). Common types include the elements (Earth, Fire, Air, Water), variants of the elements (Sand, Lightning, Weather, Ice, etc.), and forces (Light, Darkness, Life, Death, Mind, Spirit, Body, etc.). The writer is strongly encouraged to come up with their particular list of types before they start writing, but it can be done on the fly as long as they are consistent.

Magical spells are usually something akin to collectable cards, where everyone who puts some effort into it will have access to the basics for their specialty, but the more powerful the spell the rarer and harder to get it becomes. The higher-level spells are usually custom ones which are only taught by masters to their protégés or locked away in scrolls or ancient books. This is done by masters to give themselves an edge over newcomers (who wants to teach someone a spell they can use to get rid of you?) and to keep less scrupulous casters from abusing the power of magic for their own gain. Making your own spells is usually pretty hard, and often something only ancient masters can do; thus, spells are valuable collectable items for casters. (And most casters will only know a limited number of them that they cast very well thanks to practice, as opposed to a huge library.)

Magic items are usually also uncommon and expensive to make, which makes them valuable when found and people who have them tend to take good care of them. Most often, the user of a magic item needs to have some affinity for magic to actually use it, but this may vary depending on the item or setting. Items which can be used by anyone will be much more valuable and expensive than those which can only be used by a small number of people with magical affinity. Commonly, they are built around magical crystals which either power the item or act as the brain of the item, allowing it to do what it does. If this art becomes advanced enough, it becomes a type of magical technology, so be careful unless you want your setting to be a magipunk setting.

In most settings, Normal Magic and Theocratic (religious) Magic are different things. Normal Magic is based on elemental or natural forces which the casters are able to manipulate, while Theocratic Magic is either a gift from the gods (like a Cleric's ability to heal the injured), or the follower calling on gods and summoning spirits who are actually doing the casting and powering the spell. Of course, the author may choose to say that what the character thinks is the gods is still just another form of regular magic. Typically, however, Clerics function as the doctors of the setting, and their ability to heal disease and injury both allow for adventurers to quickly recover from deadly combat and for the author to explain why most people aren't dying of disease in the streets.

Religion

When it comes to religion, a typical fantasy setting is a bit of a paradox.

The default is that the gods are real and actually answer people's prayers. In fact, they're so real that they grant their followers (clerics) the ability to perform miracles like healing others and often a variety of other magical abilities. A cleric can often literally call on their god to help them out, and the higher ranked members of the religion often have some serious magical power levels.

However, the place of religion in people's lives is actually fairly weak in most of these settings. Except in the Theocracy (where it is very strong), religion doesn't seem to play much of a part in people's lives in these stories except as a plot point. Other than the cleric, most characters never mention religion and don't seem to be followers of any particular faith. This is likely a combination of two factors- one, there is non-clerical magic in the world, so performing miracles isn't as big a deal, and two, usually most fantasy writers aren't very religious themselves, so this reflects their more atheistic worldview.

In most webfiction, the Church, which is basically the Catholic Church with the names changed, is more of a social organization which performs one or more of the following social functions:

- Medical Services – The Church often runs the local hospitals in larger urban centers where church clerics who have been blessed can heal most basic injuries, perform occasional miracles, and cure some diseases. (Although never the ones which the plot calls for people to die from.)
- Education – Most schools in the setting will be run by the Church, where they will teach basic reading skills and math skills. These will usually be set up in larger urban centers, and staffed by priests and nuns who educate the young people using the holy books of their religion as the fundamental teaching texts. In a poor place, this education will be limited to the elite of society, but in a more developed place it might be available to all children. If there are Universities, these will also be run by the Church as well.
- Scribe Services – Since the majority of people are barely literate, it falls upon the educated local priests or nuns to help keep records and act as scribes for the common folk. (Who can't afford the services of professional scribes.) For a modest fee, the local clergy can help to write letters (or read ones which have come in), or help with other bookkeeping tasks. In some settings, the

Church may also be the ones offering mail/courier services, acting as intermediaries between various people and groups to pass along messages. (Which is also a great way to know everyone's secrets.)

So, as you can see, in essence, in most fantasy settings, the Church is taking on many of the functions that modern governments do, allowing some modern social amenities to exist where the government is otherwise too weak/poor to pay for them.

Religions other than the Church are usually portrayed as primitive and simple, and are based around spirits and ancestor worship. For example, elven culture is almost always deeply connected with the spirits, and they worship their ancestors as ascended gods. Dwarves are similar, but skip the spirits and go straight to devout ancestor worship.

Literacy

The big decision a writer will need to make is whether or not the fantasy society in the story has printing presses (or the equivalent) or if everything is copied by hand.

If everything is copied by hand, then books are rare, precious, and extremely expensive things which are only owned by the nobility and clergy. Most people will have never even seen a book (except maybe the holy text of the Church), and literacy rates among the common people will be very low. (They have nothing to read, or write, after all.) Shop signs will use pictures and iconographs, and if a person does need some kind of writing done, they will hire a scribe or priest to do it.

If, on the other hand, there is a printing press system, then reading materials will be less expensive and might be very common. This will lead to a more educated population, especially in towns and cities, and while most people may not be strong readers or writers, they will know the basic alphabet and numbers. There will also likely be newspapers, magazines, and books which are targeted at a broader audience, and a popular culture to go with them.

Economy

In most fantasy stories, the economy of the setting isn't really that important except as it relates to the buying and selling of things the main characters need. In relation to that, keep your system of money simple and use the fantasy standard of Copper>Silver>Gold>Platinum. The audience knows this system already, and it takes almost no effort on your part to use it. Think of a single Copper coin as being equal to a dollar in buying power, and go up by a factor of ten for each level. (Silver = $10, Gold = $100, Platinum = $1000, etc.)

Peasants in these settings pay taxes to their local lord/landowner, who then takes their cut and passes it along to their regional lord, who then takes their cut and passes it along to the central government. As a result, the central government usually isn't that rich, and the government tends to stay out of the economy and focus on the more major political issues like war and politics.

Most businesses, whether large or small, are going to be family owned and operated. Whether it's artisans who live in the city and make shoes or bread, or travelling merchants who offer goods and services between towns, they will be multi-generation operations where the parents pass down the business to the children, who will then pass it to their children. Of course, not all children can inherit the family business, or have the skills to keep it going or make it grow, and this will result in drama, splits, rivalries, and hurt feelings. (The perfect seeds for stories to grow from.)

There are likely also a few Guilds, which are groups of family businesses that have made deals or arrangements with each other to avoid direct competition and keep out newcomers. These groups may or may not have much direct power over their members, and a strong guild ruled by a single family can be as powerful as any king. (And sometimes become rulers from behind the throne, if a king ends up deeply in debt to a guild.)

Technology

The level of technology in a standard fantasy story is usually around that of early renaissance Europe, minus gunpowder. This allows for the rudimentary form of most modern technologies, but keeps things based around knights, horses, castles, and the other more medieval elements that people tend to associate with fantasy settings. In most cases, magic is replacing the lack of gunpowder, and acting as the most powerful force on the battlefield.

Very commonly, the printing press has also usually not been invented, so books are all copied by hand, and there isn't a newspaper system. (The addition of newspapers will have a profound effect on society and quickly advance it beyond where most fantasy settings want to be.) Meanwhile, steam power has been invented, but is in a rudimentary state where it hasn't come into common use yet. So, there are no trains, but one-off steam powered vehicles or devices (like airships) may be starting to appear.

Medicine will be a combination of herbal medicine and very simple healing techniques, since magic is the main way people heal each other and has replaced surgery. Although since magic isn't as effective against disease, the knowledge of herbal medicines may be quite advanced. Similarly, deformities will be something only the highest (and most expensive) levels of healing magic can fix.

There will be no refrigeration, so food will almost all be seasonal, and preserved by salting, curing, pickling or drying. Salt, spices and cooking oil will be in high demand, and treated as precious commodities. Bread and oats will be the staples, and most people's daily diets will consist of soups, stews, pottage, and other dishes which make maximum use of available ingredients. Sugar will be rare to the point of not existing (they don't have access to sugar cane, except as a rare import), and sweets will be made using fruit sugars, tree syrup, and honey.

One technology which is always present is eyeglasses (which in our world developed around the 12th century), because you need some way to show who the smart or crafty people are.

TYPES OF FANTASY WEBFICTION

The following isn't a list of all the kinds of fantasy fiction, but a list of the more common types you'll see in webfiction.

Adventuring Fantasy

When it comes to fantasy stories, Adventuring Fantasy is the original default setting. Modern fantasy as a genre is based on Tolkien and *D&D*, both of which are centered around heroic characters going on epic quests to defeat evil. In Adventuring Fantasy, the good guys are good, the bad guys are bad, and the magic is flying thick and fast. Even if it isn't explicitly said, the characters generally conform to either *D&D* character classes (Fighter, Magic User, Cleric, Rogue, etc.) or MMORPG character types (Damage Dealer, Tank, Buffer, etc.) and the standard fantasy races of Elves, Dwarves, Goblins, and such are usually present as well. The magic system itself is fairly hard and reliable, but only useable by those talented for it or gifted by the gods.

Urban Fantasy

These are stories set in an urban setting, usually a modern one or a Victorian one, which involve magic and magical creatures. They can range from stories about vampire and werewolf clans in conflict, to witch and demon hunters, to detectives with supernatural sidekicks, and everything in between. Generally, the magic is usually low-key and hidden to keep their world as close to our own as possible, but that doesn't mean it can't be powerful. There might also be magical races, but these too are usually hidden in the crowd or by magic, so that only those gifted can see the supernatural world which is right under our noses.

Magic School Fantasy

Harry Potter. This is *Harry Potter*, or another story which is trying to be like *Harry Potter* and is set around a school where young people go to learn magic. If it's set in modern times, then it happens in a secret hidden world that is all around us, and perhaps in some pocket dimensions where magical creatures live. It can also be set in pure fantasy settings where the school is one where magic users learn their craft, and the school's students include humans and non-humans together learning the mystic arts. Usually the magic is high and hard-ish, although how "hard" the system is depends on the tastes of the writer and style of the story.

Space Fantasy

Fantasy stories set in "space" have a long history, going back to Flash Gordon and his battles against Ming the Merciless and John Carter's trip to Barsoom. In modern times, the shining example of Space Fantasy is *Star Wars*, where characters use the mystic power of The Force to battle with laser swords and fight against evil sorcerers in black. In any case, this type of fantasy mixes Science Fiction and Fantasy together to produce something that feels like swashbuckling adventuring fantasy but is set against a backdrop of the stars and on alien worlds.

Harem Fantasy

This is a story where the main character's life and story revolve around meeting attractive people and purposely or accidentally getting them to fall in love with him or her. Usually set in a standard fantasy setting, it can also be combined with other types of fantasy, but the stories always end with the main character adding another cutie to their harem.

Slice of Life Fantasy

This type of fantasy story is somewhat unique to Japan, but does pop up in other places. This is a fantasy story which is usually set in a standard Adventuring Fantasy type world, but which focuses on the characters in that world living their daily lives instead of adventuring. This can range from stories about what adventuring characters do in their time off, to how the non-adventurers live, to what it's like to be a monster in these settings. These stories are often comedic, and have an off-beat touch, focusing on things like a wizard quitting adventuring to become a chef, or a goblin who dreams of learning to paint. The key here is the contrast between the fantastic setting and the characters acting like normal (if quirky) people from our world in it.

Isekai

This is a story where a character (who is often from our world) travels to another world and has to learn to survive and thrive in that new environment. This type of story is extremely common in Light Novels, and often acts as a hook to get the audience interested by having a relatable protagonist thrown into the deep end and being forced to learn to swim. See the chapter on Second Life Stories for more details.

Wuxia

These are stories about wandering heroes who interact with different clans and secret societies in settings that resemble old China. The characters usually have near superhuman (or outright superhuman) abilities bestowed on them by their training and backgrounds, and use those abilities to bring justice to a troubled land. See the chapter on Chinese Webnovels for more details.

Xianxia

Stories of this kind are specifically about a character who lives in a place where your ability to control magic (in the Taoist sense) determines your place in society. The stories are about the main character(s) starting weak and often bullied, and then displaying talent and rising quickly up through the ranks of magical society by cultivating their magical talents and related strengths. Eventually, the main character reaches the top of society, becoming a god-like figure (or actual god), and the cycle is complete. See the chapters Rising Hero Stories and on Chinese Webnovels for more details.

SECOND LIFE STORIES (ISEKAI)

The practice of sending fictional characters from our world to another is a very old one, and wasn't new when Lewis Carol wrote *Alice in Wonderland* or Mark Twain wrote *A Connecticut Yankee in King Arthur's Court* in the 19th century. After that, the immense popularity of this type of story has carried it through the ages, producing many other classics such as *John Carter of Mars*, *The Wizard of Oz*, *Buck Rogers*, *Flash Gordon*, *The Chronicles of Narnia*, *Peter Pan*, and countless others. It's a story trope which has waxed and waned in popularity over time, but always seems to be around.

However, in recent years this type of story has exploded in popularity in Asia, to the point where it's becoming harder to find a fantasy story where the protagonist isn't from our world than one where they are. Almost every possible variation of people from our world ending up in another one has been explored in Japanese, Korean, and Chinese webfiction, and the Light Novel racks are overflowing with *Isekai* (the Japanese term for the genre, which translates to "Other World") stories. In China, it reached the point where the Chinese government banned stories about time travelling characters as being a threat to public order. (Which the writers promptly got around by shifting to reincarnation stories and continued on their merry way.)

As a result, any book trying to look at Light Novels and Webnovels would be remiss if it didn't include a discussion on the Second Life phenomena and how it's shaping webfiction today.

But first, a discussion of terminology.

Properly speaking, in English, stories where a character from our world goes into another world are called Portal Fantasy, and this has been the term used for them since the mid-20th century. However, the problem with just calling these stories Portal Fantasies is that the term refers specifically to a character from our world physically travelling to another place and/or time. This leaves out a huge swath of stories where the character doesn't physically travel through time and space, but instead it's their consciousness, spirit, soul, or memories which transmigrates between realities. The Japanese and Chinese both call them "Other World" stories in their respective languages because that's a term which covers a lot more ground.

However, even the term "Other World" is misleading, because the genre can also include characters from other realities coming to our own world in some form, or journeying to computer generated virtual realities. So, this book compromises by calling them Second Life stories, as they're about a character experiencing a new life in a new reality. Whether the characters choose to return back to their world at the end or stay is a different matter, the key is they're about characters living new lives in another time, place, or reality.

Sorry for any confusion this might cause.

WHY ARE THESE STORIES SO POPULAR?

In a lot of ways, the real question should be- why wouldn't these stories be popular?

You have a relatable main character from our world travelling to another reality where everything is new, and the challenges are huge. They are the ultimate fish out of water trying to survive, and the audience's own natural curiosity about what that character will experience in this new and unknown setting pulls them in and makes them want to find out what happens to the main character. It's a perfect combination of adventure and exploration, and by the time the character finds their place in the new world and understands the rules of this new setting, the audience is attached to them and part of their journey.

A writer couldn't ask for a better set-up, especially for an epic adventure story.

It also solves so many other problems that occur in fantasy and speculative fiction set in other worlds, as the audience learns about the setting at the same time and pace the main character does, eliminating the problem of how much to tell the audience about the setting and when. The supporting cast have a perfectly good dialog-based reason to tell the main character everything they need to know, avoiding infodumps and the slow pace of exposition. Of course, they're not professors lecturing, so they'll naturally only tell the main character the bare minimum they need to know, and not a bit more, keeping a lot of the details a mystery for later on.

In addition, it makes any character into an active character with a clear goal. That goal might be to get home, it might be to survive, it might be to use their talents or knowledge to improve this setting for the better, but they're forced to do something, and that action has a natural story arc that goes with it. It's hard to be stuck in another world and do nothing about it.

And finally, this type of story has the ability to not just have a relatable lead, but one who truly represents the audience itself, and does so in a way which flatters the audience's egos. For example, if the main character uses his skills at fighting video games to his advantage in this new world, then it connects him with the audience who play those games. Or, if the main character is a master of stamp collecting, and that skill at appraising stamps is useful in this new world, then the members of the audience who collect stamps will root for him or her. This gives those audience members an extra investment in the character, and that's an investment which is hard to come by in any other genre or story situation.

So, from a writer's perspective, Second Life stories are the ultimate set-up for fantastic fiction, and have so many clear advantages, thus the real question is why wouldn't you do it this way?

THE PROBLEMS OF SECOND LIFE STORIES

There are a few good reasons not to use the Second Life trope, but probably the biggest one is that (at least in the Asian market) they've been done to death, reincarnated, and done to death a couple more times. The Japanese light novel and webnovel community alone has reached the point where to get any interest in a Second Life story, there has to be something pretty special or extreme about it. Just having a hero appearing in a fantasy kingdom and going on adventures just isn't going to get any interest anymore. Now the stories are about people reincarnated as monsters instead of heroes, or heroes with really unusual talents and interests like food appraising or organizational management. Attempts are being made at more original settings as well, since the vast majority of Second Life stories are set in a generic video game fantasy setting akin to the early *Final Fantasy* games.

In a way, this is good, because it fosters creativity, but it does mean the bar is pretty high for new writers who don't have some original take to try. (At least, in the Asian markets.) So, it can become a daunting task to figure out what is and isn't overdone and try to find a new take on things unless you're really an avid reader of the genre.

Another problem is that Second Life stories often lack depth. The main character's situation as someone from another world limits them in the types of goals they can have, and usually to pretty basic and generic ones like returning home, revenge, survival, and helping the people they meet. These are reasonable goals for someone from another place trying to make a new life, but they lack subtlety and complexity. The problem is that when the character's major life needs like food, sleep, security, and belonging aren't being met, trying to meet those basic human needs gets priority, and things like sorting their emotions out or dealing with a difficult past take a far back seat.

Not only that, but the character's outsider status, while being an advantage to the writer, also has a few big downsides. First and foremost being that, as anyone who has lived in another culture can tell you, once you're an outsider you'll always be an outsider. No matter how long you live in the community, or how well you speak the language, you will never really be one of them because you don't have the bond that comes with growing up in that community or culture. This is less of a problem in big cities, but still an issue, as people aren't as likely to trust foreigners until they get to know them. (Especially people who look odd and are from a land they've never heard of before.)

In the case of stories, this means the lead character will never really be part of the new world's culture, and always be a bit isolated. As a result, they won't really get a deep perspective on the culture, and be able to explore the setting in a way that a lead character who was born there could. You don't get to see how people grow up in that culture, and the effects that culture has on their views or outlooks as adults. (Unless, of course, the character **is** born there- see Reincarnation Stories below.)

And lastly, because these types of stories have been mined so much, there is a bit of a stigma about them. Go on a light novel or webfiction fan forum and mention you want to read some isekai stories, and watch the sarcastic and critical comments pour in like a thunderstorm. Before it's over, you'll hear every possible criticism of light novels there is, but most of them will be about the overreliance on harems, overpowered main characters, and generic fantasy settings. (The great irony being the people saying these things are also the ones reading and buying them, keeping those tropes alive...)

People will tend to look at any Second Life story warily, because there are so many bad and mediocre ones out there, and yours may really need to shine to overcome their initial resistance.

SECOND LIFE STORY CHARACTERS

In a Second Life story, the most important person is the traveler, who is normally the lead character. This lead character is generally from our contemporary world, and usually in their late teens to early thirties, because that makes them in their physical prime and gives them enough life experience to be able to deal with going to another world. They are usually on the bright side of average, but otherwise are overall average people with a few strong points that help them stand out as characters.

This average-ness isn't an accident, as the lead characters in these stories are very much meant to be audience insert characters. The audience is supposed to connect closely with them, and they very often have hobbies and interests that reflect the demographic of both the story's author and the target readership. They are supposed to be the audience, if the audience were able to have the experience they have.

The final important trait to note about them, however, is that they always have an advantage.

A great many Second Life stories are built around the hook of a character having a special talent or ability that the people in the destination setting don't, and which makes them powerful in that setting. This can be as simple as knowledge or a skill set from our world, or as complex as having magical abilities or being able to function like a video game character. In light novels, for example, it's customary for the main character to gain some weird, offbeat magical ability which doesn't make them unbeatable, but does make them stand out and give them a leg up.

And that's one of the major reasons for the advantage- to give them the ability to not only survive in their new environment, but to excel in it. These are stories about winners, after all, and watching them die of disease and malnutrition in a primitive world wouldn't be any fun for anyone, so they need some abilities to give them the edge and justify them being the main characters. If they can't thrive in this new world, then why are they there?

Obviously, the writer does have to be careful in what abilities they give the main character. The reason so many people often complain about overpowered leads in Second Life stories is because writers give in to their own power fantasies and let the lead become so strong that they turn into a lion among kittens. This can be fun if well written, but all too often it creates a boring character who just wanders through the story eliminating the competition without breaking a sweat. This goes against the desire of the audience to see characters have to use their brains and struggle, and results in audiences that will lose interest in the story after a time. Not something the writer wants.

Instead, writers are recommended to give their leads an advantage or cheat that gives them a leg up on the competition, but not one which makes victory certain, especially in all situations. A character with an exceptional talent for computer coding who applies that to learning magic might find themselves becoming a powerful wizard, but it doesn't make them a minor god overnight. Similarly, a magical talent for appraising items could let a warrior slowly amass some incredible equipment from things others have overlooked, but it doesn't make them the lord of the battlefield without a lot of hard work to go with it.

The other thing to think about when it comes to casting your Second Life story is the lead's allies. Most Second Life leads tend to be a little dull, or reserved, partly because of their reader-insert nature. As a result, the writer needs to make sure that the characters around the leads are colorful and interesting to balance off that simplicity. In most cases, it's the supporting cast that the audience will fall in love with much more than the lead character (literally, in harem stories), because they will be the lively representations of the new world the hero finds themselves in.

And that, is something the writer should remember in designing them, the supporting cast the character meets are all representatives of the people of that world. The audience will assume that most of the people of that world are like those characters, and use them as a baseline for judging the setting. For example, if the main character meets a stoic, reserved elven archer, then the audience will assume all the elves of the setting are stoic and reserved until they meet another elf who isn't. If a character isn't normal for the setting, the writer should have another character mention that to the lead character at some point, or demonstrate it in the events of the story.

SECOND LIFE STORY SETTINGS

The default setting for most Second Life stories in webfiction is a fantasy setting which resembles our historical Earth but with magical elements. Most of the reasons for this are covered in other chapters, but it is worth mentioning that just because this is the default doesn't mean it's the only type of setting available. Second Life stories have been told set in the past and future of our own world, the far future, and across multiple dimensions. Science Fiction has a long history of Second Life stories, including both the aforementioned Buck Rogers and Flash Gordon, and writers should always be looking for new takes or angles which would add spice to the Second Life story and avoid some of its clichés.

That said, there's no question that Second Life stories set in fantasy worlds sell, and sell well. Audiences find these stories comfortable and familiar because they only have to worry about learning a few new details and how this world is different from the generic one. Pseudo-litRPG settings have become especially popular, but even there, the settings are almost always based around simple early *Final Fantasy* and *Dragon Quest* type games or MMORPGS like *World of Warcraft* that are still following that same template. The bigger the change from that standard, the more the author risks alienating their audience, who would rather not have to learn complex setting details to enjoy the story.

And that, is perhaps the most important rule of Second Life story settings- keep them simple. It's easy to run away with your imaginary worlds, and to want to share them with everyone, but always keep an eye on the real focus of the story. Most Second

Life stories are character centered, so anything that gets in the way of character drama or stories should be downplayed or ignored unless you specifically want to focus on the setting or plot.

SECOND LIFE PLOT STRUCTURES

Because it can go so many ways, the Second Life story doesn't have a plot built into it. It has a hook (stranger ends up in a new land), and that hook may suggest an ending (tries to get home or settles down in the new location), but there isn't a clear plot structure that goes with it. Thus, this type of story can be anything from a murder mystery, to a Task Story, to Slice of Life, to a Romance, to a Rising Hero story, to anything in between. The hook of the character's arrival generally sets up a situation where the character focuses on survival or exploration, but this isn't always true, especially in reincarnation stories.

The most common plot for a Second Life story is one where the newly arrived hero must rise to the challenge and find solutions to some problem in order to get home or find their place in the new setting. Usually this problem is connected with why they're there (either because they were summoned, or because god/fate brought them there) and so this clear obstacle must be overcome to make their lives peaceful again. If so, this plot element should be introduced right from the start, if for no other reason than to give the story an overarching goal. That doesn't mean they have to meet the main opponent right from the start, but the character and audience should be informed that they exist and are a distant great challenge that will need to be dealt with before the character can rest.

That this is the most common plot doesn't mean it's the only one, however, or that a real overarching plot is required in all cases. Sometimes characters just wander around and have adventures, and sometimes they decide to open restaurants selling foods from our world in the other one, becoming rich restauranteurs. It's all about find a story that works for you, and having fun with it.

GOING HOME

The final thing for writers to consider when they're planning their second life story is whether this is going to be a one-way trip. The character has ended up in a strange land, and in most cases, this might mean that they want to get back to where they belong, but that may or may not be something the author wants to make an option.

One inherent problem with stories about the main character trying to get home is that it makes them inward-looking instead of outward facing. The character is always trying to get back something they lost, not going out and trying new things and exploring. This isn't automatically bad, but it does mean the story isn't so much about going forward as it is leaving wherever they are. They aren't a part of that place, they're a tourist, and psychologically they're avoiding making attachments to the place they're in because they know they'll eventually leave.

Another problem with a story built around getting home is the constant dangling of possible routes home gets old very quickly. Getting home means the story is over, so every time the main character hears about an opportunity to get back the reader is going to look at the hundreds of pages left in the story, roll their eyes, and wonder how the author is going to cheat the lead character out of getting home this time. This also means the writer has to come up with ways to have a character motivated by getting home to not constantly be seeking ways home, or have those ways be so distant or involved that they don't affect the immediate story.

On the other hand, not having a character trying to get home means they're thinking more about their life in the new place, and take their situation a lot more seriously. (Unless they're convinced this is all a dream, of course.) They're exploring their new reality, and trying to find the best way to live happily in it and with their new friends and allies.

In fact, one very common trait of Japanese Second Life stories is that the characters usually don't want to go home at all. They're people who weren't happy, or had little attachments in their old life, and this new life is a fresh start in a place where they are often respected and live a higher quality life than they ever did at home. Why would they want to go back?

In the end, whether they want to go home or not is up to the writer, but it is something that should be deeply considered at the start of the story, because it's going to affect the story's structure and the lead character's motivations in a big way. There is no right answer, but making it up as you go along is only going to result in an unsatisfying journey for everyone involved.

TYPES OF SECOND LIFE STORIES

Each variation of Second Life stories has their own special advantages and challenges that come with them, and so it's worth taking the time to look at each of the common types a little more closely. The most common types are Portal Fantasy, Reincarnation Fantasy, Pseudo-litRPGs, Second Chance Stories, Time Travel Stories, and Reverse Portal Fantasy.

Portal Fantasy

In a lot of ways, Portal Fantasy is the original type of Second Life story- a character goes through some kind of gateway to another world, like stepping through a doorway. Of course, this doesn't have to be a literal doorway, in Twain's story the main character Hank Morgan just falls asleep under a tree, and Buck Rogers is frozen for hundreds of years in a cave. But the end result is that the character, with their original physical body, is at another time and place where they don't belong.

And the fact it's their original body is the important part, because they are literally a foreigner there and unable to become one of the locals. They have knowledge, skills, and abilities that come with their original body, but they also have disadvantages- a big one being that they can't speak or read the local language without some form of help. The ability, or lack of ability, to communicate with the local people is huge, and limits their ability to not only blend in, but survive in that strange environment. This is why so many High Fantasy settings for Portal Fantasy have translation spells or rings conveniently available for use by those who meet the lead. But, what about Low Fantasy settings where there isn't magical aid available? Well then, the locals better speak the hero's language, or the lead better be a very quick study when it comes to languages.

In theory, there should also be dietary issues, and issues of what local viruses the hero is vulnerable to and what ones they're carrying themselves, but typically Portal Fantasy ignores or glosses those over quickly as minor details.

Benefits:
- The character is literally a person from our world, and because of this they connect well with the reader.
- The audience can imagine what it would be like to be in their situation more easily
- They can take items with them from our world.
- Option of going back at the end of the story to motivate them.

Challenges:
- All the basic disadvantages of Second Life stories apply to Portal Fantasy, plus the language and diet ones mentioned.
- Any health issues or physical problems from our world still plague them.

- The author needs to come up with a reasonable explanation for the transitions between worlds.
- Since it was a doorway that got them there, the character will often be obsessed with finding a way back.
- The character has advanced knowledge, but their inability to communicate and lack of understanding about the world places them at a disadvantage in using it.
- The writer has to find a way to pair them up fast if they arrive alone, to give the character a guide to the new world and someone to talk to. (Again, harder if they don't speak the local language.)

Reincarnation Fantasy

In these types of stories, the character is literally reborn into the body of a person from another world with the memories of their life in our world intact. They live in and are a part of the society they are reborn into, but they also have a secret second life that they can draw upon for knowledge, and use that knowledge (and any abilities that come with them being reborn) to give them a big advantage. There are generally four versions of this- reborn as a baby, reborn as a child, reborn as an adult, and reborn as a non-human.

Sometimes the character is reborn as a baby, in which case they need to experience the whole process of growing and dealing with a child's body. However, because this is so limiting, the story will always fast-forward to an older version of the character, who is generally viewed as a gifted prodigy by the people around them who aren't aware of the character's true nature. They then go through the interesting parts of youth like attending warrior school, becoming an apprentice mage, or other activities the story is centered around. In point of fact, this character is less a part of our world than part of the other world, and often the fact they are reborn from our world is a minor plot point which is quickly forgotten unless their old life gives them some exceptional knowledge or skills. (Which often becomes the sole reason for them being reincarnated from our world.)

In other cases, the character is reborn into the body of a young person. Typically, the body's original owner actually died (usually of illness), and the original spirit is now gone, replaced by the soul and consciousness of our lead. This method conveniently avoids the question of there being two souls or personalities in the same body, and lets the story start with the character exploring their new body and situation. Most often, the character has memories of their host's original life, although these memories may be fuzzy or incomplete. Usually, they're just enough to let the character pass as the original person without raising much suspicion, but not enough that the character doesn't need to have the setting explained to them. Another common trope is that the host body's original owner was murdered, and the new character must now avenge them or deal with a murderer who wants to finish the job.

Then there are the times when the main character is reborn as an adult, usually under a situation similar to being reborn as a young person. However, unlike a young person who is still developing and living with their family or going to school, the adult character's new host body has powers, abilities, and status of their own. The new adult body can often do things the character's original body couldn't, and part of the story will be them figuring out who they've become and getting used to the benefits and flaws of this new body. The new body also has a position in society, friends, dependents, enemies, and responsibilities that the new owner must learn about and deal with. Of course, they are also playing catch-up as well, trying to desperately pass themselves off as the original and not raise suspicions among those around them, which is much harder for an adult to do than a young person.

Finally, there are stories where the character is reborn in a non-human body. This can be another race, a monster, or even physical objects like a hat or sword, and the character now finds themselves having to deal with not just an alien body, but an alien society and environment. For example, if the character was reborn as an Orc in a fantasy setting, they now have to adjust to Orcish life and ways of viewing the world, as well as the enemies of Orcs and possible differences in lifespans. However, as a general rule, even if the character is born as a non-humanoid, like a spider, slime monster, or vending machine, they will still find a way to eventually take on humanoid form because life as a non-humanoid is too hard for the audience to relate to.

Benefits:
- The character can have a deeper view of their new world.
- A longer or shorter exploration period, depending on how much of the original body's memories the character has access to.
- Knowledge from our world is an even bigger advantage for this type of character.
- Don't have to deal with issues of language, diet, or health.
- The character now has all the good and bad points of a person living in that world, plus the advantages that come with knowledge from our (often more advanced) world.
- The author doesn't have to explain why they ended up in this body and situation, it can just be waved away as "the gods work in mysterious ways".
- The character is now stuck with any debts, tasks, or responsibilities that the original host body had, throwing them instantly into the plot.
- Can start the story with the natural friends and allies of their host body.

Challenges:

- They can't really take anything with them. (Unless the writer really fudges it.)
- One-way trip, and there isn't usually an option to go home.
- The character is less part of our world, and more part of the other world. They lose some of the reader connection because they aren't one of us anymore.
- The character may suffer some guilt because they're literally an imposter pretending to be other people's loved ones.

Pseudo-litRPGs

In a litRPG, the character ends up in a virtual world of some kind, usually a video game, but in a Pseudo-litRPG, the character ends up a fantasy world which is effectively real, but which has video game characteristics. This is a relatively new type of story which has spun off of the litRPG craze in Asian webfiction started by *Sword Art Online* and *The Legendary Moonlight Sculptor*, where now the setting has "natural" laws like a video game, but is treated like a real place.

Here are a few examples of things commonly found in pseudo-litRPG settings:
- Characters (and monsters) have levels, and as they go up in level with experience, they gain new powers and abilities.
- Characters have statistics rating their abilities, and can call up status menus to see them.
- Characters have "hit points" or other damage ratings instead of taking real damage.
- Color coded magic systems with specific spell lists that go with each and new spells which are gained by levelling up rather than studying.
- Dungeons which just exist to be dungeons for adventurers to explore, are semi/fully-sentient, and self-generate monsters and treasure.
- Guilds which exist just to provide characters missions to go on to earn money and experience points.
- Monsters leaving drop items like crystals when they're killed.
- Monsters which are spawned by the environment rather than being part of an evolving ecosystem.
- Social and economic systems that make little or no sense in real terms, but which exist to facilitate adventuring.
- Standard RPG adventuring character classes like Fighter, Ranger, Magic Users, Cleric, and so on, being real jobs and professions.
- When characters die, they resurrect at special locations.

Very often the main character was brought to the setting Portal Fantasy style by some kind of summoning, although reincarnation is still possible, and while the setting to them is like a video game it may not always be to the locals. (For example, only the summoned characters might be able to see status windows or statistics.) This also means they're there for a reason, usually because the locals needed help and the cosmos decided the lead was the right person for the job, and so rather than being randomly placed there, they are dropped into some kind of situation. This gives the story a fast start, because they're plunked right into the middle of the action, and must play catch-up while trying to deal with whatever is happening.

Also, another common trope is that the character isn't summoned alone, and they end up with a group of friends/classmates/strangers who they now have to work with to survive. The only issue with this trope is that is makes the story more complex, since the writer now has to deal with not only a new world, but a pile of new characters experiencing that world. If the writer is prepared to handle it, it can work well, but it's sometimes easier to have them meet new people in the setting, usually the ones who summoned them.

Benefits
- The issues of language (health and nutrition) can usually be hand-waved away because this setting is unrealistic to begin with.
- The writer can get creative with the laws of nature in the setting, and the audience will just go with it because this world's laws are already different from our own.
- Anyone who has played RPG video games (which is most of the audience for this type of material) understands the basic concepts of things like levels, status windows and character classes already.
- Taps into the litRPG genre fandom.
- Allows for high action "fast start" situations without the need to explore.
- Can bypass some issues of morality, because the enemies aren't natural living creatures.
- Don't need to worry about whether NPCs are sentient or not- they are.

Challenges
- The writer must plan out the rules of the setting before writing the story, or at least the basics of them.
- The writer will need to lay out the rules of the setting to the audience as soon as possible so the audience can understand them.
- If the audience doesn't know RPG concepts, they'll need to have them explained to them, or they will lose interest.

- Will turn some readers off from the start, since not everyone understands or likes this type of story.
- The other standard disadvantages that come with litRPG stories. (See the chapter on litRPGs)

Second Chance Stories

In this type of story, the main character's consciousness and memories travel not to another person, but to their own body at a different time in their lives. So, for example, a dying old man finds himself in the body of his sixteen-year-old self in the past with all his memories of his previous life, or a murdered young woman finds herself in her own body days or weeks before the murder occurs. Stories using this premise have become popular recently, especially in dramas and romantic comedies, where characters go back in time to fix the mistakes that lead them to a bad end or where they made choices they regretted. Often, they learn that those choices they thought were bad also caused good things to happen, and come to appreciate the life they had before.

However, there is a variation of this type of story which pops up in fantasy webfiction as well- the main character from a fantasy world (not ours) who highjacks their younger self's body to fix the mistakes of the past and prevent future disasters. There, they use their knowledge of the future and skill sets as a tool to try and alter history and usually amass power very quickly to achieve their goals. Of course, the more they change the timeline, the less useful their knowledge of future events becomes, so it creates the paradox that by working to prevent a bad future, they become less able to prevent that future from happening.

These types of stories also often turn into wish-fulfillment stories, where the lead character is doing the types of things the audience members would do if they could only go back. Or, where the character gets to take revenge on all the people who wronged them the last time around, and uses their knowledge of the future as a weapon to achieve their goal.

Benefits
- Second Chance stories set in our world where the second chance is the only magical element are easy for general audiences to accept and work well for dramas.
- There are no issues with language or culture because they know it already.
- Natural audience interest if the character and their goals are relatable.
- Engaging stories if the character is trying to do things like solve their own murder or prevent other bad things from happening.
- Can work for stories of any length.

Challenges

- There's not much need to explore or ask questions because they already lived this life.
- The character's much younger self is usually pretty weak or lacks the freedom and resources to do what they want to do.
- The character's memories of the distant past need to be kept pretty fuzzy.
- The writer must decide whether the past can be changed in this story (creating new timelines), or if the past is set and will try to fix itself.
- The character can quickly become overpowered relative to their setting if they have too much of a knowledge advantage.
- The character will need to hide their future-ness from the people around them or else they'll be treated like an imposter or exploited. It can be very isolating and lonely.

Time Travel Stories

In webfiction, time travel is generally just a plot device to get the character (as opposed to their consciousness) to another time, where they will have their adventure or experiences. This is different from stories where the character can travel through time at will or via a magical police box, because the trip is usually one way or they return at the end of the story. As a result, the character doesn't get to use time travel as a "superpower," but instead only have the knowledge, skills and abilities from their own time to work with.

In essence, these stories are usually historical fiction, with a fantasy element thrown in, or Portal Fantasy science fiction where the character ends up in a future setting due to some form of suspended animation or accident. In the past, their knowledge of the future creates a difficult balancing act (depending on whether the future can be changed without erasing themselves), and in the future their knowledge of the past usually gives them something that has been lost by future generations to act as an advantage.

Benefits

- The writer can play with what-if scenarios of the past.
- The writer can send the technology of today with the character, for good or ill.
- The character feels more real and physically in danger, since it's their actual self travelling through time.

Challenges

- The character is physically in the past, and so may have to deal with language, health or cultural issues.
- The author must decide from the start if history can be changed and what happens if it is.
- The author must think about the most effective way to get the character to the other place and time, and how that method of transport affects the character and story.

Reverse Portal Fantasy

Sometimes, the present world is a little boring and needs livening up, in which case Reverse Portal Fantasy brings characters from other worlds, times, or realities to our own world. Most often, these are characters who are great figures in their own reality, but who may or may not have the abilities that made them great in ours. In addition, they are also often fugitives, fleeing from a bad situation or circumstance in their place of origin, and now find themselves on our world trying their best to survive or fit in.

Generally, the focus of these stories is going to be on the "fish out of water" situation these characters find themselves in, since we already know the setting well. They let us see our own world with new eyes, and this creates a lot of opportunity for introspection and comedy as these characters are held up as a mirror to our own society. Of course, they are often also tragic figures, and their time in our world is time spent healing and recovering for when they return home, which is what generally happens at the end of their stories.

Benefits
- Lots of comedy and drama opportunities.
- Works well as Slice-of-Life stories or Action stories.
- Instant storyline- they usually want to get home.
- Almost always have enemies following them, so built-in antagonists come with the story.

Challenges
- The character from another world needs to be paired up with someone from our world to be their guide.
- The ending usually involves them being torn between their new life in our world and returning home, leaving the friends and lovers they made here.
- The writer has to explain how they got here.
- They have to hide from the authorities.
- If they retain their magic or power, why don't they just take over our world?

LITRPGS

Coined by Russian author Vasily Mahanenko, the term litRPG is short for Literary Role-Playing Games and describes a type of story where the main setting of the story runs on a set of stated game rules. Most often set inside virtual computer-generated gaming worlds, the main characters in these stories are typically people who are "playing" the game, and are aware they are playing by the rules of a game rather than "normal" reality. They are most often people from our own modern world, and we the audience are watching them learn the rules and overcome challenges as they level up and try to beat the game in some fashion.

HISTORY

While the idea of writing stories set inside computer generated worlds started with the early video games which flourished in the 1970s, the first popular example of this type of story is likely Disney's 1982 film *TRON*. In that movie, a computer programmer is sucked into a video game world, and forced to learn the rules of that world in order to "beat the game" and survive. Although primitive by today's litRPG standards, *TRON* brought the idea of people entering virtual worlds into the popular consciousness and started the ball rolling.

The next major event in litRPG history was the release of *Legendary Moonlight Sculptor* by Heesung Nam in 2007- a South Korean webnovel that took Asia by storm. In it, a young man named Lee Hyun attempts to beat a virtual reality RPG in order to pay off his family debts. Its popularity resulted in an explosion of litRPG stories being written in Korea, and thanks to translations, the genre spread to Japan, China, and Russia as well. *Moonlight Sculptor* showed the potential for this type of story, and slowly different takes on this idea began to flourish in online gamer communities.

In 2009, a Japanese writer named Reiki Kawahara wrote a book called *Sword Art Online* for a Light Novel contest. The story was about a group of gamers trapped in a virtual reality game world where if they die in the game their body is killed in the real world- and they can't log out. Obviously, these gamers can survive if they beat the game, and the main character Kirito sets off to do just that. *Sword Art Online* became a megahit book, and the 2012 hit anime adaptation that soon followed spread the idea of litRPG stories across the planet, reaching people who would never normally read a litRPG novel.

Meanwhile, as the *Sword Art Online* anime was still being produced, an American writer named Ernest Cline wrote a book called *Ready Player One* in 2011 that captivated the American science fiction community. Combining the simple story of a young man trying to beat a video game quest in the future with a heavy dose of 80s nostalgia, the book found a wide audience, and it popularized the idea of stories set in games to the English-speaking world. It would eventually become a movie in 2018, but by that time litRPGs were already flourishing everywhere.

Over in Russia, the aforementioned Vasily Mahanenko released his own book, *Survival Quest*, in 2012, and also came up with the term litRPG to describe the types of books he was writing. This is the first recorded use of the term, which would later spread to the rest of the world. *Survival Quest*, and *Alterworld* by D. Rus, would later be translated into English by Magic Dome Books, and sold on Amazon's Kindle to a wide ebook reading audience beginning in 2014 and 2015. These two Russian litRPG books were extremely popular, and helped prove that litRPG books could sell in English, and sell well.

Since then, the litRPG genre (which is already massive in Asia) has only expanded and continued to explore new territory. It will likely continue to grow in the future as a whole generation raised on video games combines their love of gaming with their love of adventure to tell new stories.

GENRES

LitRPG is not a genre itself, but a meta-genre- a type of story which can be combined with other regular genres like science fiction or romance to produce a particular type of story. While there is technically a "standard" litRPG story (a hero in a virtual reality fantasy game trying to beat it), that is still basically just adventuring quest fantasy with a game element added to it. In reality, litRPG stories can be of any genre or story type, just as long as the story is one where there are clearly stated game mechanics ruling the setting and how it functions. People have started to write everything from litRPG westerns to litRPG erotica, and everything in between.

That said, of course, fantasy stories are the touchstone of litRPGs; it's where they came from, and make up the majority of litRPG stories as people do their own takes on the meta-genre. People connect litRPGs with fantasy, and they fit well together because the type of people who like to read litRPG books tend to be the same types of people who like to play video games, at least in English. In Japanese, people have started to use litRPG elements for many different kinds of stories, and they have a wide variety of different takes on things.

Here is a list of a few common types of litRPG stories:

- **VRMMORPG Stories**- The main characters are playing a fully immersive Virtual Reality Massively Multiplayer Online Role-Playing Game (VRMMORPG) while their real body sits back in the physical world. Effectively a Second Life story, but it's a game and everyone knows it's a game. Almost all the story time is spent in the other world, with little to no time in the real world. (*Sword Art Online, Alterworld, Survival Quest*, etc.)
- **litRPG Lite Stories**- The story is set in a game world with rules, but the premise that it's a game is quickly shoved into the background and mostly ignored after the introduction. These stories are usually just an excuse to tell a Second Life story without having to explain the setting logically. Often, they're actually slice-of-life dramas, romances or comedies that just happen to take place in a virtual world as a gimmick to add gaming humor or make them feel different from a "real" fantasy story.
- **E-sports Stories**- The story is about competitive gamers, usually playing an online RPG, which is often VR-based but not always. The drama tends to take place in the real world, while the action takes place in the virtual one. Usually fairly balanced between virtual world and real-world time. (*The King's Avatar*)
- **Augmented Reality Stories**- The story takes place in our world, but with elements of a virtual world laid overtop of it. The players are playing a game which is superimposed over the real world, adding game-like mechanics to the real world through the game interface. (*Yu-Gi-Oh!*, SIGHT)
- **Pseudo-litRPG Stories**- these are stories where the characters are transported to a fantasy world which functions like a game for the main character(s), but which the local people think is real/normal. Usually there is a question whether the setting is real or not, but it is often left unanswered. The main character usually has access to a game interface, but only player characters can see it. The rest of the population thinks that this is how things always are. (*Grimgar of Fantasy and Ash, Overlord, No Game/No Life*, etc.)
- **Puppet Park Stories** - These are litRPG stories where the main characters are adventuring in some form of theme park or artificial setting in the future. The character is using their real body to interact with robots or androids, but game-like mechanics may be present. (*Westworld*)

CHARACTERS

Main Characters

As a meta-genre, there really isn't a typical litRPG hero, but one thing that most litRPG heroes have in common is that they're almost all gamers- people who play games. Not only that, they are usually master gamers because their incredible talent for playing games is normally the thing which allows them to be the hero when they are in the game setting. They might not start the game as a master gamer, but their abilities will soon manifest, and they will eventually dominate the game and their environment.

These stories are ultimately still a form of power fantasy, so the audience wants to see how someone beats the game, not is beaten by it. The character can have setbacks, but they need to win, and win often, so they can develop and improve. Frequently, they are also extremely lucky, finding or earning a few key items or cheats near the beginning which allow them to advance quickly through the levelling and ranking system while surviving against tough opponents.

Opponents

As is typical of serialized webfiction, litRPGs don't usually have a main opponent, or at least not one who appears before the end of the story. Most litRPG stories are about the main character learning the game and overcoming a series of challenges of increasing difficulty, but these challenges usually aren't linked by a single overall enemy. This is mostly done because the writer doesn't know where the story will end, and doesn't know how long it will be, so introducing a main opponent right from the start isn't practical. If there is a main opponent, they will be a distant far-off foe that will only be vaguely mentioned at the start of the story and then occasionally from time to time, but not actually appear much or at all before the final arcs.

Instead, the lead character will encounter a series of "level bosses" who stand between them and their short-term goals, and who usually go up in difficulty as the story goes on. There may also be a mid-range level boss who takes the place of the main opponent for the first half of the overall story, and then is beaten in an epic battle to show how far the main character has gotten (while still having far to go). These level bosses also tend to have equipment, or their defeat will provide other things the main character will eventually need to defeat the final boss when the time comes.

These opponents aren't always part of the game world, and in many stories commonly some (or even most) of them will be rival player characters. Sometimes they are solo villains, or sometimes they are whole guilds who hate the main character and want to see them fail or be punished. If they are from guilds, they are usually mid-to upper ranked members of the guild's leadership who can bring the power of the guild to bear in different ways. (Such as blocking the character's access to resources, hunting them, or even laying traps for them.)

Supporting Cast

In litRPG stories, the main character will usually gain a couple friends who will help them along the way. Typically, there is a main love interest who they meet near the beginning, and then encounter a few times before they finally get together near the end. Along the way, they will meet other attractive wannabe love interests (think harem) who fall for the main character, but who the main character isn't that interested in because they're focused on their goals of winning the game. (Usually romance is something the main character considers a distraction.)

The main character will also usually have a guide character around who exists to explain the world to them (and the audience) as the story goes on. This guide character might be a buddy, an attractive cutie (who usually isn't the main love interest but wants to be), or quite commonly a non-human character like a magic talking book, a ghost in a ring, or an ancient animal spirit, and acts as a secret companion/source of information.

Background Characters

Settings in litRPG stories are typically populated by "smart" Non-Player Characters (NPCs), which means that despite being artificial, they act like "real" people. Writers do this because populating a world with NPCs who can only say the same few set lines would be pretty boring, so instead they treat the setting as a "fake" fantasy setting where the local people think this is a real and normal world. Like the hand-waving done around VR technology, the Artificial Intelligences of games are assumed to be good enough to simulate real people's behaviors.

The NPCs are often aware of the setting's status as a game, but don't care or think about it. (Their programming doesn't allow them to.) They are almost always archetypes to keep things simple (ranger, thief, innkeeper, bartender, etc.) and are usually linked to geographic locations within the game, often having a story role they play with whoever comes along.

A Note about litRPG Characters

In most litRPG stories, the characters are people from the modern world (or near future) who end up inside a game world they need to navigate for whatever reason. As a result, they know they're in a game, and they tend to act differently than they might in the real world. Anyone who has played an MMORPG like *World of Warcraft*, or seen HBO's TV series *Westworld*, knows that real people put in a fantasy world without social constraints tend to act in very primal ways. While they might often act reasonably towards other player characters (who they could have to deal with in real life), they will often treat the NPCs as toys and behave in cruel and destructive ways towards the setting. (Acting out of a desire for a feeling of power, or boredom.)

One example of this is that players in MMORPG type settings tend to take slights extremely personally, and even small things can result in blood feuds because another player has gotten in the way of their personal power fantasy. Accidental killings of a character (even ones who respawn with little to no effect later) can produce enemies that will constantly harass and hunt down the player who they feel was responsible, no matter how much they apologize. This can turn into abusive and bullying behavior online and off, and such players can make great villains for stories.

Another useful way to use the difference between players and NPCs comes down to the old adage of judging people by how they treat service workers. In this case, how they treat NPCs. If the players treat NPCs as playthings, it shows their true cruel nature, while if they treat them well, this shows a more positive side to the characters. "Good people" who torture NPCs because it's "just a game" aren't really good people.

PLOT

The typical litRPG is a Rising Hero Story where the main character has a simple quest (beating the game world) and the whole story is built around the character trying to survive and achieve that goal. This can play out in different ways depending on the rules of the game, the main character's level of comfort and ability with the game, the character's own personal limitations, and the difficulty level of the game world.

Most often, the character starts the story weak, and often at a disadvantage compared with other players or the world around them. This makes the audience more sympathetic towards the main character, since they naturally want to root for an underdog, and gives the story a strong sense of jeopardy as the character is in a dangerous situation where they could die at any time. As a result, the early phases of the story are both thrilling and keep the reader interested in seeing how the main character will survive in such a tough situation.

At some point during the opening stages, the main character typically gains some form of advantage not given to other players. This might take the form of a guide character (who helps the main character maximize their progression), a special skill or spell, a special rare character class, an artifact or item, special allies, or even knowledge of a game flaw or cheat. They usually earn this advantage (but not always), and it will be this thing that allows them to zoom up the ranks, and take on progressively more powerful foes, once the story shifts into high gear.

Speaking of which, once the "tutorial" ends, and the main character (and audience) know and understand the rules of the game, and their place in it, the story shifts out of the survival phase and into the "grinding" phase, where the character begins advancing quickly through the levels of the game. They are more comfortable with the world now, and so the focus becomes about gathering power, making allies (and enemies), overcoming challenges, finding items, and levelling up. They will almost always do this with amazing speed (even for the game) thanks to their hard work and whatever advantage has been given to them in the story.

Obviously, other people will notice the hero doing this, and so the hero starts to develop a reputation and gain allies and enemies. They will be approached by clans and guilds who want them to join up, which they may or may not do, and some people (or groups) may start to hunt the character because they want whatever the advantage is the main character has. At this point, the character will often have to decide on whether to form their own organization out of their friends and allies, move up the ranks in an existing one, or just stay as a solo player.

At the same time, the character is also facing progressive challenges from the game itself, as they face bigger and bigger obstacles and foes designed to test higher powered players. These challenges will often be made more difficult by recurring enemies, who may turn up when the player is least able to deal with them after defeating a powerful test. The main character will often only escape these surprise attacks due to allies, luck, or thinking-ahead, but it will show that despite the character's growth in power, there are still dangers lurking out there.

Eventually, once the character has achieved high level/rank, they will have to deal with their enemies (either because they are trying to defend something precious, or tired of being harassed), and this will usually turn into a major story arc near the end where all the character's power and allies are gathered to face the powerful enemies they've made. Generally, it will take time to build up the allied forces, and the enemy will know they're coming, so it will turn into a hard fight. This fight will almost always result in the character losing friends, allies, power, or the advantage that let them progress so fast. Now they've paid a heavy cost, and seem to have won.

Some stories will end there, but often there's one more final story arc, where the character has to beat the game world itself and the final boss(es) that go with it. They're stripped of a lot of their power, but still have everything they built up over time while playing the game, and that ability (and those resources) will be what allows them to march into battle with the final game world boss and win. Frequently there is also something precious at stake, like the ability to revive lovers and friends who were lost during the previous big battle, and this comes with a time limit that forces the character to act before they're really ready. The final challenge will be what tests them, and by beating it they show how far they've progressed and changed.

Once they win, they're given their rewards, and usually the game world itself has also been changed for the better. The hero is now able to settle down with their friends and just continue to enjoy the game as a game rather than a puzzle to be beaten, or move on to something else. Either way, they're a winner, usually both in the game, and often in real life due to some prize money.

Of course, this is just the "standard" litRPG plot, and you can actually use any type of plot with it, on a story by story, or story arc by story arc basis. You could do a Romance where the focus is on the relationship between the main character and their love interest(s), or a detective story where the character is trying to solve some great mystery in the setting (like which player character stole an item from their clan)- the only limit is your imagination.

SETTING

LitRPGs are most often set in the near future, where everyone (or at least large numbers of people) play some form of virtual reality online game that allows them to live as a character in another world. Obviously, this technology is more advanced than we have today, which is why it's set in the near future, and it also allows the writer to hand-wave away issues like semi-sentient NPCs and the costs that would be involved in playing such a game. After all, how does an average person afford a fully immersive VR capsule that plugs directly into their brain? These systems would be far outside of an average person's salary, but in order for the story to work, they need to be as common as personal computers are today.

Some stories set in modern-day side-step this by acting as if the game was a VR simulation, when in reality the characters are just playing normal modern online games. The events which happen are dramatized as if they were far more advanced games than they really are, making it a fantasy representation of the game's events to liven it up. This is especially common if the players are playing e-sports, or involved in real-life drama outside of the game, and lets the game be part of the story in an interesting way.

Naturally, litRPGs run on rules and game mechanics, and the most common game mechanic you will find in any litRPG story (and in fact almost the thing that defines it as a litRPG story) is the ever-present game menu. The main characters are almost always able to access a game menu of some kind which lets them view their statistics, options, skills, abilities, spells, and other important game information. It also usually lets them communicate with distant players through messaging, access game documentation, get information on other players, access maps, and sometimes even access game forums. This ability to reach outside of the game world and see the mechanics behind the scenes, and interact in a meta-game with other players takes the game to a whole other level.

Often, online players can also see a simplified version of the menu in their field of vision with important information about their own characters (like health points, stamina points, maps, current equipment, etc.) and important information about other characters (name, level, profession, health status, etc.) which helps them to navigate the game. This will vary with the game, but it's the reason why it's hard for characters in games to sneak up on each other unless there are special skills or magic used, because they'll see each other on their maps.

What system of rules the game setting uses will depend on the story (see below for some generic suggestions), but there will always be rules, and the player knowing those rules and how to make the best use of them is often what makes them a master of the game. All complex game settings will have tricks, loopholes, and flaws in them, and players (and their opponents) can make use of those tricks and flaws to accomplish their goals. However, always remember not to pull a Deux ex Machina and just have a trick or flaw come out of nowhere to save the character unless it's something that gets them into more trouble later on. The use of special tricks and rules should be foreshadowed, or at least implied as possibilities before they come into play to avoid making them seem like the author cheating.

Anyone who wants to write litRPGs should spend at least some time not only reading litRPG fiction, but also playing a few games, and learning the common terminology and ways in which both the games and the players of the games work. Just like knowing the rules of baseball doesn't tell you everything about how it's played, knowing the rules of a typical online RPG won't tell you how players navigate those rules and make use of them. There is a lot of strategy and tactics involved in playing online games, and even if your game is fictional, you still need to know the common styles of play and elements which almost all games of certain types have.

For example, game players generally divide almost all characters into three combat roles during play- Damage Dealers, Tanks, and Support. Damage Dealers (which includes Ranged Damage Dealers (Wizards, Archers) and Melee Damage Dealers (Warriors, Rangers, Thieves) have strong attacks but are weaker in defense, while Tanks are tough and strong in defense, but weaker when it comes to attacking, and finally Support characters are great at neither attack nor defense, but have abilities to make Tanks and Damage Dealers stronger. When facing Mobs (low to medium level enemy NPCs who attack in groups), Tanks will draw the Mobs' attention while the Damage Dealers hurt them, and the Support characters cast spells to heal the Tanks and make the Damage Dealers stronger.

As you can see from this example, playing these games can be a science and an art, and while you might not need to know the information from this example to write a litRPG, it helps to explain the underlying logic of why most groups of player characters consist of an Armored Warrior (Tank), Archer (Ranged Damage Dealer), Magic User (Ranged Damage Dealer/Support), and Priest (Support). A finely balanced and coordinated team of experienced players are a force to be reckoned with, and are often much more powerful than a single opponent who is several times their level.

Doing your research before you write a litRPG story can save you a lot of time and embarrassment, and most of all, help you come up with more interesting story ideas while making your setting livelier and more interesting. There's nothing worse for gamers than reading fiction about games written by non-gamers, as it almost always rings false. Do your homework before you try to play in a new genre.

WHAT IF YOU DON'T WANT TO LEARN GAMING STUFF?

Well, first, without the rules being part of the story, it really isn't a litRPG, it's a fantasy story set inside a virtual world. It might follow some gaming ideas or tropes, but it isn't actually a litRPG, which requires the game's rules to play a role to count. You can do this if you want, but don't think you can really call it a litRPG story without someone complaining.

Second, the way most light novels seem to handle this is by writing Pseudo-litRPGs. These are stories set in what may or may not be a virtual world, but where the setting functions like a game despite everything seeming real. Often whether it's a game or not is unknown to the main character (and reader), and answering that question may be part of an overall greater story. It might be because it's all a game, or because the gods of this world simply set it up using their own rules that are different from our world. (Or it may not matter at all.)

These stories basically run like typical fantasy stories (often Second Life ones), but the setting has lots of game elements built into it without technically being a game.

So, for example, there are character classes, characters level up, monsters are spawned by the environment (rather than being natural creatures), and other standard game tropes. But, at the same time, the people are flesh and blood, death is death (unless someone has a handy resurrection spell), and the only ones aware of it being game-like are any imported main characters and the audience. Think of it as a game, but only the main character(s) are in on that fact.

Doing it this way not only eliminates the need to focus on rules, but also makes it more accessible for non-gamers who just want a fun story. In addition, it takes all the player-character drama out of the story, so there's no need to worry about guilds, clans, or other meta-game issues, and you can just focus on the adventures and drama of the main story.

A simple guide is that if it's a litRPG, then the rules are important, but if it just uses a game-like setting without many rules being involved, it's a Pseudo-litRPG. The truth is, the vast majority of light novels are Pseudo-litRPG stories, with only a very few like *Sword Art Online*, *Log Horizon*, and others being true litRPG type stories.

LITRPG AUDIENCES

As might be expected, the main audience for litRPGs is gamers, and people who play online, console, or tabletop RPGs. However, a lot of this will depend on how "rules heavy" the story is, and how much it involves detailed gamer culture. Generally speaking, the lighter the amount of rules, the more accessible the story will be to a general audience, while the more detailed it is about gaming culture and mechanics, the less general appeal it's going to have.

It's the difference between a book like *Survival Quest*, which involves combat that has lines like, "*You have received 15 points of damage. Your current Hit Points are at 32.*" And, which goes into detailed skill and profession trees, or a story like *Ready Player One*, which has no actual discussion of damage or even advancement in rules-based terms. One of them is very much about the experience of playing a game, while the other is simply a fantastic story set inside a virtual world. Both of them are perfectly good ways to present the story, but they have different goals and a different approach and that determines what kind of audience each of them is going to appeal to.

Rules heavy stories are going to appeal more and primarily to gamers and members of their niche, which are very happy to read such stories and can be loyal customers. However, writing a more universal story can appeal to a general sci-fi reading audience, but also might make it appeal less to a gaming niche crowd, so it's a fine line for writers to walk between being appealing to both audiences. This is a decision that the writer should make early, as it will affect their readership and marketing for the story.

CHALLENGES OF WRITING LITRPGS

Making the Audience Care

LitRPGs have the unusual challenge of having to work harder to make their readers care about the characters and situations than most types of stories do. This is due to the problem that the story is often about a character playing a game- which means they have multiple lives and chances to overcome tasks and obstacles. And this has the potential to really kill the tension of the story because it can feel like there's no real danger or weight to anything, and nothing is really at stake for the main characters. Audiences want to feel like the story events mean something in the lives of the characters, and with litRPGs it's very easy for them to say, "Well, it's just a game, so why should I care?"

Sword Art Online famously got around this problem by having a situation where the players were trapped in the game, and if they died or logged out, their real body died. This created incredibly high stakes for the characters, and made their every move potentially life changing, which made the story instantly gripping and fascinating for the audience. This is also perhaps why some Japanese writers like writing pseudo-litRPGs, because those stories are set in "real" worlds with the natural consequences that come with that. However, the author doesn't have to go to such an extreme (unless you want to) to give the story weight and stakes.

Here are a few possible other ways to add consequence to the character's in-game activities:

- The lead is trying to use the game to pay off real life debts.
- They're unable to leave/respawn due to the victory conditions of the game.
- Losing their life in the game means losing a bet.
- The game rules change at a certain point in the game. (As their level goes up, for example, their ability to return to life becomes more difficult.)
- Losing lives means losing experience levels/abilities and having to take time to regain them.
- New lives cost real money, and the character is penniless in real life.
- Losing a life means downtime, which the character can't afford because they're in some kind of time limited competition.

- They're forced to live inside the game, so it's effectively their reality.
- If they die, they go back to a really bad save point. (Like a trap they escaped from.)
- There are only certain save/spawning points in the game, so dying means losing a lot of progress.
- To accomplish some real-life goal, they need to beat the game.
- Winning in the game affects the outside world.
- They're getting paid the longer they can last in the game.
- They're getting paid the longer they can last in the game on a single life.
- They're getting fame the longer they last on a single life.
- If they die, they lose clan/guild membership.
- If they fail, other people will suffer because of it.
- They don't know what will happen to them if they die, but probably it isn't good.

As you can see, it's all about coming up with some reason that playing the game isn't "just a game" but an important act which the main character must do or bad things will happen. Limit the character's ability to treat the game casually, and the audience will also be more engaged in caring about the character's success despite the world not being "real."

Other Types of Games

One interesting idea is whether a litRPG story must be based around a Role-Playing Game, where characters take roles and play characters, or if other types of games could work as well. Could you do a game-based story where the characters are part of a shooting game, a platform jumper, or even a puzzle game? Could you write a story about a character who finds themselves playing a role like *Pac Man*?

The answer is yes, you could in theory do any type of game, and even with litRPG stories, the types of games people build stories around do vary. Sometimes the stories aren't set in free and open worlds, but in settings with very limited roles for the characters and game mechanics that only allow limited kinds of actions. For example, combat might be expressly forbidden, or characters might be only allowed to think or act in certain ways.

However, the trick is that as soon as you inject characters into a game situation, you're making the story an RPG of sorts because there's a dramatic element at play. The character is automatically taking on a role (aka role-playing), and they're going to be interacting with other characters at some point in most stories. This means that there's a dramatic role-playing element happening, and even if the game itself isn't truly an RPG, the RPG elements take over that game story. Even if a character found themselves as a general in a Real-Time Strategy game stuck in a single command tent on a battlefield or starship bridge, they're going to be interacting with their subordinates and opponents, which means role playing, just to play the game and fulfill their goals.

That said, you could do an entire story about a single character (or small group) solving puzzles inside a virtual environment that is otherwise "dumb." For example, a character playing the role of the lead in *Pac Man*, learning the patterns of the mazes and avoiding computer-controlled ghosts, but it's going to be a pretty limited story in terms of drama and possible interesting situations.

How much should role-playing play a part?

As anyone who has played online RPGs knows, despite the name, most players don't make any effort to really roleplay their characters. Most players act and behave in the game like the people they are in real life (just with even fewer personal filters), and mostly treat the setting as something to be abused, and other players as either entertainment or obstacles. This drives people who do want to roleplay nuts, because they're trying to pretend to live another life in a fantasy world, while the people around them won't shut up with the endless swearing, real-world trash talk, and discussions. Listening to the chatter of most gamers playing an online game is more like hearing the Friday night discussion of a group of friends playing a tabletop game of Monopoly or Poker than hearing the discussion of a group of characters in another world speak.

Thus, when writing a litRPG the writer needs to consider whether the characters are going to talk like real gamers, or they're going to talk like people who are making some effort to roleplay their characters in the setting. These two things will produce very different tones in the story, because if they speak like real gamers it will be a constant reminder that this is just a game (see "Making the Audience Care" above) and reduce the world to just being a game board instead of being a real world. On the other hand, expecting that the players of a game would spend all their time roleplaying and never deviate into out-game discussions and talk like real people is pretty unrealistic.

There is a happy medium in between, which is where most virtual reality litRPGs seem to try to aim. In that approach, the players tend to talk like real people who have been sent to another world (like it's a Second Life story), but use only a little slang, cursing, and don't overdo the meta-gaming discussions. Instead, when they do talk about the rules, it's something which is relevant to the current plot (often setting up something which will happen later so the audience understands it), and come across as very focused and dedicated people who aren't fooling around and take the game they're playing very seriously. This isn't unreasonable, as the story is happening in a virtual reality world, and the players are fully immersed in the game, and it **is** real to them, so naturally they'll treat it more seriously than they might if it's just a character on a computer screen.

That, of course, will depend on the writer and the story, because some stories might work better with lots of out-game talk and more modern slang and references. Just remember, however, that too much real gaming culture will turn off some more casual readers, and might even remind some litRPG fans of why they quit playing games to read books in the first place!

The Laws of Nature

One of the fun aspects of truly virtual worlds is that they don't have to follow the same rules or laws of nature which the real world follows. As a result, authors should feel free (within limits) to push the envelope in terms of what can happen in their settings and explore how those changes affect the characters and players in that setting. LitRPG settings don't need to obey the laws of physics, so impossible things in our world are no problem there.

For example, how would a no-dying rule affect things? In theory, it would make the setting very peaceful as nobody could hurt each other. On the other hand, it might just shift the natural conflict in games to other forms, like social and psychological warfare as people still try to out-game their opponents. It could also produce situations where a character couldn't die, but needs to die to escape from something like a trap. No-dying might be the one thing that makes slavery of PCs possible, because they are trapped by physical barriers they can't get around, and can't escape their prison by dying.

What about a litRPG setting where everything is settled using a sub-game? Like Chess or Rock-Paper-Scissors? This changes the rules so that suddenly being a badass combatant with swords or magic doesn't matter, it's the skill in the sub-game that does. One benefit of doing something like this is that it allows for a more "peaceful" or strategic setting for telling different kinds of stories like romance or comedy. The light novel *No Game/No Life* is a beautiful example of this, where all conflicts must be settled through games and bets and violence isn't an option because god thinks violence is dull.

Just remember to keep things simple, and not get too wild with the setting's deviations from reality. The audience already accepts game settings and virtual worlds, so they can handle some changes built on top of those ideas, but if you go too extreme you'll start to lose them. One really big change and its consequences might be as far as you want to go.

Keeping the Audience Interested

Stories like litRPGs usually run on three basic big dramatic questions:

1. Will the character accomplish their overall goal? (the story's Spine of Action)
2. What challenges will the lead face, and how will they overcome them in interesting ways?
3. What cool new abilities/options/equipment/allies will they get as they advance, and how will that change the story?

The first question is straightforward and not worth discussing further, but the second and third dramatic questions are very important to think about when writing litRPGs. Since most litRPGs are task-based stories about problem solving, most of the interest in the story will be generated by introducing challenges for the main character to overcome and then watching them come up with entertaining, creative, and clever solutions to solve that challenge. This gives the reader a vicarious thrill as they feel part of this process of out-thinking enemies and overcoming obstacles, all the while thinking "What would I do?" and then watching how the lead does it to see if their solutions were correct.

And, this vicarious thrill is made even stronger by the advancement system that the story uses where each time the character overcomes a challenge, they are rewarded with new equipment, new levels, new skills, and/or new abilities. Each of these abilities then changes the game/story slightly, because now the character has new options to add to the mix and can handle different types of situations.

For both the character and reader, new levels and defeating challenges is like Christmas morning, because suddenly they get a shiny new toy (or toys) to play with and both the character and audience are now trying to answer the exciting questions "What does this do?" and "How does this change things?" They get to feel the joy of new possibilities opening up, and the anticipation that comes with having a new tool in their kit and wanting to try it out.

Thus, when writing these kinds of stories, writers should always be aware of what method they plan to use to keep their audience interested. Just like in real video games, the character and audience need to be rewarded on a regular basis to keep them interested, motivated, and engaged with the story so they keep coming back for more.

Game Mechanics

One of the things that litRPG writers sometimes struggle over is what kind of rules system to use in the in-story game world. Many of them either default back to a thinly veiled version of their favorite online Role-Playing Game or they bash together a rough and simple system based off either *Dungeons and Dragons* or an early console game like the original *Final Fantasy* titles. This is fine, and it often works well, but it's worth thinking about what the different components of game rules systems are and how they affect writers and players.

Attributes

One of the first things early game makers like Gary Gygax and Dave Arneson (the creators of *D&D*) realized was the need to quantify how weak and strong different characters were in different ways. For example, traditional *D&D* games ranked characters in the attributes of Strength, Dexterity, Constitution, Intelligence, Charisma, and Wisdom. In each of these areas, humans rank a 10 or 11 on average, with the normal range being within 1-20. These are then use to determine calculated attributes like Hit Points (how much damage you can take), Carrying Capacity (how much you can carry), and the number of spells you could cast per day (for magic users). This set of attributes was chosen because they felt it allowed a fairly well-rounded view of a character who could do anything a real person could do, or more.

Similarly, the early *Final Fantasy* games were based off *D&D*, but simplified it for a video game world where the character's actions were more limited. Thus, early *Final Fantasy* games all used some version of Strength, Agility, Vitality, and Magic, each of which start in the low teens but can grow with experience into the hundreds. From these came the derived statistics of Attack, Defense, Hit Points, Magic Points, and so on. The main difference here is that unlike *D&D*, where the character's attributes changed very slowly over time and had limits, the attributes in *Final Fantasy* went up with each level depending on the character class chosen.

From these original systems grew the systems used for RPGs of all kinds today, and this will probably not change in the near future. Even in future virtual reality online games, characters will likely be rated using attributes like Strength, Agility, Toughness, and Intelligence because each of those four key attributes can directly be used to affect their abilities in the gaming world. The first three are all key parts of combat (Strength- your ability to do damage, Agility- your ability to hit and not be hit, and Toughness- your ability to withstand damage and keep functioning) and the fourth attribute usually governs magic and non-combat skills. Most games add or subtract some other game-specific attributes depending on what the designers think is important or is needed to play the game, (for example there are no mental attributes in early *Final Fantasy*, because it's the player's own intelligence which matters in the game, not the character's.) but the core parts are always there.

One other major consideration with attributes is what kind of ranking system to use. Most online RPGs have followed Final Fantasy's lead and use a rising number system for attributes that ranges up into the hundreds to represent wide growth potential. However, a trend in Japanese and Korean litRPG stories has been to rank characters using letters instead, using something like attributes being ranked F>A (with F being lowest and A being highest, just like in school) and each rank being double the level of the one before it. Usually there are also AA, AAA, S, SS, SSS ranks above A, to represent higher levels beyond the norm as well. Usually, this is only used in litRPG-lite stories, where they want a rough comparison in attributes, but aren't too hung up on actual hard numbers.

If, however, you want a system where there's lots of room for improvement, and the numbers do matter a bit, then sticking with the generic *Final Fantasy* type number ranking system is probably the way to go. It was designed to make players feel like they're seeing real large improvements as they go up, and it will have a similar effect on audiences. Also, seeing characters with attributes ranked in the hundreds or thousands gives a real sense of scale, especially when your character's highest starting attribute is only 15.

In addition, three other derived attributes which will almost always be present in RPGs are Hit Points, Endurance Points, and Carrying Capacity.

Hit Points (aka HP, Health Points, Hits, Damage Points, etc.) are a measure of how much damage a character can take while still stay active, conscious, or alive. In combat-based games, this is required information, and the toughest players will be the ones who tend to survive the longest in a fight. This number is usually based off your Constitution/Toughness/Stamina attribute, and is also modified by things like level, character class, skills, special abilities, and sometimes equipment. Usually these are regained by time and healing magic/items.

In many game systems, as you lose hit points you feel other effects, like penalties to actions or being slowed down. This usually happens at key percentage like 50% or 25%, and will be there to represent blood loss and the character being on their last legs. In a virtual reality game, this would probably be represented by pain (if the players can feel pain), or finding their actions slowed. Amusingly enough, a quirk of many online RPGs is that unlike humans, some monsters actually get bonuses and become tougher as they get closer to zero HP to represent their death throes.

Endurance Points (aka Magic Points, MP, Health Points, Qi Points, etc.) are a measure of how much energy the character has available to carry out their actions. If used for everything, they'll usually be called Endurance Points or Energy Points, and if just used for magic and special abilities, they'll be called something like Magic Points or Mana Points. In either case, these will be based off the character's Toughness and their Intelligence (or Magic Ability) attribute in some combination. They too are also modified by things like level, character class, skills, special abilities, and sometimes equipment. Usually these are regained by time and resting.

In game systems, the main reason for having these points is to keep the characters from using their magic or special abilities non-stop. If the wizard is a magical Gatling gun, the rest of the adventuring group can quickly become pretty useless, and nobody would stop using their special killer sword move every time if that's what does the most damage. So, in order to force players to pace themselves, and add more variety to the game (and keep magic users from dominating things), system designers introduced Magic Points. Also, having spells and abilities use points encourages strategizing about where and when to use them, and how to use them most effectively.

Carrying Capacity (aka Equipment Capacity or Encumbrance) is a number which is based on a character's Strength, and represents their ability to carry a limited amount of weight on their body. This attribute is often forgotten about by non-game designers, but is actually pretty important because if it isn't there players will turn themselves into walking armored battleships bristling with weapons and equipment of all kinds. Adventuring players pick up a lot of things during their travels, and having a weight limit forces them to think about what's important and focus on certain items instead of being walking junk heaps.

Some games give everything a weight, and let the players deal with it (like real life), while other games give players a certain number of "slots" for different kinds of weapons and equipment and ignore weight in favor of just saying they have a limited number of things they can carry, period. (With things like bags expanding this number, and magic bags expanding it infinitely in some cases.) It will depend on how self-sufficient the game designers want the characters to be, and whether the players are expected to carry things like rations and water.

Character Classes

Another early RPG innovation which has stuck with the online gaming genre is Character Classes, or specific jobs which players select when characters are created. By using these job archetypes, it allowed for quicker character creation, and gave everyone a clear and balanced role in the party. Also, when combined with characters coming from different fantasy races, it became a simple way to add variety to the group by having many different combinations in terms of roles and Special Ability trees.

The traditional *D&D* character classes are Bard, Cleric, Thief, Fighter and Magic User, and these still tend to cover the basics of most fantasy RPGs today, with the exception of Bards, who have been jettisoned for being useless in most online RPG settings. The other four classes all have combat roles, and since Bards don't have a direct combat role, they're not usually part of a party. In most gaming settings, they've been replaced by Monks or some other form of unarmed martial artist character.

As characters of different classes go up in level, they get different bonuses and Special Abilities depending on their class. In some settings, the player is stuck in the Character Class they chose at the start for the whole time they play that character, while in other systems characters can have more than one class. If characters can have more than one class, usually they start each new class at Level One, regardless of what their current level is in their main class. Then the main class and the other new class(es) go up together naturally as the character rises in level, with the experience points of the character divided between the two classes. (In other words, they go up half as fast in each class.)

For example, if a 30th level Fighter decides to find a teacher and learn magic, they become a Level One Magic User, and then when they go up a level, they become a 31st level Fighter/2nd level Magic User. However, if it normally took them 10,000 experience points to go up a level, it now takes 20,000 because their points are being split between both classes. (This is why most players don't multi-class, because it kills their progression speed.)

Character Levels

Most gaming systems work on the concept of Character Levels, which is an idea that goes hand-in-hand with Character Classes. Using this system, characters are given a rank depending on how experienced they are and how long the character has been an active adventurer. This system was originally created so that *D&D* characters could be matched up against monsters and enemies who were their equals and to avoid slaughters. (On either side.) Today it serves much the same purpose, letting everyone know in a simple and quick way how they rank compared to the people and world around them.

For example, if you're a Level 20 character, and the average level of the monsters in the dungeon you're entering is Level 30, then you know to just turn around and find someplace else to explore. Similarly, if a Level 5 thief wants to join your Level 60 party for an adventure, you can politely point him in another direction, because he'll die during the first monster encounter.

Players advance through levels by gaining experience points for each opponent they defeat or mission they complete, with the higher the difficulty challenges being worth higher numbers of experience points. Once their experience points reach a certain number, they automatically go up in level, and their attributes, spells, and special abilities go up accordingly as well. This is how characters are rewarded for killing monsters and going on adventures. (Besides money and loot.)

Generally speaking, levels start at one, and then go up to some number the designers choose between fifty and three hundred. The reason for the maximum number is to have an end to the game for those players who reach their cap, and so that the developers don't have to design areas or opponents in the game which are stronger than that level. Also, each level requires more experience points to achieve than the one before it, making levels successively harder to climb up the level ladder.

As a rule, the greater the number of possible levels, the less experience points you need to go up a level, while the fewer the number of possible levels, the more points each one requires. This is to keep the game interesting for players (who want a constant thrill of going up each level), while keeping them playing for the longest possible time (to make money from them).

Of course, levels also serve another purpose among player characters by letting them know who they need to respect and who they don't need to take seriously. While the character's level doesn't always equal the player's skill level, they often do go together, so higher level players will often ignore things coming from lower level characters unless they know them. Similarly, players will try to recruit characters of roughly the same level into their clans or guilds, and are always keeping an eye out for promising stars.

From a writing point of view, the thing to remember is that the audience is there to enjoy the thrill of watching the character advance, and slow advancement means the audience isn't getting their thrills. It's generally best to have the main character(s) advance a lot at the early levels, and then when the advancement scheme slows down have them face many high-value targets so they keep moving forward quickly even though the experience point requirements are higher. Don't let the character wallow at any level for too long, because the audience wants to feel rewarded with progress.

Speaking of rewards, when the character reaches new levels, give them some options and don't just automatically have them get set results. It's always better if the character is making choices (so the audience thinks about what they would do too), and to offer them different branching paths they must choose between. For example, when they become a Level 10 Archer, they can choose to follow the Sniper path, or the Scout path, each of which offer different special abilities and bonuses in the coming levels.

Magic

Most modern RPG systems use fantasy settings, so naturally magic is going to be part of any system. Magic systems in RPGs are always what author Brandon Sanderson would call "hard magic," which means they're built around clearly defined sets of rules and principals, and function almost like another form of science. You cast the spell doing whatever is required, spend a few magic points, and get the result you want pretty much every time. Some games might have an aspect of spell failure based on the character's skill level, but that's usually more of a minor inconvenience at most. Spells either work or they don't and generally have fairly consistent effects.

First level characters start off knowing a few spells, and then depending on their character class, the type of magic they focus on, and their natural gifts, they work their way through a tree of available spells. For example, a fire mage starts off knowing spark, and then they can learn smoke or lesser flame, and after they learn lesser flame, they can learn greater flame, then lesser fireball, then greater fireball, and so on. Different types of spells have pre-requisites, and you have to learn the basics and the simpler forms before you can learn the advanced ones. Usually these are purchased with points which you get when you go up a level, and can choose which spells to improve.

Magical items in most settings function like modern electronics, and are about as reliable. They require some form of power source (typically magic crystals, which may or may not be a commodity in the setting) and have a few built-in spells that they perform. Some more advanced items, called Artifacts, are much more powerful (being made with ancient magic) and may have extra requirements to use or limited uses, but have rare or spectacular spells that go with them. Naturally, these are highly sought after.

Most online RPG settings are very high magic environments, where there are magic shops everywhere, and things like magic weapons and armor which can enhance your abilities are pretty common. Things like scrolls (limited use spell items) and potions (one-time spell items, usually affecting the user), are carried by almost all adventurers and few would be caught without a few healing potions or Scrolls of Teleportation (to a pre-selected site) in case things go bad in the field.

Special Abilities

When early fantasy games were being made, it became clear fairly early on that there were issues with how powerful different character classes were. At lower levels, the warrior classes dominated, while the magic using classes were almost useless. At mid-levels, the warriors and mages were almost equal, and both had their uses in a fight or adventuring situation. However, at the higher levels the magic using classes, with their wide variety of powerful spells, made warriors almost useless and left them crying in the dirt.

On the other hand, modern RPG games want to start all characters on roughly equal footing, and keep them there so that players stay happy, keep playing, and keep paying! So, modern RPG wizards start with some useful spells to keep them from being hopeless, and everyone has access to Special Abilities which grow with their level and experience. This way, all character types become better and more powerful in their own ways, and no one group dominates at any particular experience level.

Special Abilities come in many different forms, from special attack moves, to skills, to enhanced senses, to the ability to transform, to innate magical spells. One character might have the ability to eat rocks, while another is impervious to cold, while another has a special multi-hit sword strike, and another just knows how to sew amazing looking clothes. They may (or may not) require some kind of magic or endurance points to use, and often have a limited number of uses per day.

Who gets what Special Abilities will usually depend on a few factors. First, the race of the character, as most races have innate sets of special abilities that make them unique, and new ones often appear as the character goes up in level. Also, it will depend on the Character Classes of the character, since most Character Classes will have skill trees or special ability trees they can access and learn as their characters go up in level.

Typically, Special Abilities either go up with use or experience level. If they go up with use, then the character gains the ability at Level One, and then as they use it the ability will slowly go up in level until it reaches Level Ten. At that point, the ability may have reached its limit, or the player may now be able to access a new improved version of the ability which can continue to grow. (Spider Line Level Ten becomes Spider Web Level One, for example.) Similarly, some games have Special Abilities go up with experience level, either growing with the character automatically, or with the player getting points when they go up each level that can be spent on improving special abilities of their choice (Or buying new ones.).

Note: In litRPGs, Skills are almost always lumped under Special Abilities. This is to avoid cluttering up the character's information display with lots of useless data. After all, most characters would probably learn dozens or hundreds of skills as they go up through the levels, but there's no point in listing them all. Instead, it's better to just have a few key "Special Abilities" that are the highlights of what the character can do and are easy for the audience (and author) to keep track of.

Combat

Role-Playing Games evolved out of tabletop Wargames, so it's in their DNA to be combat focused. Also, since most RPGs are about characters fighting and battling monsters and other enemies, combat tends to play a big part in most RPG stories, including litRPGs.

RPG combat is a very simple affair- one character attacks another with a weapon or spell and the other character tries to evade it. If they fail to evade, the target takes a randomized number of Hit Points in damage, with armor subtracting from that number before it's applied to the target's personal pool of hit points. For example, if Mighty Marvin hits a dragon with a sword, and does 24 points of damage, we subtract the dragon's natural armored skin rating of 20, and Marvin does 4 points to the dragon's personal 1000 Hit Points. (Good luck there, Marv!) Any attack that does less than 21 points on any single hit does nothing to the mighty beast.

Although spells, Special Abilities and magic items can come into play, it really doesn't change much in terms of the basic mechanics of fighting. Also, characters tend to hit much more than they miss in combat (unless their target has some special dodging ability), so most combat usually comes down to who can deal more damage to the other side faster than their own hit points run out. The character with the higher level tends to have more hit points and deal more damage, so they're usually the victor unless other factors like teamwork or strategic use of magic is involved.

Magic in combat tends to perform three roles– One, it acts as a ranged attack like an arrow, but much more powerful and often affecting multiple targets. Two, it is used to paralyze or impair enemies so they can't move or fight back, allowing the close-combat characters to get in and use their powerful attacks to do more damage without being hurt. Three, it is used to "buff" or support fighting allies by temporary raising attributes, giving them temporary special abilities, or healing damage they've taken. This is why with careful use of magic, a team of characters can take on much stronger opponents than they might be able to handle alone.

In most games, when characters reach zero hit points, they die and are out of play. If there's a wizard or character with the ability to resurrect them, they might be brought back during or after the battle, but in most games, they have a time-out period and find themselves teleported to some nearby town or save point. They may or may not have all their equipment, and it's very common for games to randomly leave some of their items behind as a penalty which other players can pick up. Other possible effects of dying include loss of experience points/levels, needing to pay in-game money to resurrect, or even other characters needing to do some kind of action or quest to bring them back to life.

One final consideration for litRPG combat is to decide whether you want to include actual game combat information in your story. Lines like, *"You have taken 60 points of damage, you have 32 remaining,"* which you see in some litRPG books can help to add to the gaming feel of a litRPG story. On the other hand, they can also make everything feel very mechanical, and take some readers out of the story as well, since now they're just watching two countdown clocks to see who dies first.

Another issue with the numbers is that once the character gets to higher levels, fights can take a long time, and nobody wants to read pages that look like accounting spreadsheets, not even hardcore gamer types. So, including all the information about who takes what and how much can quickly turn from something to add flavor into a bore for the audience and a chore for the writer who has to keep track of it all. All of this for very little payoff, since most readers just want a cool story, and the numbers aren't really as important as who wins in the end and how they win.

One solution to this some litRPG writers use is to show the numbers only during the early parts of the story when the character only has a few hit points and fights are fast and deadly, and then quietly phase the numbers out as the story goes on. After this, they only show the numbers when they're really big, or can enhance the feeling of combat or danger (like the character is really low on Hit Points or struck a huge blow), but otherwise just describe the effects, leaving numbers hidden. (Good advice when writing litRPGs in general!)

WRITING E-SPORTS STORIES

While some might debate including e-sports stories as litRPGs, since they are stories built around players playing games and immersing themselves in game worlds with clear mechanics, there is a strong case to be made for saying that (some) e-sports stories can be litRPGs. If you want evidence of this, you need go no further than *The King's Avatar*, a very popular Chinese litRPG webnovel and animated series which combines e-sports and the other common elements of litRPGs to produce an exciting story. Also, even the original Korean litRPG story that started it all, *Legendary Moonlight Sculptor*, has strong e-sports elements to it, with the characters dealing with both real-world guild drama and in-game competitions.

So, what makes e-sports different from typical litRPG stories?

First of all, while many litRPG stories focus on the in-game world almost exclusively, e-sports stories are equally or mostly set in our own real world. E-sports stories are about people playing some popular game, typically an online RPG, and how their lives revolve around the game they're playing, both in and out of the game. These are typically people who are professional game players, or want to be, and so they've dedicated their lives to playing this game not as just a hobby, but as a job, and so they're focused on climbing the ranks inside and outside the game.

And that's another important aspect of e-sports stories- a lot of the character drama and conflict is about things which have nothing to do with the world in the game. The e-sports world is a place of cutthroat competition, where teams, guilds, clans, and companies are in constant war with each other for the best players, the top spots, and (of course) the big money. Like other professional sports, e-sports players can make a lot of money not just from team owners, but from winning competitions, and the coveted corporate sponsorship deals. In China and Korea, top-ranked e-sports players are also celebrities on the levels of singers and movie stars, and they get the perks that come with that celebrity like appearing on TV, commercials, and getting invited to exclusive clubs and parties.

So, with all this being true, you can see how fierce the competition is for the top spots, and how hard it is to stay in those top spots once you're there. To make things worse (again like real professional athletes) e-sports players also have a limited lifespan before age catches up with them, and a talented new kid with faster reflexes is always waiting to steal their spot. In fact, it's worse than being a professional athlete, because at least they can last until their thirties, while a pro-gamer might retire in their early twenties and should be thinking about setting themselves up for their eventual retirement from the early days.

Another big aspect of e-sports stories is the game itself is usually just a battleground as opposed to a world to explore. The NPCs don't need to be semi-sentient (unless you want them to be) because the real drama is about player versus player, and to a limited extent, player vs. world in the form of monsters, quests, and other challenges. The world is a place of competition, as opposed to exploration, and the goal of the game is to figure out how to hack, exploit, and use the setting to make yourself the top player in and outside of the gaming world. Level in the game isn't as important as other rankings, like being part of the top guilds, teams, and lists of most valuable players. The game is a means to real-world success, not the other way around.

As a result, players are always looking to find the best paths to achievement. Most will do it by mastering the rules of the game and its mechanics, but others will do it through good old-fashioned networking and playing social politics. Any system which involves people making judgements about who is best and worst can be hacked, and often the people who get credit for things aren't the people who actually deserve the reward. A team captain might present themselves as a genius leader based on their squad's great success, but it might be the rest of the team which are actually the geniuses, and she's just the face of the team so she gets the credit. Also, never underestimate the power of sucking up to those in authority, as attaching yourself to powerful people has been how many successful businesspeople have gotten to where they are today.

One last point to consider when writing e-sports games is how to write the actual game parts. There are two clear approaches with this, and this is probably where the line between an e-sports story being a litRPG or not appears. The first approach is to write the game parts like a sports report does, describing the action and events from an objective third person observer point of view, the way you might describe any game or competition. This way focuses on the point of view of the audience and players, and describes the events from their perspective. If it's done this way in the story, then probably the story is not a litRPG, but in fact a sports drama which revolves around an electronic game. (Even if the game they're playing is an RPG-like game like *Diablo*.)

On the other hand, if the story is from the point of view of the characters inside the game, as though the game world was a real world they were running around in, then the story would likely qualify as a litRPG. (Especially if the game itself is an online RPG.) It's the immersion of the characters inside the game world as if it were real that makes a litRPG story, even if the characters themselves are acting and talking like a bunch of players of a sport. So, while the players might discuss everything in meta-gaming terms (damage dealers, tanks, noobs, mobs, buffs, etc.), they are still involved in the setting and interacting with the setting, which both makes the game world feel alive and immerses the story inside it.

SHOULD YOU WRITE LITRPGS?

There is the old writer's saying of "write what you know," and rarely is this more true than with litRPG stories. Each author should decide whether to write a litRPG story (and what kind) based on their own background. For example, if the author is more of a casual gamer (or not one at all), trying to dive into writing a story that requires you to not only understand your setting but to actually know its laws of nature (game mechanics) can be pretty daunting. You can, of course, take the litRPG-lite option, or write a Pseudo-litRPG, but even those still require you to understand basic gaming principals and rules.

On the other hand, hardcore gamers who know the hidden key commands in their favorite games might be the perfect people to dive deep into the mechanics and enjoy the puzzle of figuring out the mechanics as they go. LitRPGs might be a natural fit for them, and they would be able to explore their passions with this art form. That said, the danger with hardcore gamers is that since they understand it so well, it might be hard to write something that will interest non-hardcore gamers.

Finding the right balance for you, between your own comfort level with game mechanics and the needs of the audience is the key to being a successful litRPG writer. Don't be afraid to do a lot of research (gaming and reading) before you strike out on your own path, and write what you love, because that passion will inspire readers as well.

TASK STORIES

The Task Story is a story where the main character is trying to accomplish a goal and following a pre-existing set of steps or ideas (a task) to do it. The task part comes from the fact that the lead character is typically given a job to perform by circumstances or an outside force, often trying to manage or create something. This type of plot isn't very common in North American media, but is extremely common in Japanese media, and some other Asian media as well.

There are five common kinds of task stories:

Creating – The character is making something new, be it a book, a car, a civilization, or a business empire, and the story is built around the character following the steps needed to create that thing. The end goal of these stories is the creation of that thing.

Managing – In these stories, the character manages a system of some kind. This is different from a Building story because the system was usually not created by the main character and already exists when the story starts. Most typically, the character is thrown into a system in chaos and expected to sort the system out and expand it, with the end goal being a system which is running better than before and is self-sustaining.

Restoring – Something that has been lost must be rebuilt or re-created, and the character is trying to find a way to do it. In many ways, this is a variation of the Building story and the Managing story, but unlike both it has a clear mystery element to it. What went wrong the first time? And, how can the character learn from it and avoid the same mistakes? The end goal here is re-creating what existed before but doing it better or understanding why it failed in the first place.

Learning – The character is exploring a new or unknown subject and learning about it. The story is about what the character uncovers and learns as they discover new things about their subject. This includes mystery stories (learning the identity of an unknown killer), mapping a new world, or even stories about scientific exploration. The end goal here is understanding the subject and often mastering it.

Teaching – The character is sharing information or skills with others to improve the students' situations. The story is built around the character trying to find the best way to teach others information, or the character using information or skills they have they work with others and help them improve their own situations. The end goal is that another character (or characters) and the audience gain useful knowledge or skills.

Each of these approaches will produce a different take on a story. For example, let's say our hero is whisked off to a fantasy kingdom and given a task to perform...

In *Creating Task Stories*, the story would be centered around a character who needs to create a kingdom-wide communication system in order to strengthen the security of a country where they have appeared. Using their knowledge of communications from their background as a computer programmer, they create a semaphore system and later a telegraph system.

In *Managing Task Stories*, the story would be built around the character being given the responsibility of running a small failing city-state and turning it into a successful economic enterprise by using their knowledge from Adam Smith's *The Wealth of Nations*.

In *Restoring Task Stories*, the story would be built around the main character rebuilding a trade alliance that once allowed this region to thrive, but has since fallen apart. Using diplomacy, and their background as a stock trader, the character tries to re-create an alliance and learn why the last one failed to survive.

In *Learning Task Stories*, the story would be built around the main character trying to find a cure for a disease which is ravaging the land using the scientific method to explore the nature of the disease and possible cures.

In *Teaching Task Stories*, the story would be built around the main character using the skills and knowledge they get from their smartphone's extensive textbook library (which they never bothered to read before) to improve the lives of a kingdom's people by teaching them things that make their lives easier like crop rotation and making concrete.

As you can see, each of these takes the same core idea of a newcomer to a fantasy land, and puts a new spin on it by matching it with a different type of task story goal. This allows for stories which unlike the typical "gather the items and kill the evil lord" quest-type stories, are built around creative and positive goals. It doesn't matter whether the character is restoring a kingdom, managing a dungeon, building a gang, starting a business, or even forming an army. In a task story, the character is following a preset bunch of logical steps or ideas to produce something or manage something, and this gives the story a shape and structure.

This may be why the Japanese are so fond of it. Unlike the conflict-driven version of the Three-Act Structure which Americans tend to use, this is a structure which doesn't require conflict to generate reader interest, and is ultimately about creativity and community. A character sets out on a constructive quest of some kind, and by their own hard work and working with others builds something, restores something, or adds something to the world or community which wasn't there before.

The reader interest comes from the dramatic questions of "Will they succeed?" And, (more importantly) "How will they succeed?" Especially since the characters are most often engaged in a task that would be difficult or daunting for most members of the audience. The key when writing these types of stories is answering those questions in the most interesting ways possible, while not letting the story just turn into a textbook with a plot. It's all about keeping it engaging so the audience doesn't notice that they're actually learning something as they go.

TASK STORY OVERALL PLOT STRUCTURE

The overall story structure of Task Stories usually looks something like this:

Act 1– Setup

- The main character, setting, and situation are introduced in a way which establishes both the main character's motivations, goals and their ability to achieve those goals. Often the goal will be something pretty big for that character to accomplish and this will be laid out clearly for the audience so they wonder how the main character could possibly accomplish it. The main character's major resources (knowledge, materials, equipment, people) will be established here too, usually with emphasis on the people, since the character will need help.
- Normally in the opening story, the main character will accomplish their first small step toward the goal as a way to show the audience their ability and establish that it is possible, just extremely difficult.
- The lead will begin (with or without help) breaking the task down into smaller steps that need to be accomplished in order to reach their goal, which is information they may or may not share with their allies and the audience. They will definitely declare what the next bigger step to be accomplished is, and lay out any mini-steps needed to accomplish that. With this in mind, they will begin gathering resources and working toward solving those goals.
- During this stage, we will usually get a more complete idea of the main character's motivations and it will often come from some event or circumstance linked with their past. (Often somewhat tragic, but not

always.) Their relationships with their allies will also be established and the motivations behind those characters also revealed.

- Usually any major long-term opposition the main characters will need to overcome are also established in this phase, as are any weaknesses the main characters have.

Act 2 – Action

- With their first big step accomplished, the main characters will start to move towards the future.
- Each story arc of the story will generally follow the Short-Term Task Stories structure outlined below, with the difficulty of the tasks increasing with each one, but also the main character's abilities and resources.
- New unforeseen events will happen that will alter the character's plans and methods to reach their goal, but the goal itself will never change. If there are lucky or fortunate events, they will be balanced by greater problems that they will need those resources to overcome. The character will always succeed, but mostly by using their head and thinking creatively rather than brute force or power.
- The character will often be faced by big moral decisions as a result of their actions, and run up against the Law of Unintended Consequences. Nothing comes easily or without a price, and the character will need to pay some big ones (social, emotional, financial, moral, personal, etc.) to keep advancing towards their goal.
- If they are going to change the setting in some significant way, there will be those who will naturally be opposed to the changes the character is going to make, and these people will actively work to stop the character from succeeding. They may even have perfectly justifiable reasons for not wanting the main character to succeed, as not everybody likes change, and there will always be winners and losers in any shift. Also, the what the main character is doing may not be clearly right or wrong, but helps a majority at a cost to a minority.

Act 3– Result

- Finally, the main character will reach the final step needed to accomplish their goal, and this will coincide with the biggest challenges they have ever faced in making it happen. Everything that can go wrong will go wrong, and any mistakes they made will come back to haunt them in the worst possible ways and times. They will often be separated from many of their tools and major resources, and forced to finish the step based on raw skill and determination. However, all the good they did will also come back to benefit them, and this will be what helps to boost them over the finish line.

- With the goal achieved, and the world a different place (and possibly the main character a different person) the lead character will settle down to enjoy the fruits of their labors and bask in their success. That is, until the next challenge comes along...

This overall structure will work for most task stories, but you should remember that this is an overall story, and it doesn't tell you how each individual story or arc should be structured or presented. In most cases, individual story arcs could be built around any other plot structure, however the most common one used is the one below.

STORY ARC TEMPLATE FOR TASK STORIES

This is a generic plot pattern for writing and planning Task Story episodes and story arcs.

Act 1- Setup

1) The main characters are situations are introduced, including their story arc goal.

2) The main character faces a problem in accomplishing that goal... (pick one or more of the following)

- A task they need to do to accomplish some larger task.
- Someone else creates a situation they need to fix.
- Someone else needs their help to perform a task.
- Someone/something is trying to damage/destroy what they've made.
- They don't have what they need to complete something they're doing.
- A new problem which has just popped up due to something they did previously.
- They lack the knowledge to complete something they're doing.
- They need help to do what they're trying to do.

So, they figure out what they need to do to solve the immediate problem (or to figure out how to solve it).

Act 2 – Action

3) But a complication appears! To accomplish their main goal, they (or someone they know) are going to need to... (pick one or more of the following)

- o   Accomplish the goal in limited time
- o   Accomplish the goal with limited resources
- o   Build something
- o   Convince someone/something
- o   Deal with a personal issue related to friends or family
- o   Defeat someone/something
- o   Find someone/something
- o   Learn something
- o   Teach someone something
- o   Overcome some personal flaw in themselves or someone else

Act 3 – Result

4) The main character and their allies try their best to solve the problem by using clever and creative solutions to further complications that arise, and... (pick one or more of the following)

- o   By helping to solve another character's problems, the main character solves their own.
- o   By other characters opening up emotionally, they give the lead character the strength/wisdom to overcome their own issues.
- o   By working together, they accomplish what the main character couldn't on their own.
- o   The main character ends up digging deep and finding the solution to the problem inside themselves by overcoming or accepting something they didn't before. (Unlocking some special strength.)
- o   The main character has a series of experiences which make them see things in a new light and provide a solution to their problem.

5) Thus, they have moved closer to their end goals, and... (pick one or more of the following)

- o Become closer with someone else in the process
- o Become stronger/more skilled
- o Built something new
- o Learned something about themselves
- o Learned something new

In addition, the structure of a task story is going to also be dependent on two more major factors- Is the focus on the task Intense or Casual? And, is the task being followed Clear or Unclear in nature?

INTENSE VS. CASUAL

In an **Intense Task** Story, everything in the story is structured around a process and the steps involved in finishing that process and achieving the end goal. In this type of story, the task story's steps aren't just the core of the story, they ARE the story, from top to bottom. The characters exist to represent the parts of the tasks and different aspects of that task, the setting is structured entirely around that task, and that task directs 90%+ of the plot.

For example, if the character is building a car, everyone in the story will be related to car building or affect the character's attempt to build their dream car. The settings will be garages, auto parts shops, race tracks, car shows, car dealerships, junk yards, and other places related to building cars. The plot will be about each step involved in building the car, from finding a chassis, to restoring an engine found in a junk yard, to customizing the body, to dealing with the main character's wife feeling jealous of the time spent on the car, to testing the new car and finding problems to be fixed, to taking it to car shows, and so on. The whole world of the story is going to be built around that central creative task.

In a **Casual Task** Story, the creative process is there to be a structure which unifies the story, characters, and setting, but not everything in the story is connected to it all the time. For example, if it's about a character building their dream car, then some of the chapters will be about the steps involved in the car's creation, but others might be about the character's history with their father, some might be stories about the adventures the main character gets into with his car-building buddies, some might be about the local politics of the car-building community, and some might be about the main character's relationship with his rebellious teenaged daughter. A Casual task story very often goes into slice-of-life territory, or into other types of stories which are character driven. Instead of being about the central plot of creating/learning/teaching/managing, the story is about the characters involved and their lives, with the task just there to give the overall story a dramatic spine and direction.

Some subjects naturally lean towards Intense stories while other subjects lean towards Casual stories. Exploring a new world is probably an Intense story, but collecting baseball cards is more likely to be a casual type of story. However, most tasks could be either, or some shade in between. You could do a Casual story about random character encounters the lead has as they explore a fantasy world, or an Intense story about the world of a baseball card trading and the rivalries that happen as different people try to compete to finish sets of rare cards. It's all how you want to present it and what works best for you.

CLEAR VS. UNCLEAR

The other major influence on the plot structure is whether the task being performed is one which has a clear set of steps to reach its goal or is unclear about how the final goal is reached. In a **Clear Task**, everything the character needs to accomplish the goal is laid out already, and the character just needs to follow those large and small steps to complete the task. This specifically refers to the overall goal, and whether the ways to accomplish that goal have been clearly mapped out. In this case, while there might be a little wiggle room on some steps, the right way to accomplish the goal is already known and the character just has to follow them, just like a step-by-step guide, a playthrough manual, or even a strategy guide might lay out. This doesn't mean that following or accomplishing those steps is easy, but it does mean that they and their optimal order are clear. (For example, first you build the foundation, then the walls, and the roof comes last.)

Clear tasks are a great advantage for writers because the writer just needs to learn the steps just like the character will, and then show how the character deals with executing them and the situations that surround trying to accomplish those steps. It also makes the end-point of the story very clear, and usually any online or printed guides you can find will include plenty of common mistakes for the character to make, adding drama and interest to the story.

Unclear Task stories are when the character has a goal, but there is no clear pre-set path to reaching that goal. Instead, the character must feel their way through, usually by using one or more smaller task stories approaches to solving the problems along the way. An example of this might be a character who has to travel a long distance but has no money, so they begin learning tricks from street hustlers and gamblers to earn their survival money as they go. This would be an Unclear Casual Learning task story, with each story being about how they learn a new card or coin trick that will get them money and through their current challenges. The tasks learned and used are the tricks and cons, and those are helping them work toward their overall goal in a general way.

Unclear task stories can be harder to write, since they require the writer learning a lot of smaller skill sets, but they have two clear advantages- flexibility and variety. First, since there's no pre-set route for the character, there's no pre-set route for writing the story either. The writer can do whatever is easiest for them or interests them, and use the kinds of plots for stories and arcs that they feel most interested in exploring. If they want to have the character learn knitting in one story and cooking in another, that's perfectly fine, as long as it fits with the story themes and goals. Which leads to the second big advantage- variety. While Clear task stories are locked onto a set of railroad tracks and passing each clearly defined station, the Unclear task stories can wander off the beaten trail and offer a wide selection of stories and plots which fit under the large umbrella of the story's goals. One story they're learning how to rotate crops, the next how to patch a thatched roof, but it's all still about living in a medieval setting.

By combining the different elements of a creative task story with different genres, situations, and characters, it's possible to create a wide variety of unique plots and stories that offer the audience something more than the usual adventure and romance that fill so many books. That isn't to say there isn't adventure and romance in these stories (if the author wants), but they offer another approach that doesn't follow the cookie-cutter genre types and brings something new to the story and the audience.

OTHER CONSIDERATIONS

The Human Factor

Stories place an emphasis on friendship for a reason- not just because it's hard to become accomplished in life by yourself, but because it's much more interesting when you do it with other people. Whenever possible, there should be a human element involved in the main character completing their goals. Watching someone decide to build a table and then build it isn't that interesting unless you're trying to learn how to build a table. Watching someone try to guide someone else to build a table is much more interesting because of the human complications which result.

Never forget the human challenges in projects either, as doing and creating involves a lot of stress on the creatives and those around them. It isn't just human interactions and different ideas and opinions that cause stress, but time limits, personal issues, lack of sleep, poor communication, sabotage, accidents, and lack of skill or ability. Then there's the social factor- since creatives are members of society, and they and the people they need often have families and social networks that need to be cared for and maintained. And finally, health is an issue that's easy to overlook but can come back to bite you if it's ignored- many a project has failed because someone got sick at the wrong time or their performance suffered due to poor health. If character's lives go out of balance in one way, it can throw many other parts of their lives out of balance as well.

Many of the things that go wrong in task stories happen because of a human factor, or the solutions involve dealing with other people. That way the characters are forced into emotionally difficult situations of one kind or another, where they most grow and develop as people. This makes the story appealing to more than just people interested in the subject at hand, and is where universal and interesting drama comes from.

Opponents

You might think it would be difficult to come up with opponents for stories built around task story structures, but actually that isn't true at all. The Laws of Physics say any action is met with an equal and opposite reaction, which is also going to be true for anyone trying to change things. There are always people who benefit from the status quo in any system or organization, and they will see people who are trying to change things as a threat. This doesn't mean they are evil or wrong (although they can be), it means that they're the winners in the current setup, and naturally they won't take kindly to the lead character messing things up. There will always be natural opponents in any task story, because change is scary and unwelcome to some.

The opposite is also true. There will always be people who lose under the current system and who will see the lead's changes as a positive thing and an opportunity to change their status. They're naturally going to support and encourage the lead in their work, and make good friends and allies the main character will need for help along the way. Of course, while their goals align with the main character, that doesn't mean they are good people. Some of the greatest challenges a character who wants to change things can face will come from inside their own camp, as they deal with people, they need but who have other agendas or different ethical standards. Some of the greatest organizations in human history weren't destroyed by their enemies, but by infighting, power struggles, poor organization, and poor management.

Research

This type of story is often heavily research-intensive on the part of the writer. Even if the character is doing something fictional, like running a dungeon, the writer still has to understand or come up with the basic principles of dungeon ecology, and more importantly, organizational management. (How do organizations function? Where do they go off the rails? And so on.) Knowing these things alone will tell the writer what challenges the characters will face and give them plenty of story material to work with while at the same time giving the reader something extra to enjoy about the story.

The great advantage of these stories is, of course, that the writer doesn't need to come up with the tasks, the challenges, or often even the settings. All the knowledge they need is there on the Internet, and with just a little research the author can find out more details about any task than they can possibly use. Yes, some tasks might involve taking free online courses from *Coursera*, *edx.org*, or others, but most tasks have *YouTube* videos for learning the basics and the common challenges. Procedures can also be learned from games and other ways, or even the writer actually trying to do the task themselves in real life.

Of course, following the maxim "write what you know," writers making their first attempts at task stories are advised to base the stories around skill and knowledge sets they already have or find interesting. If you're into collecting baseball card sets, then write your story around that. If you've always wanted to learn computer programming, write your story around that. But that doesn't mean it has to be mundane, as you can also do it with a twist- the baseball cards being collected are the keys to a hidden secret treasure map, or the magic system of the fantasy world the lead finds themselves in works like computer code. Think about how to put a creative spin on what you already know (or are passionate to learn) as a way to bring more value to the story and make it unique to you.

The thing to remember, however, is that the author doesn't need to be a master of this subject, they just need to know more than their audience about it. As long as the writer understands the basics and can build on those well enough to impress their audience and use it to structure and enhance their story, then it's all good. Don't think you need to spend years of your life studying a subject before you write a story about it. You can, but while you did, other writers likely published several similar books and moved on. Just jump right in there, learn what you need to know, and get those stories flowing!

CONQUEST STORIES

The conquest story is as old as mankind itself. No matter how much or little we have, we always want more, and the conquest story is about characters who reach out and seize their dreams. Sometimes the character is a poor peasant girl who gets whisked off to the Imperial Palace and must fight her way to the top of the pecking order in the women's quarter. Sometimes the character is an ambitious young man who dreams of being his company's CEO someday, and will do whatever it takes to get there. And sometimes, it's a space fleet admiral trying to subdue a galactic empire in chaos and restore order and civilization to a million worlds.

Whether it's taking over a company, a country, an organization, or a galaxy, or if it's set in the past, present, or future, all stories of conquest are essentially the same- a character with a goal of conquest must face and defeat a series of challenges that stand between them and that goal. They must gather resources, allies, and information and use them to move up the food chain, facing ever harder challenges as they work their way to the top. Sacrifices have to be made, prices will be paid, and their will to achieve their dream will be tested time and again. In the end, they will stand at the summit of their victory, looking out over what they have accomplished, and smile a bittersweet smile, proud of how far they have come, but having paid a steep cost to be where they are.

But, would they do it all over again?

In a second.

These are the stories that answer the ancient question of how you get to the top, and they do it with the simple words- "Work hard. Do what it takes. You too can succeed."

Although not as popular as they once were in our civilized world, stories about conquerors still resonate with audiences everywhere. Watching the underdog rise and seize command speaks to something inside our more primitive hearts, and inspires us to dream big in our weary everyday lives where power is often the last thing we have. We like to think the best will rise to the top, and dream of being among those best-ready to seize the world and make it our own.

But, of all the different types of stories writers can tackle, the conquest story is perhaps the one which requires the most planning and forethought. There are easier ways and harder ways to go about writing this kind of story, but that will largely be dependent on the skill of the writer and their pool of knowledge. Because, if there is any type of story that requires a lot of skill and knowledge to pull off well, it's the conquest story.

CONSIDERATIONS

There are four basic decisions that each author has to make when they plan to write a conquest story, and depending on how you approach each of these, it will have a huge effect on the way the story plays out. These four basic decisions are: is this a story of *War or Advancement?* Is it a *High Intensity or Low Intensity conflict?* Is the situation going to be one of *Perfect or Imperfect Information?* And finally, is this going to be a *Tactical or Strategic conflict?*

Any one of these can and will determine a lot about how your story plays out, and choosing the right mix from the start is crucial to make sure the story goes the way you want it to and is one that you can take from start to finish.

WAR VS. ADVANCEMENT

The first decision anyone who wants to write a story about conquest must make is whether this a story about someone climbing the ladder within a structured organization (Advancement) or if this is a story about someone trying to seize power, resources, and territory among loosely organized groups (War)? While there is a lot of overlap between the two, fundamentally these are two different stories- Advancement is about conflicts inside groups, whereas War is about conflict between groups.

Stories about Advancement take place inside businesses, bureaucracy, organized crime, politics, the military, imperial harems, school councils, and any highly structured organization. They are usually stories about someone who starts near the bottom of that organizational pyramid, and then uses one method or another to work their way to the top. At risk is their career, their future, and their dreams, and they put all of them on the line to move up the ranks- defeating, outwitting, and overcoming rivals, jealous superiors, and an unfair system that pits friend against friend and gets only more vicious the closer you get to the top chair.

How will the main character overcome the challenges of rising in an organization designed to only allow the best (or most ruthless) to advance? How will they get around the boss who hates them? How will they deal with their rival stealing their ideas and presenting them to the board? How far are they willing to go to get their major project approved when there's six other contenders and the project manager winks and gives them the pass to a hotel room?

The key to Advancement stories is that they happen within a structured system- which means there are clear rules for how things are done. Whether the main character decides to follow those rules isn't really important when planning the story, but understanding that those rules exist is. Those are the rules that the main character must bend, break, and overcome to move upward, because that's where the story is going to come from. Those rules say what the character can and can't do, and they determine the rewards the character will get for managing to succeed, and the punishments if they fail. The organization's rules and structure are the maze the character must navigate while dealing with rivals and other challenges. And, if they fail, or get trapped in a dead end- they lose.

Also, each level of a structured system has gatekeepers- the ones who decide who passes, who moves on, and who stays. These literal "level bosses" are the people the character must please, avoid, work around, and do whatever it takes to get past. Worse, these gatekeepers are not always the boss, but sometimes the people who have the boss's ear, and may be rivals the character is dealing with on a daily basis. This is where the organization's rules come in, because while they sometimes work against the lead, they can work for them as well- saying what the requirements are to advance and limiting what the boss can and can't do. A clever lead can use those rules to help in their struggles with gatekeepers, but so can their opponents, and sometimes it's a case of who thinks of it first.

Meanwhile, stories about War happen between businesses, organized crime groups, high schools, clubs, and anywhere you find groups (or individuals) in conflict where there are few or no rules. Because there aren't many rules, it means that there is no clear path to advancement beyond domination of others. The main character either wins, and dominates others, or they lose, and are dominated- and to be dominated in war usually means death or worse. War is a shark pit, and only the strongest and most crafty will survive.

Of course, while war might not have clear rules, it does have goals, strategies and prizes. War is usually fought over territory or control of resources (or both), and so the aim will be to seize territory or resources and exploit them while keeping someone else from doing the same to you. Organizations need resources to survive, and those with the most resources are usually the strongest, so the ones who have the most resources in war tend to be the victors. Taking resources, and exploiting them, is the key to winning a war, and those are a basic set of rules that transcend any conflict.

Writing War stories is about knowing three things- the players, the map, and the resources. Who the people fighting the conflict are, and their strengths and weaknesses, will determine how they fight and how they act as the war progresses. Similarly, the geography (even in space) of the battlefield will determine what each side can and can't do, and who is naturally in conflict with who due to being near or far from each other. Finally, which locations have the best and/or most important resources will determine the places where battles will happen and what the most critical things each side needs to possess are. These are basic concepts that any audience can understand, and how they're laid out determines a lot of how the war will be fought and the story will play out.

Finally, if the difference between Advancement and War is still unclear, think of it this way- Advancement stories are Vertical, they're about characters moving up in status to gain power. On the other hand, War stories are Horizontal, they're about a character spreading out and taking control of the things around them to gain power. Visualized in this way, the difference should be easy to remember.

HIGH INTENSITY VS. LOW INTENSITY

Someone once said that timing is everything, and this applies to stories too. One of the factors to consider when planning a conquest story is the intensity of the conflict which the story is going to be based around. In a High Intensity story, the conflict is going to be constant as the threats to the characters never lets up. This is the situation you find in games, like chess or poker, where every single move made counts towards either victory or defeat, and there's rarely a chance to breathe, much less think. It can also occur in stories where characters are in a series of high-pressure situations or a single long situation where loss or failure can occur at any time.

On the other hand, Low Intensity conflict is gradual and ebbs and flows in intensity depending on the situation, allowing the people involved time to rest, think, and contemplate. This is situations like naval warfare, where the ships take long periods of time to travel from place to place, but at their destinations might be involved in high intensity fighting. It can also be stories where the conflict is real, but the stakes are either not high or gradual- like life in an imperial palace or some office environments like accountants or architects. Those would be very low intensity compared to the offices of lawyers, politicians, or tax officials.

Generally speaking, most stories are a mix of High Intensity and Low Intensity conflict, but it will depend heavily on the style and goals of the story. In most War stories, the intensity is high because the story is often skipping from battle to battle, with just brief interludes before the next crisis or mission because time is critical. On the other hand, Advancement stories tend to be Low Intensity because the story is all about the interesting moments between long periods of hard work and the company grind. The set up for Advancement stories often requires a lot of negotiation or investigation (i.e. talking), leading up to the big (but brief) moments where the action happens.

Of course, neither of these is always true. You can do a High Intensity story about a Lawyer clawing their way to the top of the firm, or a Low Intensity story about a feudal lord competing economically rather than militarily with his neighbors. It's all in the way you choose to present the story.

PERFECT INFORMATION VS. IMPERFECT INFORMATION

In Game Theory, a Perfect Information situation is one where all parties involved have equal access to all information about the state of affairs. A game of chess is a Perfect Information situation, for example, because in a game of chess each side can see everything the other is doing and has equal access to all aspects of the game. This means that in chess, the game itself isn't a factor in who wins or loses, but instead the skill of the players is what counts because the knowledge of the conflict itself is equal. It removes the game as a factor in victory, and makes everything about the people playing the game.

In reality, Perfect Information situations are rare outside of games, although in situations which include advanced scrying magic/sensory technology, or extremely skilled spies or information sources, a temporary Perfect Information situation might result. It can also happen in a warfare situation conducted in an open space such as a plain, the ocean, or space, where everything is visible to both sides. However, even in these situations, if it is possible for one or both sides to hide information from the other, an Imperfect Information situation will still result.

An Imperfect Information situation means that both sides lack equal knowledge of the state of affairs, and this is the normal situation in real life. In trade, business, politics, interpersonal relationships, and even war, both sides rarely know everything the other side knows, and are usually working to keep it that way. After all, everything you know that the other side doesn't gives you an advantage, and information is power, especially in conflict situations. Most conflicts are won or lost based on the quality of information each side has about their opponents, as that information is what will lead to them making good decisions or bad decisions about what to do.

For writers, Perfect and Imperfect Information situations are something to give some thought to. If the focus of the story is going to be on the characters as strategists, then the more equal the information they have about each other the better. This makes the story into a battle between minds, and like Chess, removes many of the other factors of war by making their knowledge of the battlefield equal. On the other hand, if the story is going to be about tricks and deception, where each side is trying to use information as a weapon, then the less high-quality information they have about each other the better, because that allows for more uncertainty.

In addition, Perfect Information situations can be harder for writers to work with. A situation where everyone can see everything means it's very difficult to pull any kind of tactical surprise on your opponent. Space Warfare is a good example of this, barring cloaking devices and FTL jump drives, in space there is nothing between you and your opponents, so against a familiar enemy you know exactly what you're dealing with hours or even days before you come into conflict. You know when and where the fight will come, and you know if you will likely win or lose long before the enemy is in range of any weapon you have. This means that Space Opera writers have to come up with all sorts of ways to add tactics and surprises to a battle which was determined before the ships ever encountered each other.

But then, some writers like this kind of challenge or situation, and that's good too.

One final thought- a common cliché in Conquest War Stories is the chess/poker/whatever master who is also a battlefield tactical genius. However, in reality, while being good at strategy and tactics in a game is definitely going to help you in other types of conflict, being good in Perfect Information situations does not necessarily translate to Imperfect Information scenarios. A chess master is working with perfect knowledge of the game and a finite number of moves, while the real world is much messier and often missing key details that they need to make the right call. Not that you can't still have your lead be a chess master, but you might think about how other Imperfect Information games or skills may be a better fit for your main character.

TACTICAL VS. STRATEGIC

The final thing to think about when it comes to your Conquest Story is the nature of the way conflict is going to play out. If the conflict happens at a Tactical level, then the focus is going to be on characters directly fighting each other to accomplish their goals. This may come in the form of military battles, but could also be duels, sports, games, meetings, courtrooms, or any other type of conflict where the opponents are directly facing each other. These are usually tense high intensity situations, and ones where each side is making move after move to try and outfight or outwit their opponent.

On the other hand, a Strategic level conflict is about a battle of resources – allies, money, information, combat units, spies, and whatever else they have. Here, the character is using their resources to oppose the other side's resources to accomplish their goals. The main character is a strategist, not a fighter, and is usually far away from the actual conflict as it's carried out. Their job is to put the right people at the right place, at the right time to win, not do the fighting themselves.

Simple examples of this are ship captains and soldiers, who fight at the tactical level, as opposed to admirals and generals, who fight at the strategic level. All of them are fighting a war, but the captains and soldiers are going to be on the front lines doing the work, while the high-ranking officers are going to be far away, making plans and overseeing the operations. For one side, the conflict is direct and personal, while for the other it's a less personal affair where they will often send people to die never knowing their names.

Both of these approaches can work equally well in conquest stories, and many stories will have elements of both, but the writer should prioritize one over the other from the start. A Tactical Conquest story will have strategic elements, but is first and foremost about direct conflict, while a Strategic Conquest story will have battles, but is first and foremost about indirect conflict through resources. These stories will play out differently from each other, as Tactical stories are High Intensity, whereas Strategic stories are Low Intensity, and tend to occur over much longer periods of time.

That said, it isn't uncommon for a story to start out as a Tactical story, where the character is a scrappy fighter, or up and comer with no or limited resources who must do everything themselves, and then slowly shift to being a Strategic story as the character gains more resources and a higher position. This is a natural, realistic progression, and can be one way to keep the story fresh over time by having it shift in focus as the character grows and matures.

However, natural as it is, there are a few dangers with this approach.

First, the shift from being a Tactical story to a Strategic one fundamentally changes what the story is. If the audience is showing up to enjoy a story about the meanest badass fighter who ever lived, and the story is now about him standing around in rooms staring at maps and drinking tea there's probably going to be a disconnect. It becomes harder and harder to justify the main character taking a personal hand in battle when they have great amounts of resources available to them. Even if they would risk themselves, their subordinates would do anything to stop them from going out and getting themselves killed, something that would cause the army to fall apart and ruin everyone's day.

Of course, if the main character is a walking battleship of power, and the strongest on the battlefield, then yes, they'll probably have to go out and face the enemy's champion at some point. And, this becomes a good excuse to skip them fighting the foot soldiers and get them involved in the big fun battles, but not every story or setting has this option. In a non-magic setting, where one hit can kill anyone, leaders are better off at the back of the army than the front, and that can be a challenge to write well.

Which leads to the second "danger" of shifting from a Tactical story to a Strategic one over time, and one which should also be considered from the start- do you, the writer, have the skill set and interest to tell that kind of story? Strategic stories are much harder to tell well than Tactical ones, which is why we don't see them as often. To tell a Strategic story well, you must be able to come up with interesting ways to present indirect conflict, and to tell grand events as they play out. Not only that, you, the writer, have to be able to come up with strategies and tricks the characters will use, believable ones that impress your audience.

That's going to require research, and hard work on your part. Lots of it.

If these "dangers" make it sound like you'd rather stick with a Tactical story and leave the command post work to other characters, then make sure early on in your character's rise you introduce support characters who are experts at handling those parts of the Conquest. An aide who's a wiz at accounting, a master staff officer, or someone who will be a great prime minister of the new empire, can allow the main character to keep fighting the battles personally while only having to worry about the messy details when it's relevant to the plot.

AUDIENCE AND PRESENTATION

Like any conflict-based story, the writer needs to think carefully about how they're going to present the conflict to the audience. Conquest Stories work best in clearly structured environments so the audience can understand and track their progress. The more the audience understands the rules of the conflict that's playing out in front of them, the better they will be able to enjoy and appreciate the story you are trying to tell. If the audience doesn't understand the game being played, it will be difficult for them to understand why the main character's clever move left everyone in awe, or enjoy the twists you have planned.

What this means is that in Conquest Stories, the writer needs to give extra care to lay the situation out to the audience, spoon feeding them details if necessary. If the "game" being played is a real-world one, like moving up the company ladder, then there might not be a lot of explanation necessary except when setting up situations which are specific to that company. For example, if the character is going to use a clause in the company constitution to prevent their boss from firing them for exposing the boss's corrupt practices, then you need to talk about the company constitution existing and what role it plays long before that scene comes up. That way it doesn't come out of the blue like a *Deus ex Machina*, and the reader will feel it's a natural twist in the story.

Similarly, if the situation is a primal one that transcends time and space, like fighting for survival or resources, then the audience only needs to be told what makes this situation special and different from what they already know. The audience will want to know who is involved and why they are competing, but beyond that, the details needed are only ones which are there to set up the story events and make the whole thing run smoothly.

On the other hand, if you have a highly complex scenario like a full-scale war, or an advanced game, then a lot more explanation might be needed. In this case, the best practice is to only tell the audience what they need to know at the time to understand what's happening or going to happen, and nothing more. You don't want to overload your audience with facts and information, because that will likely bore or confuse them, or both. Instead, you need to give them the details they need to understand the immediate situation and then move on with the action.

And the audience should never be left out on what's happening because one of the keys to telling an exciting and interesting story is making sure that the audience knows more than the characters involved in the story do. If the audience understands the challenges that the main character faces, then they are more likely to be engaged and question the main character's chances of winning.

Not only that, it creates tension.

Alfred Hitchcock, the legendary suspense filmmaker, famously gave this example during an American Film Institute seminar:

"There is a distinct difference between 'suspense' and 'surprise,' and yet many pictures continually confuse the two. I'll explain what I mean.

"We are now having a very innocent little chat. Let's suppose that there is a bomb underneath this table between us. Nothing happens, and then all of a sudden, 'Boom!' There is an explosion. The public is surprised, but prior to this surprise, it has seen an absolutely ordinary scene, of no special consequence. Now, let us take a suspense situation. The bomb is underneath the table and the public knows it, probably because they have seen the anarchist place it there. The public is aware the bomb is going to explode at one o'clock and there is a clock in the decor. The public can see that it is a quarter to one. In these conditions, the same innocuous conversation becomes fascinating because the public is participating in the scene. The audience is longing to warn the characters on the screen: 'You shouldn't be talking about such trivial matters. There is a bomb beneath you and it is about to explode!'

"In the first case we have given the public fifteen seconds of surprise at the moment of the explosion. In the second we have provided them with fifteen minutes of suspense. The conclusion is that whenever possible the public must be informed. Except when the surprise is a twist, that is, when the unexpected ending is, in itself, the highlight of the story."

So, as Hitchcock demonstrates, the audience knowing more than the characters is often essential to making the story lively and interesting. Very often, conquest stories take place in what are Imperfect Information environments for the characters, but are near Perfect Information environments for the audience. This way, the audience can feel concerned for the character they know is walking into a trap, but can't do anything but watch in horror, allowing the writer to control what the audience feels about the situation.

Of course, this doesn't mean that the writer of a conquest story (or any other kind) must always play fair with the reader. Hiding or omitting key information to set up a surprise is another important tool in the writer's toolkit, and writers often pull a slight of hand on the audience and make them think one thing is happening when another really is. Although, these twists too should generally be foreshadowed in some way, so that the audience can look back and see that there were clues all along, they just missed them. That way it seems like the author is playing fair, even if they really weren't.

This is also why most conquest stories are presented in Third Person, not First Person. Third person lets you show what the different parties are doing and gives you the flexibility to show and not show what each character is up to. This lets you present and edit the information like a film editor, focusing on key details and skipping what isn't important in favor of what's interesting and relevant.

First Person, on the other hand, locks you inside a single (or limited number) of perspectives, and makes it much harder for the writer to show what the opposition is planning. (The character can only accidentally overhear so many conversations.) It also makes it harder to hide information about what the lead character is doing from the audience, which makes tricks and surprises on the audience more difficult to pull off well. But, despite these challenges, First Person does have a few advantages- first, it makes the audience bond with the main character more, and makes the story a bit more intense, which is a major plus. Second, as the support characters explain things to the lead, they're also explaining things to the audience, which is a great way to avoid infodumps. But, the most important advantage of First-Person narrators in conquest stories is that it's a great way to avoid moral responsibility.

There is an old saying that you can't make an omelet without breaking a few eggs, which refers to the idea that big projects get messy and complicated, and sometimes people get hurt in the process. A character engaging in conquest, whether War or Advancement, is going to hurt a lot of people as they do so, and might even get more than a few killed, depending on the story. Viewed from some perspectives, this is going to make them seem immoral and unethical, but if the audience is inside their heads and understands what they're doing and why they're doing it, it makes it harder to judge them harshly. We know the young feudal lord is just trying to bring peace to the land, so we accept that even in his position we might have to make some of the hard choices he does, and we forgive him doing things that might otherwise be pretty unacceptable. We know the princess had to poison her handmaiden who was caught by the evil count before the girl gave up the princess's secrets under torture. We know these things because we're inside their heads, and we're them, and it makes it a lot easier to stomach, even if it's still not ethical.

We might not always like these characters and the choices they make, but it's much harder to hate them when they feel like a real person who is making understandably hard decisions. You can achieve much the same effect using Third Person close, where we can hear the characters' thoughts, but nothing beats First Person for putting the audience up close and personal with a troubled lead.

Thus, Third Person stories will produce something more sweeping and cinematic, while First Person will produce something more intense and personal. Which one you use, or a combination of both, is up to you, and should be determined by the nature of the project itself.

CHARACTERS

Characters in conquest stories tend to be clearly split between active and passive. The active characters are the combatants, the ones who will be fighting over power, whatever form it takes. The passive characters will be the ones supporting them, following their lead, or forming the bodies they step over on their path to victory. Both have a role to play, but the reader should never be in doubt which character belongs in each group.

Lead characters, and their opponents, in conquest stories are by necessity aggressive and ambitious. If they weren't, they wouldn't be the lead character in this kind of story. It doesn't mean they always start off that way, and sometimes they are made this way by experience and circumstance, but in their hearts, there is always a spark waiting to be kindled into a raging fire. All that is needed is fate to blow on that ember, and it turns into an inferno that threatens to rage over the world.

That said, lead characters in conquest stories are almost always good people at heart, at least at the beginning. This goes back to the idea that in order to connect with the audience, there must be something about the character the audience can relate to. They must either be able to support the lead's goals or ideals, or see the lead as doing the things they wish they could do. This is why so many leads in conquest stories have one or more of the following traits:

- Grew up poor
- Are coming into the story at a disadvantage
- Want to prove to someone they can accomplish their dreams
- Want to take care of their parents/friends/loved ones in style
- Have a dream to be something better
- Have a dream to change something for the better
- Want revenge, having been badly wronged

Every one of those traits is something that the audience will be able to understand or sympathize with, and most importantly, turns the character from a bully into a noble figure who is just trying to make the world a better place in their own way. This is important, as without this kind of positive spin, the character can easily come across as evil or unlikable because they're doing things that aren't normally seen as acceptable in society.

And it isn't difficult, because the audience is already conditioned to look for these things, as so many action movies use them as justifications for why the main character does awful things, and if you give them even a hint of these traits the audience will happily go with it. This is how a typical action hero can murder a dozen security guards just trying to feed their families because that hero is trying to get revenge on their boss, and everyone cheers the action hero as they do it. After all, they're between him and his goal, so screw the guard's wives, children and parents- they shouldn't have gotten in his way!

Giving them a sympathetic background also helps to soften things as the character starts to do things which may be less noble as they get closer to their goal and the fighting gets more intense. It's easier to forgive a character who has to betray trusts and sacrifices their morals and beliefs when we know they're doing it for what they consider the greater good. As long as the character struggles a bit in their decisions, and questions their direction from time to time, the audience will be able to let a lot pass. That doesn't mean they can't go over to the dark side in the end, just that they can't spend the whole story there or the audience won't have an easy time supporting them.

Their opponents should be much the same way, impassioned characters with clear goals, and sometimes even noble ones, but who have taken the wrong path or already fallen prey to their darker desires. Evil lords and ladies who are evil for the sake of being evil are boring, but ones who think they're doing the right thing, or are doing the right thing in the wrong way are interesting mirrors of the main character that the audience will understand and connect with. So, always look for ways to have your opponents represent the darker side of the challenges the lead character is facing, it will bring more life and depth to the conflict.

Finally, the quality of the supporting cast in conquest stories is critical to the success of the story. The most precious resource that would-be conquerors gather is allies, and it is almost impossible for characters, no matter how competent, to gain power without help. The character can't do everything and be everywhere, and they need the help of trustworthy allies to do what they can't do and be where they can't be. A leader is only as good as the people they gather around them, and the quality of the people who join the main character will be a major factor in how other characters and the audience views them.

Plus, half the fun of conquest stories is the cool and interesting supporting cast who gather around our hero and provide color and comic relief. Often, they are reflections of the leader, and each has a trait that the leader either lacks or needs to work on. In addition, they provide the skills the leader needs to run their operation, and there will always be a right-hand person there to deal with the messy and boring details so the leader can focus on the fun and interesting parts. Just remember to avoid cast bloat by having too many support characters involved at the same time.

STORY STRUCTURE

As noted at the start of the chapter, whether the story is about Advancement or War, the story is largely the same. A character has goals and limited resources, and then comes up with strategies to use those goals and resources to carve out their piece of the available pie. Along the way, every move they make either brings them closer or farther away from accomplishing their goals, but they're always trying to move forward and find the path that will lead them to victory. As they get closer, the challenges get bigger, and eventually they face their penultimate challenge that will decide everything.

However, there are some small differences between how Advancement stories play out and how War stories play out, so it's worth looking at each separately.

ADVANCEMENT STORIES

Stories about Advancement, or going up in an organization, are built around the character navigating a controlled and structured environment. Each level of the organization has its own rules and requirements, and the character must figure out how to advance within that structure if they want to move past it. While in reality, this is typically done by working hard and proving your worth to the company, in fiction there are normally two other ways that characters rise- talent and ambition.

In some stories, the main character is highly talented, and in fact they are so good at their job that they naturally move upward in the organization. These characters don't even need to try to do anything to advance, because by being so valuable to the organization they're naturally promoted for doing their job. For these characters, the focus of the story is usually on them overcoming their rivals, and as they defeat each rival their rise naturally occurs. They will have to deal with jealous bosses blocking their way from time to time, but usually the company leadership actually likes them because they're making the organization a better place.

Alternately, there's the characters who plan to rise on pure ambition. These characters are still usually good at their jobs, but aren't so gifted that their rise is guaranteed, and may be part of an organization which doesn't fairly reward based on merit. So, for them the only option is to use opportunities and whatever they can do (or are willing to do) to ensure their rise within the organization. Difficult bosses block every turn, and the people at the top see them as a threat to be eliminated or a pawn to be used against other members of the leadership. For these people, the road will be hard, but by not giving up, they can achieve their dreams.

You will find Advancement stories about both types of lead characters, and naturally there are stories where the main character is both super-talented and ambitious. However, most stories tend to lean toward one side or the other. Either the main character just needs to worry about how to solve their immediate problems, and can leave advancement to luck and proving their worth, or the main character has to fight for every rung up the ladder of success and actually doing their job is often an afterthought in the games of office politics.

In either case, the actual structure of the overall story will tend to look like this:

Act 1 – Setup

- The major characters, setting, situations, and controlling ideas are introduced.

- We are introduced to the main character in a relatively short story arc where the character is trying to accomplish some short-term goal that sets them up for the stories to come. For example, the character is facing their first important assignment, or given some kind of test to get hired. Usually the main character appears to be losing, but then pulls the fat out of the fire to impress everyone.
- Usually the character's past and motivations are revealed through flashbacks, although some important details are left for later stories or only hinted at.
- The main character's first ally will usually be introduced as part of this story as well, which is usually a sidekick character of some kind with potential to be something greater. (Although some stories reverse expectations and have the potential sidekick turn out to be the real first opponent, or working for the opposition.)

Act 2- Action

- In the next story arc, the main character faces their second major challenge, the main opposition is also introduced and set up so the audience comes to understand the real nature of the challenge the main character faces. In the Introduction we saw a small piece of the organization, but now we see the whole monolithic monster the character is going to try to climb atop of.
- This look at the real challenge involves the main character facing off against an opponent who, while still not very strong, represents the true challenge the character has ahead of them. For example, they face off against a character who is a minor member of the vice president's posse, or get on the wrong side of a powerful eunuch's aide.
- From this encounter, the main character (and the audience) is reminded how hard this is all going to be, but the experience usually just drives them to try even harder.
- If the main character is going to make a tragic mistake that will come back to haunt them later, this is usually where it will happen.
- After that, the main character begins grinding their way to the top, with each level and challenge they face becoming harder and more complex. Along the way, they gather more and more allies and resources, which make them a bigger player in the organization and more confident in their abilities and position. However, they also make more enemies and become a bigger threat to those already in power.

- As the main character rises, they are noticed by more and more of the higher forces in the organization, who will either try to recruit, block, or occasionally enable their rise. These players will tempt the main character, but the lead will turn them down in the end or use them for their own benefit- the lead only works for themselves, nobody else.
- The lead will also receive the rewards, perks, and problems that come with advanced status. These can be seen as little reminders of what they'll get when they reach the top.
- The lead is also pulled at by social forces, which tempts them to stop and just accept what they've accomplished. The main character **must** be tempted to stop at some point, preferably before they hit the third act. Then decide to keep going and push on into the final phase.
- Also, towards the end of this act, the lead will usually have to make some kind of final sacrifice, where they lose something or someone important to them as a result of their ambitions. This will be their fault, and the result of the choices they made, and symbolizes the price that success comes at.

Act 3 – Result

- At this point, the story is almost finished, and the lead character faces their final, greatest challenge that stands between them and their goal. Usually this involves dethroning the person who currently sits at the top, or facing off against another rival for an empty top position.
- All the main character's ghosts come back to haunt them, and all the good they've done comes back to reward them as they face their final challenge. Usually they must make a final choice between their dream, and some other good option, where they are offered one last chance to turn away, but take their dream anyway.
- Having achieved their dream, the lead receives some physical, tangible symbol of their victory- be it the Love Interest, a symbolic object like a medal or throne, a certificate, or a crown. There will always be some symbol of their victory, often one first introduced right back at the start of the story. (For example, they promised to marry their high school sweetheart when they reached the top, or the throne they cleaned as a slave is now where they sit.)
- The lead's story usually stops right after their victory to end on a high note. After all, drudgery and lots of paperwork are what usually actually follows victory of this kind. However, if the story wishes to continue, it can shift from an Advancement story to a War story, as they focus their ambition outside the organization. Alternatively, the organization might be eaten by

another organization and then the character must claw their way up through the new levels of power in the bigger organization. There are always sequel possibilities.

Notes on Advancement Stories:

- Individual Advancement stories and story arcs will be based around the character trying to accomplish whatever it is they need to do to move up to the next level. This might be one big task, or a series of tasks, it might involve a professional challenge, or it might be a personal challenge. Usually in the early stories, when the character's position is weak, it will be about them defending themselves from people trying to eliminate them, but as they go up, they'll gradually go on the attack.

- Not all main characters end up on the advancement ladder through direct ambition. Sometimes they end up on the ladder by accident, and stay because of anger, stubbornness, boredom, or someone pissed them off. Although generally, at some point, they must decide to actually try for the top seat, for whatever reasons.

- In organizations, there are always lines of power and factions which have existed long before the main character arrives. Often, a big test in the main character's skills are to deal with opponents at their level while not antagonizing more powerful opponents before they're ready to face them. If they anger the wrong district manager or local lord, their career could come to a sudden end, and in some organizations, angering the people at the top could be fatal.

- The higher up the food chain of an organization they go, the more intense the competition becomes, so having some patrons and mentors watching out for leads at the higher levels can be key to their survival. There needs to be someone or something keeping the higher ups from just getting rid of the upstart main character, and often the main character is going to need guidance from a more experienced voice.

- The main characters also need to be on the lookout for other ambitious, but compatible, people who they can pair up with and work alongside as allies. They don't have to be best friends, or work together forever, but people will be their greatest strategic resource in most situations. Even rivals and enemies can become temporary (or permanent) allies in the right situation, if their interests align with the main character against some other person or group.

- Organizations can sometimes be almost Perfect Information situations, where because everyone has spies everywhere and the environment is so small, it's hard to do things without others noticing or being aware. This makes it easy for the lead to find out what their opponents are doing, but it also makes it hard for the lead character to do things without their opponents noticing as well.

WAR STORIES

Unlike Advancement stories, which are often conflicts between people who know each other, War stories are most often conflicts between strangers. At the same time, however, War Conquest stories are also about conflicts between groups, so the main character is very rarely alone in either their goals or their efforts. The character is usually part of a team, perhaps one they assembled themselves, or which is assembled for them, and they (and their team) must figure out how to best seize their aims and make their ambitions into reality.

This difference means that in War stories, the main character actually spends most of their time among their allies, and only rarely actually encounters their enemies face to face. (Depending on the situation, of course.) Most of the drama in a War story will play out between either the character and members of their team, or between distant enemies who likely only know each other by name and reputation, and who battle indirectly through their subordinates.

In many ways, a War story is a puzzle story, where each side is trying to solve the problem of how to defeat their opponents while taking as few losses as possible. Both sides are dependent on spies and sources of information which are critical to making the right decisions because the one who has the best information often wins in situations where the information about each other is less than equal. At the same time, having the ability and resources to exploit that information is also critical, and going to war without careful preparation is a very lethal recipe for disaster.

The overall structure of a War Conquest story is harder to pin down, because the nature of the war being fought and the players in it can change so many things. A defensive war is different than an offensive war, and a small-scale war between tribes won't be the same as a large-scale space fleet battle. But, since the fundamental factors of people, resources, and territory don't really change with time or the conflict, a rough outline for an overall War Conquest story would probably look like this:

Act 1 – Setup

- The main characters, setting, situations, and controlling ideas are introduced.
- The main character is introduced in a short arc which sets up the character, and the circumstances surrounding the reasons for war to happen are presented. Usually the main character is a talented young tactician or fighter who sees a land in chaos or out of balance and wants to make it right. Heroes usually arise during troubled times, and the main character sees themselves as the solution to the troubles the land faces.
- During the opening arc, the lead will usually encounter some crisis situation, often one which represents the land itself being out of balance, and this crisis becomes both the excuse and the first step the character takes onto the road of becoming a conqueror.

Act 2 – Action

- After that, in the next story arc, the main character faces their second major challenge, the immediate opposition is also introduced and set up so the audience comes to understand the real nature of the challenge the main character faces.
- This is where the character tries to make their first conquest, usually succeeding in either gathering some new allies or some resource that will be the springboard to their future expansion. This might be a silver mine in old Japan, a rum factory in the prohibition days, or an abandoned mining outpost to use as their first star base. It will be the thing that lets them begin to gather more power and attract others to them.
- From this encounter, the main character (and the audience) is reminded how hard this is all going to be, but the experience usually just drives them to try even harder.
- If the main character is going to make a tragic mistake that will come back to haunt them later, this is usually where it will happen.
- The main character begins a series of campaigns trying to accomplish their goals, with each new opponent and challenge becoming more complex. As they seize more key resources and gather more allies, they become a respected power, which in turn brings more allies and enemies who see them as threats to be dealt with.
- If the land is in chaos, then the main character usually tries to create a zone of stability- a safe secure space under their rule where order is restored. This

has the advantage of attracting capable people who can help the lead, but also tends to attract a lot of displaced refugees from the more chaotic parts who are trying to survive. These refugees are a huge drain on the lead's resources, but the main character can't get rid of them because it would be unethical, and a public relations disaster too. This is when the reality of trying to be more than just a rebel leader, but actually the leader of a country begins to sink in, but if the lead can find a way to turn this into a good thing, they'll profit from it in the end.

- As the main character rises, they are noticed by more and more of the larger forces in the land, who will either try to recruit, block, or occasionally enable their rise. These players will tempt the main character to join them, but the lead will turn them down in the end or use them for their own benefit- the lead only works for themselves, nobody else.

- The lead will also receive the rewards, perks, and problems that come with advanced status. These can be seen as little reminders of what they'll get when they reach the top, and the challenges that come with it.

- The lead is also pulled at by their loved ones and successes, which tempt them to stop and just accept what they've accomplished. The main character **must** be tempted to stop at some point, preferably before they hit the third act. Then decide to keep going and push on into the final phase.

- Also, towards the end of this act, the lead will usually have to make some kind of final sacrifice, where they lose something or someone important to them as a result of their ambitions. This will be their fault, and the result of the choices they made, and symbolizes the price that success comes at.

Act 3 - Results

- At this point, the story is almost finished, and the lead character faces their final, greatest challenge that stands between them and their goal. Usually this involves dethroning the person who currently sits at the top, or facing off against another rival for the top position.

- All the main character's ghosts come back to haunt them, and all the good they've done comes back to reward them as they face their final challenge. Usually they must make a final choice between their dream, and some other good option, where they are offered one last chance to turn away, but take their dream anyway.

- Having achieved their dream, the lead receives some physical, tangible symbol of their victory- be it the love interest, a symbolic object like a medal or throne, a certificate, or a crown. There will always be some symbol of their victory, often one first introduced right back at the start of the story.

- The lead's story usually stops right after their victory to end on a high note. After all, drudgery and lots of paperwork are what usually actually follows victory of this kind. However, if the story wishes to continue, it can shift from being about collecting power to maintaining it, or dealing with the natural problems that come with trying to hold a large political union together. And, naturally, there is also that other kingdom across the sea that seems to be preparing for war...

Notes on War Conquest Stories:

- Individual stories and story arcs are generally either about acquiring something (resources, allies, information, territory), protecting something, or honoring treaties and alliances. Usually at the start of the story it will mostly be about trying different methods to acquire things and people, and occasionally being on the defense as the main character's group is still weak. As the story goes on, the focus will shift from gathering power to maintaining and developing it, including supporting allies and dealing with internal strife. What conquests occur become larger and more complicated when they happen, and are big expensive affairs.

- The main character may have been forced into this role by circumstances, but they will stay out of a sense of duty or stubbornness. Occasionally, they will be motivated by revenge, but this will be tempered as they find themselves responsible for more and more people underneath them and are chained by the responsibilities of command.

- Capable lieutenants are a conqueror's greatest resource, and they will do whatever it takes to get the best people working for them. Each of these lieutenants is a vital piece of the main character's equipment, and the loss of any one of them weakens the lead significantly. On the other hand, the main character grows more powerful with each capable person who joins them.

FINAL NOTES

As mentioned above, writing conquest stories look simple, but is hard on the writer compared with many other kinds of stories. It requires a lot of preparation and foresight, and just like a military campaign, the conquest story's success is often determined before the opening page is written. On a simple level, the conquest story seems like one about beating up each boss and levelling up, and they can be written than way, but unlike a typical battle story, conquest stories are typically stories where the bravest and smartest person wins, not the strongest or most powerful. (Troves of magical weapons and arms aside.)

This means that a conquest story writer should take the time to not just take in stories about war and conquest, but actually study some of the classics. These are a good place to start:

- *The Prince* by Niccolò Machiavelli
- *The Art of War* by Sun Tzu
- *The 36 Stratagems* by An Unknown Chinese Author
- *On War* by Carl von Clausewitz

In addition to these, spending some time playing strategic games (if you haven't already) can be a good training ground. Chess was created to simulate battle in ancient India, and is always worth learning if you don't already play. *Go* (aka *weiqi*) is another ancient wargame (the oldest still played, actually), and was created to simulate war in ancient China. It's easy to learn (go to Playgo.to for an animated tutorial) but epic in scope, with many smaller battles making up a greater war, and can teach a lot about military strategy that chess cannot.

And naturally, on the computer games front, there are many games like *Starcraft, Civilization, Homeworld,* and others which can be a fun way to learn different approaches to conquest. The crown jewel of these being the *Total War* series by Creative Assembly, which are some of the best military and conquest simulations produced to this day.

ROMANCE WEBFICTION

Humans are social animals, and our fiction is just as dominated by stories about relationships as our real lives are. It's no surprise then, that Romance is the single best-selling fiction category in the world, and outsells everything in both print and electronic formats. People can't get enough of stories about human relationships, if for no other reason than we're trying to find out ways to make our own real-life relationships better (or work).

Webfiction is no different, and at least in the English webfiction world, Romance and dramatic stories aimed at a youthful audience tend to dominate the charts. Legions of young readers who are still figuring out their own lives, and how to interact with others, devour stories built around human relationships as fast as legions writers can produce them, and the writers of those stories can gain masses of loyal fans overnight with the right story.

And that, is both the best and worst thing about writing relationship stories.

There is a huge demand for them, but there is also a lot of competition in writing them. Everyone who has read more than a handful of Romance stories has realized that there's a fairly simple pattern to them, and thinks they could write them too. This means standing out as a Romance writer can be pretty hard at times, just because of the sheer number of people trying to write these kinds of stories. That can be a real challenge, and is perhaps one of the biggest ones a new Romance writer will face.

However, it's also a problem that can be overcome with a little planning and understanding.

So, let's begin.

TOP 10 THINGS YOU SHOULD KNOW BEFORE WRITING ROMANCE WEBFICTION

Here are ten important things that anyone who wants to write romance webfiction should know going into it. This isn't a complete list, but covers the major ideas that any romance webfiction writer should know before they jump in and start writing their own.

1. Not all women's webfiction stories are romances.

While the majority of webfiction targeted at women and girls are romances, not all webfiction stories for girls are romances. Especially with webfiction for tween girls, the focus is often more on friendship, self-discovery, and adventure instead of romance, which they're still growing into. And, even among webfiction for older girls and women, there are still many popular series that have romance only as a subplot and instead focus on monster hunting, career building, getting revenge, and other interests. Romance may be the queen of women's webfiction, but other popular genres exist as well.

2. Romance is both a genre and a plot at the same time.

While the action, comedy, or horror genres all have many different kinds of plots that go with them, Romance is one of only two genres (the other being mysteries) which are expected to follow the same plot no matter what. In a romance story, two people will meet, are attracted to each other, overcome obstacles, and then unite as a couple in some semi-permanent way. If a story doesn't follow these beats, then that story isn't a romance, it's a drama.

3. The ending to romance stories is written before the story begins.

The audience doesn't want a happy ending to a romance story, they demand it. (And leave bad reviews if they don't get it.) The main character must fall in love, and they must unite with their love interest at the end- full stop, no questions asked. The only dramatic questions that exist in a romance story are how they will get together, and who they will get together with. (If there is more than one possible romantic partner.)

4. If the romance isn't the focus of the story, it's not a romance.

Many stories have romance in them, but to be considered a romance the romance plot must be front and center in the story. A story about two characters building a school in a slum who fall in love isn't a romance, it's a drama with a romance subplot.

A story about two characters who fall in love while building a school in a slum is a romance, because the romance is the focus. It's a small distinction, but it makes a big difference- in the first example the focus of the story is on building the school, but in the second example the focus of the story is on how the couple get together. In a romance story, everything that happens in the main plot is connected to the relationship of the characters, and is developing that relationship.

5. The most popular romance plot is "Beauty and the Beast."

If there is one plot that dominates romance, it's the plot of the powerful and wild alpha male with the broken heart who is healed by the love of the female lead and restored to society. If you look at a list of male love interests in romance stories, you will see a long list of kings, pirate captains, CEOs, werewolves, vampires, billionaires, lawyers, surgeons, presidents, and other powerful high-status men who act like jerks and tyrants when we first meet them. But, of course, every one of them is an emotionally damaged and scared little boy on the inside, and by breaking through their tough exterior and healing their wounds, the female lead wins their love and becomes their partner. It's a tale as old as time, and it still sells well today.

6. The male lead must always be honest with the female lead.

Even though the male lead might be a jerk, a playboy, a bully, or someone who makes the female lead's life a living hell, the one thing they will never do is lie to the female lead. This is very important to making the end of a romance story work, because if the female lead (and the audience) can't believe it when the male lead professes his love at the end, the whole story will fall apart. The male lead can be a liar who tricks and cheats everyone else in the story, and they may even cheat on the female lead with other women, but their word (when they give it) must be their bond, and they must never break it when she's involved. If they do, the whole house of cards will come down and the audience won't buy the ending.

7. Romance is all about "balance."

While princes picking up peasant girls and whisking them off to castles to be queens works fine for children, more mature audiences know that real lasting relationships are about communication and respect. If that peasant girl who becomes a queen doesn't show she's worthy of the role, the king is going to get bored of her pretty quickly, and things will sour fast. At the end of a romance, the audience needs to believe this couple will last, and that means that both sides must have shown they're worthy of each other's love. They have to bring equal value to the relationship, and even if a billionaire falls in love with a cleaning lady, she has to prove she's his equal by the end of the story in some way.

8. In romance stories, the main opponent for the lead is the love interest.

In stories, the main opponent is the person who stands between the main character and achieving their final goals. In a romance story, that person is the lead character's love interest- they are the one who must be convinced to enter into a long-term relationship with the lead character at the end of the story for the ending to happen. This doesn't mean there can't also be rivals and villains in a romance, and there often are, but the main opponent of the story will always be the love interest because it's their heart that is the key to finding love happily ever after.

9. The rules are the same regardless of the genders of the people involved.

While most romance stories are about male-female relationships, there are other possibilities as well, and LGBTQI are extremely popular. However, even in those same-sex pairings, one character usually has more masculine traits than the other, and one character will have more feminine traits. Thus, a "Beauty and The Beast" plot basically plays out the same whether both the leads are female, or both the leads are male. One will be active and assertive, and the other will be more passive and accepting, because this combination is the most balanced and results in working relationships in fiction and real life.

10. Men like romance too!

While romance is clearly a female favorite genre, according to a 2017 survey by the Romance Writers of America, 18% of Romance novel readers were actually men! While they might not always admit it, men too want to know more about human relationships, and can enjoy a good love story just like their sisters can. However, men, and especially the young male readers of romance webfiction, tend to like a heavy dose of comedy with their romance. Romantic comedies that have a few sexy and awkward situations can be a big hit with guys, although they don't care as much as women for stories that deeply explore feelings and heartbreak.

ROMANCE AUDIENCES

The audience for romance webfiction is one that changes a lot depending on the age and other demographics of the target audience. Younger audiences like simpler, more chaste and idealized romance, while older audiences prefer something more nuanced and complex with heavier doses of tragedy and sexuality.

However, what all these audiences can agree on is that they see romance stories as a way to escape their daily lives and plunge into a beautiful and exciting fantasy world where true love wins out. In fact, if there's one major rule to romance, it's that true love must always win.

True love has to win in fiction, because if it doesn't win in fiction, how can it win in real life? Romance readers want to be re-assured that "love finds a way," and that "true love is waiting just around the corner." These stories promise them that if they put their hearts into it, and weather the storms of life, they too will find happiness and fulfillment in the arms of the perfect partner. They sell a dreamlike version of reality to audiences whose lives are anything but dreamy, and who want that extra comfort that only a romance story can give.

So, when you're trying to reach a romance audience, always remember that you're selling them a fantasy, and part of that fantasy is keeping them happy and comfortable. That's the winning formula to writing successful romance, and keeping them coming back for more.

ROMANCE THEMES

Romance stories always have a single central theme- "Love conquers all." If they don't have this as their main theme, then they're not a romance story but something else with a romance subplot. This isn't bad, it just means that the story isn't about the romance, but something else.

However, romance stories can and often do have other supporting themes that go along with them and add spice to the story. A "pure" romance story is rare, and most romance webfiction pair the main romance story with some other theme to give it a more unique flavor and style. For example, common secondary themes in romances include "being true to yourself," "finding the courage to follow your dreams," "love takes courage, but it's worth it," "accepting people for who they are," "love versus family duty," "the power of love to transform your life," and so on.

When planning your romance story, you should always think about what the secondary theme of the story is going to be, and how it will be expressed in your characters, situations, and the ending of the story. If the secondary theme was, "finding courage," then the main character will probably be a fearful person, at least when it comes to relationships, and then the more she opens herself up, the better her relationships will become until finally she takes the biggest step of all with her love interest at the end of the story.

ROMANCE CHARACTERS

Characters in romance stories can be divided into three categories- the female lead, the male love interest, and rivals. Other types of characters exist, like best friends, mentors, wise grandmothers, annoying bosses, and the other people who fill out a character's supporting cast, but they are all dependent on the type of story being told. These three, however, are crucial to the success of a romance story and must be planned with care.

The Female Lead

The main thing you need to remember about the female lead in a romance story is that they're stand-ins for the reader. The reader needs to not only sympathize with them, but connect with them on a deep level, because they're not just a character, they're a mask that the reader puts on to experience the events of the story. The deeper the connection, the more intensely the reader will feel the experiences the main character has, and go through her emotions with her.

So, a lot of the success of a romance story will depend on how well the creator can make the audience connect with their lead character. How to do this has been discussed in other chapters, but one of the main ways that romance webfiction do this is by having female leads that have positive traits that are traits that the audience either has, wishes they had, or thinks are good to have. On the other hand, the female lead should not have any major negative traits that might distance her from the audience and make it harder to relate to her.

First, female lead characters in romance webfiction generally have four basic traits in common- they are smart, assertive, tenacious, and good hearted. They are smart because their brain is their greatest asset in the story, and they will need it to overcome the obstacles that get thrown their way. They are assertive because audiences respect assertive characters, and it makes them easier to write because they're doers who actively try to solve their problems. They are tenacious because unless they have a great inner strength and don't give up, they won't be able to achieve their goals and make their dreams into reality. And finally, they are good hearted because it will be their pure heart that makes the male lead trust them deeply and wins the day at the end of the story.

They may have other positive traits, but these are the ones which almost every female lead has and which will end up being crucial to the story's success. It's hard to find a successful romance webfiction where the lead female character (or feminine character) doesn't have these traits to some degree.

On the other hand, they must not have traits that will make the audience dislike and distance themselves from the lead character. Traits like being dishonest, cheating, stealing, abusing others, or being passive or greedy will turn audiences off if they're a major part of the character's personality and not balanced out in some way by positive traits. Audiences don't want to connect with characters who don't share their values, and they won't root for male love interests to get together with female leads that they don't like.

The Male Love Interest

Just as the audience must empathize with the female lead of the story, they must fall in love with the male lead for a romance story to work. Thus, the male leads in romance stories are idealized alpha-males of some kind who represent the fantasy lover of the female lead and the audience brought to life, and in need of their help.

The key traits that every male lead in a romance story should have are that they should be strong, attractive, trustworthy, and a winner. They need to be strong because they will be called on to show inner strength by not giving up when things get hard, and physically strong when they need to protect the female lead. They need to be attractive because the audience needs to find them as appealing as the main female lead does. They need to be trustworthy (for the female lead) because if their word can't be trusted, how can the main character settle down with them at the end of the story? And finally, they must be a winner at the game of life, or someone who is on their way to becoming a winner, so that they're desirable as a romantic partner. This means they must hold (or have the potential to hold) high social status within the culture they belong to, and be worthy of the female lead's attentions. (Nobody wants to date a loser.)

Also, there are two more important traits a male love interest needs in a romance story- they must be emotionally incomplete, and a reflection of the female lead.

They should be emotionally incomplete because it's the reason why they need the female lead. This emotional incompleteness can be a personal flaw, it can be damage done by previous relationships, or it can be just something missing from their life.

Regardless, they are missing something from their life that only the female lead can provide, and through providing it when nobody else can, the female lead is like prince charming showing up with the glass slipper to prove she's miss right.

In addition, the male love interest should be a reflection of the female lead- their balanced opposite who brings out the best in them when they're together. If the female lead is quiet, the male lead is talkative. If the female lead is impulsive, the male lead is thoughtful. If the female lead is fearful, the male lead is brave. He is the one who brings balance to her, and her life, which is how he shows he's the right person for her.

Rivals

In most love stories, there is a rival male or female character (or both, or several) who are trying to get in the way of the lead couple getting together. They are there to add drama, give the audience someone to hate, and add a little uncertainty to how the whole thing will turn out.

The thing to understand about romance rivals is that they're actually funhouse mirror versions of the lead couple. They represent the things that the lead couple are looking for, but in the wrong way, not the right way. For example, the female rivals will be women who are charming and attractive on the surface, but underneath are cold hearted and the worst kinds of women. Similarly, the male rivals are usually alpha males gone bad, who are physically abusive, manipulative, and dishonest. They seem handsome and charming on the surface, and to be mister right, but underneath they're deeply flawed in bad ways that will only break the female lead's heart if she goes with them.

These rivals will tempt the lead couple, and might even get them to lose faith in each other, but will always fail in the end because true love will find a way to get the main couple back on the right path.

ROMANCE PLOTS

The tricky thing about romance stories is that the audience knows the ending (or a version of it), right from the beginning of the story. There are no huge surprises in a romance story (with one exception, see below), because the audience is there for a very specific ending, and if they don't get that ending, they're going to be very, very unhappy.

For a story to be a romance story, the ending is already written before the writer even begins- the main couple gets together and commits to each other for the long term, forsaking all others. It doesn't have to be marriage, it doesn't even have to be forever (sometimes, "for now" is good enough), but the key is that the story will end with the leads pledging their hearts to each other in a way which makes it clear that this is going to last.

If the ending is anything else, then that isn't a romance story, it's a romantic drama, which is another kind of story. A romance is about finding love, accepting love, and gaining love- it's that simple.

That doesn't mean other kinds of stories can't also include romance (most do), but a story which **is** a romance, and where the romance is the point, is a very particular kind of story. So, if you're planning to write one, you should always remember that your ending is already written for you, and your readers will riot (and write bad reviews) if you don't give it to them. (Because it breaks the fantasy that they too will find love and happiness with that perfect person someday.)

Some people might think this puts the writer in a difficult position- after all, how do you write an interesting story when the audience already knows how it's going to end? But the truth is romance stories aren't about the ending, they're about the journey and how those two characters get across that finish line. The audience is there to find out how the characters get together, not whether they do.

The audience's interest in romance stories is in seeing how the characters overcome challenges to get together. The bigger the challenges, the more the audience is interested in seeing how the main characters overcome them. These challenges can come from within the couple and outside the couple, and most stories have a series of these obstacles that stand in the way of the couple getting together.

Challenges from Within the Couple

There are two types of challenges that come from inside the couple- personal flaws and couple flaws.

Personal flaws are issues that one member of the couple has and which affect their relationship. These can include the following:

- Addictions
- An overdeveloped sense of duty
- Attachment to a parent or relative
- Bad habits
- Being a devout believer in an ideology
- Being a devout follower of a religion
- Being a ninja
- Being a workaholic
- Being physically or mentally disabled

- Being too attached to fictional characters
- Being uneducated
- Doubts about themselves or others
- Emotional scars from previous relationships
- Fears
- Goals they're unable to give up which interfere with the relationship
- Having a mental illness
- Having a serious illness
- Loving webfiction or anime too much
- No sense of fashion/style
- One side has no interest in personal improvement
- Poor personal hygiene
- Pride
- Stubbornness
- The inability to adapt to new environments
- The inability to admit they're wrong
- The inability to change
- The inability to choose the best partner
- The inability to commit
- The inability to communicate with others
- The inability to forgive
- The inability to give up standards of living/lifestyles they are used to
- The inability to have children
- The inability to hold steady employment
- The inability to keep pets
- The inability to let go of past events
- The inability to let go of past relationships
- The inability to perform sexually
- The inability to trust
- The inability to use technology

Any of these can seriously affect one or both people in a relationship by making it hard for the other person to have a relationship with them. However, these are not the only issues- there are also couple flaws which specifically affect their ability to have or maintain a relationship with each other. These include the following:

- Different hobbies or interests
- Different relationship goals
- Different relationship styles

- Different sexual tastes
- Different styles of fashion
- Different styles of living
- Different styles of work
- Different tastes in food
- Differing sex drives
- Habits that drive each other crazy
- One person being overly critical of the other
- One person just isn't interested in the other as a romantic partner
- One person not liking children/pets
- The couple are unable to use the same language to communicate
- The inability to communicate well
- The inability to satisfy each other sexually
- The side they bring out of each other when they're together
- They have conflicting worldviews about politics, social change, religion, or pizza toppings

Any of which can affect their ability to be together as a pair, or to interact with each other well. Not a few of these have been deal breakers in many relationships, and all of them offer potential as reasons why a couple is unable to get together in a story.

Challenges from Outside the Couple

Being in a relationship and bonding with another person is hard enough, but on top of that there are many external forces which prevent, harm, and even destroy relationships. These outside challenges keep couples from being together, and a few of them includes the following:

- **Biology** - there is some external biological reason they can't be together, such as drug treatments, surgical procedures, infectious diseases, or genetic manipulation
- **Chance** - one side never gets the opportunity to get close with the other
- **Custom** - cultural or family traditions keep them apart
- **Duty** -having to perform a task, fulfill a promise, take care of someone, do a job
- **Education** - one side's education level keeps them from getting together with the other
- **Emotion**- they are surrounded by people who hate one side or the other, or are afraid of one side or the other

211

- **Family** – their families stand between them getting together, usually by not liking the partner or their family members
- **Geography** – distance, borders, walls
- **History** – their personal, cultural, or family history keeps them apart, for example their families fought on opposite sides of a conflict, or relatives harmed each other
- **Honor** – a vow or promise which prevents them from getting together with the other person
- **Intent**– one or both people is being forced to harm or take advantage of the other person in some way
- **Law** – laws keep them apart, for example one of them is a fugitive or criminal, one is already married, their relationship is illegal, one person is a slave, etc.
- **Money** – one side needs money to get together with the other, for example dowries, buying the other person's freedom, having enough money to meet some standard or requirement
- **Optics** – not being able to be seen together without facing censure or creating a false impression
- **Other Lovers** – one or both of the main couple are being pursued by other people, or in love with other people.
- **Politics** – gang, tribal, local, or national politics prevent them from getting together with the other person, for example wars, revolutions, belonging to rival organizations, belonging to different political parties, belonging to an underclass
- **Race** – their racial backgrounds keep them apart
- **Reputation** – the poor reputation of one side (deserved or not) keeps the other one from getting together with them
- **Rules** – one or both people are bound by some external rules which prevent them from accepting the other person
- **Status**– there is a large gap in status between the two which prevent them from getting together
- **Work**– their jobs keep them emotionally, physically, or socially apart in some way

These outside pressures put a lot of strain on relationships, and make a couple finding happiness with each other an even bigger challenge than it might normally be. Just remember that these, like the flaws listed above, should be used in ways which are consistent and reflect the themes of the story.

Also, if you're looking for excuses to shove a couple together who wouldn't want to be together, and keep them there, then the above list can be used for that too! Every one of those above reasons can push a couple together as much as it can pull them apart, and keep them together until they figure out how to love each other the way you want them to.

However, if these long lists leave you confused and unsure of which challenges you want to put between your poor star-crossed lovers, then you can always fall back on the big five:

Top Five Relationship Challenges!
1. **Doubt in themselves or each other**
2. **Family troubles**
3. **Other lovers**
4. **One person just isn't interested**
5. **The inability to change**

This quintet is so popular you will find them everywhere in romance stories, especially Asian ones.

However, there is one other way which creators keep audiences interested in romance stories besides the normal challenges of getting and staying together—competition.

WHO WILL THEY END UP WITH?

While it's clear that the main character will get their happily ever after ending in a romance story, what isn't so clear is who they'll be spending that ever after with! This is the one thing that the writer is actually allowed to play with about the ending, and in fact is something that can keep audiences interested and guessing until the very end.

Love triangles, squares, hexagons, and do-decahedrons are as common in romance webfiction as stars in the sky, and they're an important tool in a romance serial writer's toolbox. Audiences can get antsy very quickly if they feel an author is just stalling a couple getting together to stretch a story out for time, but if there are several different suitors then sometimes it isn't so clear in whose arms the main character belongs. This lets the story go on for some time without worrying about dragging because the main character is reasonably exploring possibilities with different partners and trying to determine the best one.

It also turns the story into a bit of a contest, as each suitor tries to prove they're the best partner for the lead character, and the audience is left to judge with whom the main character really belongs. This was the classic formula that propelled *Boys*

Over Flowers into its top spot, and has made harem webfiction (one boy pursued by many girls), and reverse-harem webfiction (one girl pursued by many men) into industry standards.

Thus, between how the couple gets together, and who they end up with, a creator keeps the audience interested and turning pages.

ROMANCE WEBFICTION STORY STRUCTURES

Like other serialized entertainment, romance webfiction function on two levels–the overall story and the individual stories. The overall story is the story of how a particular pair of people end up together, while the individual stories represent the smaller steps the couple takes in their slow dance towards leaving the story together.

The structure of most romances is a natural and universal one- boy meets girl, they overcome problems, and they end up together. This is how real (successful) relationships tend to work, and the audience knows and expects it to go this way. However, writing a good relationship story isn't quite this simple because if the story is just about the author coming up with random reasons to keep the main pair apart in an effort to make the story last as long as possible, then the reader is going to feel like they're in a relationship where the other side is never going to commit. They'll be bored, restless, and eventually they're going to be the ones to head for the exit.

This is why it's important to plan and write the romance story in such a way that the audience can feel there is actual progression happening, and it's a natural progression which is playing out the way they'd expect based on the situation and circumstances. That doesn't mean there can't be twists, reversals, and exciting turns, but it does mean those should be used sparingly, and preferably set up or foreshadowed long before they actually happen.

The best way to structure a relationship story is to set it up so that each story (or story arc) of the tale is centered around the characters dealing with one of the obstacles or problems which are keeping them apart, and growing closer together through the experience. The Overall Story of the relationship is built around the steps the characters must go through to go from being apart to being together, and each smaller story inside that greater story represents the actual steps of that journey from A to Z.

Thus, a typical Overall Story structure for a romance serial will look something like this:

Act 1- Setup

- The lead characters and their situation are introduced and we're shown that they're right for each other. Typically, the audience (and sometimes the leads) know they're meant to be together from the start.
- The first story arc is about introducing these people who belong together, and then showing why they can't be together.

Act 2 – Action

- The second story arc happens, expanding the world the characters live in, their supporting casts, and detailing the magnitude of the problems which stand between them.
- They usually confront one of the less major problems and overcome it, showing that they have the potential to be together if they work at it.
- Usually one of them admits their feelings to themselves, and sometimes the other person (but is rejected).
- A series of escalating challenges appear, each one representing a reason the couple can't be together, and each one is (at least partly) overcome at the end of the arc, bringing them closer together.

Act 3 – Result

- They overcome the final challenge, usually one which forces them to either get together or forever be apart, and walk into the future together.

This gives you, as the writer, three clear story arcs which need to be told (Introduction, Development, Conclusion) and then a more flexible number of story arcs which play out between them (Activity). Each of the Activity story arcs being about a particular problem that stands between the pair and how it's resolved, thus keeping the plot moving forward. So, say there are three things keeping them apart - family, emotional baggage, and work - one arc is about the family issue, one arc is about the emotional baggage issues, and one arc is about the work issue, and each one of the problems is solved in some way which brings them closer together. This is a simple approach which gives the story a clear and finite structure and progression that the audience can feel and see.

Often, each of the individual Story Arcs will look something like this:

STORY ARC TEMPLATE FOR ROMANCE STORIES:

Act 1 – Setup

1. Characters and situations are introduced.

2. The main character of the story has a problem and... (pick one from the list)
   - They try to recruit others to help them solve it, and they do.
   - They try to solve it themselves with some success.
   - They try to solve it themselves and fail, but others notice they need help and offer it.

Act 2 –Action

3. A larger obstacle appears... (pick one from the list)
   - Something unexpected happens that complicates the situation.
   - They try to solve it and make things worse. Now must dig themselves out.
   - They try to solve it and succeed, but then the unexpected happens and they must deal with it.

Act 3 – Result

4. The main character and allies try their best to solve the problem by using clever and creative solutions... (pick one from the list)
   - By working together, they accomplish what the main character couldn't on their own.
   - They end up digging deep and finding the solution to the problem inside themselves by overcoming or accepting something they didn't before.
   - They have a series of experiences which make them see things in a new light and provide a solution to their problem.
   - By other characters opening up emotionally, they give the lead the strength/wisdom to overcome their own issues.
   - By helping to solve another character's problems, they solve their own.

5. The main character's overall situation improves a tiny bit as a result of this experience, and... (pick one or more from the list)
   - They grow closer to their love interest emotionally.
   - They grow as a person, making them more ready to be in a relationship with others.
   - They understand their love interest better, making them better suited to be their partner.
   - The audience feels more strongly that these two belong together.
   - Their relationship becomes more balanced.
   - On rare occasions, their relationship becomes worse, but in a way that will eventually lead to their relationship improving through later story happenings.

Notes:

- This plot is used for individual story arcs of a romance serial story. It doesn't work so well for the Overall Story of a relationship because the goal here is limited/slow change to give the feeling the relationship is moving forward while still keeping the main characters from admitting their feelings for as long as possible.
- The main character of the story arc doesn't always have to be the main character of the series, in fact it's good to switch it up and offer different perspectives on the situation. Sometimes it's the series lead, sometimes it's the series love interest, sometimes it can be a rival character, and sometimes it can be one of their friends. This can really pad out an episode count.
- Usually each romantic lead character has at least one major personal flaw that prevents them from truly bonding with the other character or admitting their feelings. Through shared experience they get to know each other and by doing so move closer together. It's about trust, and the endgame is being able to admit your feelings because you feel the other side has the same feelings.
- At the end of most episodes, they will feel closer to their love interest. This may be consciously or unconsciously, and if they are young teens, they may not really understand these feelings and it will lead to them being confused and more unsure.
- Unless it's near the end of the overall story, something will always keep them from confessing. Usually their own fears or being rejected or insecurities.
- Usually the problem of the story arc is emotional/personal, not an enemy or opponent. There is something they're not willing to do but they must do it or

overcome it to succeed in this situation. The problem of the story arc is there to make them confront their personal flaw and force them into facing it. The way they overcome the problem should always reflect the theme of the story.

- The opponent in these stories is usually the situation which forces them to do difficult things, or their own friends/allies who work to keep the main character on track in an effort to help them overcome the problem.

- When a main character is faced with a problem in this plot, they will often try to solve it in a way which is linked to their personal flaws. The entertaining part comes from them trying to solve it the wrong way, and then finally accepting they need to use the right way to solve it at the end. (A way which they knew all along, but weren't willing to do because it requires more effort than they want to put in.) An example of this is a lazy character who tries to solve the problem in a lazy way, which seems to work, but really makes things worse, and then they actually end up having to work harder than they would have if they'd done it right in the first place.

- This plot works equally well for conflict and non-conflict-based stories. In a non-conflict-based version, the main character usually solves their problem themselves by hearing the thoughts or seeing the experiences of others. Inspiration from others leads to them to a solution, and no direct opponent is needed or other characters to conflict with.

- The feeling of change at the end comes from change happening to a particular character, but not necessarily a change in the situation. Maybe the character is a little more confident, or wiser, or has learned something about themselves. These kinds of changes lead up to a major change, and changes in the situation, and feel like real change, but don't change the real status quo of the story.

- For larger story arcs, you can do a series of these types of smaller stories which are linked together by characters, situations, time or location. These arc collections usually culminate in some small, but real change in the situation or character's feelings to feel satisfying.

- A common variation of this story is the Harem story, which will rotate the main character's interactions with a group of cuties. Each story arc will be about a problem the lead solves along with a new or previously introduced cutie, leading to positive feelings between them, then the story jumps to another member of the harem for the next story. Usually the main character is solving the cuties' problems, which leads to them bonding with him or her.

ROMANTIC COMEDY

Another popular type of romance is stories where there is a large dose of comedy to go alongside the romance. These stories are popular for many reasons, not the least of which is that they appeal more to both sexes, but mainly because they lighten the story and present a happy, positive world the audience can escape to for a few hours a day.

Romantic comedies are largely driven by their casts and the interactions of those casts, often drawing heavily from the slice-of-life genre. They are also usually linked more heavily with a setting, exploring the ins and outs of that setting while at the same time serving up a heaping helping of love and comedy. So, for example, a school romantic comedy might be about the odd members of an astronomy club and the situations and relationships which come from those people interacting together as they try to explore the heavens. (And spend a lot of times out in the dark countryside huddled together in blankets waiting for celestial phenomena.)

A typical romantic comedy will usually have a lead couple, but also a few other couples in the supporting cast, and will alternate between focusing on the leads and the secondaries as it plays out to extend the story. The supporting cast, of course, represents the good and bad sides of the main couple, and their relationships will make the main couple reflect on themselves and their own connection. In the end, of course, the main couple finally admit their love for each other, but not before the rest of the cast and the setting are as familiar to the reader as their own lives.

ROMANCE SETTINGS

Because romance stories are so hyper-focused on characters, the setting in romance stories is mostly just there to provide an interesting backdrop for the drama to play out in front of. Or, when it does become involved, the setting is there to either push the characters together or keep them apart.

The most common places for romance webfiction to happen are schools and workplaces because those are both familiar environments for the audience. Using familiar environments has two big advantages- first, since the audience also lives in those environments, it makes the characters and situations feel more familiar to them, encouraging sympathy. And second, it lets the creator skip a lot of the worldbuilding and go straight to the important parts that make the characters' little world special or unique and reflect the themes of the story.

219

Here are a few places romance webfiction are often set, and notes about them.

School Romance

Since most webfiction characters are young, a large amount of romantic webfiction is set in schools, mostly high schools with the occasional middle school, college, or university. The school in these stories provides a place where the students need to meet on a regular basis (forcing them together), but also acts as a miniature society with its own rules and customs. (Which can keep them apart.) The school also provides a rhythm to the story, as the characters progress through the school system and deal with the recurring stresses and challenges that come with school life. And finally, the school can even pull the characters apart, as graduation looms, creating a natural deadline for their time together.

Common Obstacles to getting together at school include rivalries, school social politics, school policies, different social status, poor reputations, the need to study, part-time jobs, gangs, family, competing romantic partners, and school officials.

Workplace Romance

These are stories about finding love at the workplace, or through work. This work can be anything from cake decorating, to making films, to working on the international space station. The job in this story acts as the thing that brings the leads together and then pushes and pulls on their lives as they try to find a new balance with each other. The workplace is also the arena where the story will play out, and will prevent the leads from avoiding each other- forcing them to confront their feelings.

Common Obstacles to getting together include differing workloads, jealousy, rivalries, ambition, different levels of status within the company, different levels of social status, personal finances, personal goals, and office politics.

Palace Romance

Romances of this kind are almost always between an emperor, king, prince, or other high court official and a female character of lower nobility, or peasant birth. Typically, the female lead enters the palace with some purpose, sometimes as a concubine, nurse, or maid (for peasants), or as a teacher, doctor, or cook (for low nobility) and catches the eye of the male lead. They then begin a romance where everything and everyone says they shouldn't be together, but the female lead overcomes the challenges and, in the process, proves her worth to the king and his court. Typically, he has to make a large sacrifice for her at some point near the end, but this helps to convince everyone of his sincerity, and she becomes his first lady.

Common Obstacles to getting together usually include status differences, social politics, national politics, war, vows and promises, finances, promised marriages, family objections, cultural traditions, rivals, attitudes towards women, infertility, and legal restrictions.

ROMANCE NOTES

While they are simple at heart, romance stories have more than a few things creators should think about.

Chemistry

It isn't enough to just assume the leads need to be together because they're the main characters in a relationship story. You have to give both the characters and the audience reasons to believe that these two people belong together forever. Whether you want to call it chemistry, a spark, or resonance, the two leads need to bring out something in each other that they don't have with any other characters in the story. This can be different sides of their personalities, this can be vulnerabilities, this can be forgotten memories, or even old habits, but there needs to be some special connection between them that the audience can see and feel.

Also, being attracted to each other is nice, and being compatible in their life goals is good, but the real connection happens on a much more subtle level. It's the little things the characters do as they interact that will indicate whether they belong together or not. Things like considering the other person's feelings when they don't need to, putting the other person first, and showing extra care for the people and things that the other person considers important. Sometimes these things are subconscious, especially at the start of the relationship, but characters taking actions like this show their inner feelings about the other person and what that person means to them.

Finally, good verbal chemistry is important as well. People in love not only listen to each other, they mirror and echo the words and ideas the other person expresses. There is a dynamic energy to their conversations because each side can't wait to express their thoughts and help the other person express theirs as they work as a team. When they're together, they aren't two separate people talking, but two parts of a single mind working in natural synchronicity.

Vulnerability

"The best way to find out if you can trust somebody is to trust them," Ernest Hemingway once said, but for many people this isn't so easy. Trusting others means letting your barriers down and being vulnerable, but that means also risking being hurt, not such a simple thing for people who have been hurt in the past or have their own emotional issues. But unless both sides let their defenses down and trust each other enough to let themselves be open and risk being hurt by the other person, true deep love can't actually develop. If one side doesn't open up, then the relationship is unbalanced, and is likely going to fail because of that unstable nature.

For writers, this means that a big part of writing relationship stories is often about the characters lowering their barriers to each other, which is often a slow and difficult process. Trust comes with time and understanding each other, and these personal barriers are something that the characters will often need to work through as part of the story.

Going it Alone

Not everything in a story can be solved by the main couple together, and sometimes one member of the couple (usually the lead) will need to take time off from the relationship to solve their own problems. Especially with deep, personal problems, one of them will sometimes have to go and deal with it on their own before they come back ready to be part of the relationship again. In this case, the story/arc will be one which forces them to confront their problem and either solve it, or give them the key to working toward solving it. Not everything can be fixed overnight, and sometimes a little personal space might be needed.

In cases like this, the writer should generally not be afraid of time-jumps. If a character needs six months, then wrap the other time-sensitive stories up (or tell them during that period), and then jump the story into the future to when the characters are ready to be part of the relationship story again. Always remember that this is the story of the relationship, not the people, so if there are gaps in the people's lives where nothing important happens that's fine, because we're there to read about the interesting parts of the relationship. Just do it as smoothly as possible, and not too often, as the audience will get annoyed with regular unscheduled time-jumps that feel like the writer is skipping past what could be interesting stories just because they don't know how to tell them.

Ending it All

All good things must come to an end, and the lead couple need to get together at some point (or permanently go their separate ways) or the audience is going to be pretty unhappy. They started this journey to see the story of how these two people got together in an interesting way, and if the author doesn't deliver, or takes too long to finish what they started, the audience is going to get tired and restless. This is why it's important to know from the start where the endpoint will roughly be so that you can work towards it in a natural way.

Remember there are three criteria for a good ending- it must be reasonable based on what happened, earned by the protagonist, and surprising in some way to the audience – and when the time comes to deliver those three things, the writer must be willing to finish the story and walk away. Don't keep a story going for the sake of keeping it going, but instead finish it and write a new story that the audience will enjoy just as much, maybe better.

This is why it's important to know how long you plan the story to run, and the steps the characters will need to go through right from the beginning. By setting everything up, the audience will be able to feel the progression, not just hope for it or guess at it, and the whole thing will feel much more satisfying. In addition, it will also feel earned, because the characters really did the work, and the writer will have time to plan an ending that the audience didn't quite expect, but still works out happily in the end.

A perfect place to close the curtains and call it a night.

SLICE-OF-LIFE STORIES

Someone once described life as "long periods of boredom punctuated by exciting moments of screaming terror," and while most stories are built around those "exciting moments," there is a place for stories built around "long periods of boredom" as well. Those so-called periods of boredom are where the small realities of our lives occur, and they make up the bulk of time we spend as living beings. They aren't empty, but instead filled with trivial moments and a constant stream of choices being made, just ones that aren't epic or life changing, so they're ignored or forgotten.

But, where there are choices, there is story.

The term "slice-of-life" was first coined by 19th century French playwright Jean Jullien to describe a type of theatre where we see random pieces of the lives of characters without plot, story development or conflict, like we're looking at random "orange slices" without seeing the whole "fruit." The idea was to capture the lives of the characters in a pure and natural way by removing them from the structure of plot and just showing them living as pure individuals uninfluenced by ideas of story.

However, in the last hundred or so years since Jullien's time, the term has shifted to mean not the separation of character from plot, but instead stories about characters living everyday, mundane lives just like the rest of humanity. slice-of-life now refers to a meta-genre of stories where characters are freed from adventures, mysteries, quests, and other great dramatic genre plots, but instead are doing what normal people do- work, sleep, study, relax, play games, commute, shop, fight, cook, and the hundreds of other small and large activities that make up our daily lives.

Slice-of-life stories are about the common, the mundane, the ordinary, and the routine.

But that doesn't mean they're boring- not at all.

The slice-of-life story looks at the mundane aspects of life, and then lets us see them in new and interesting ways. Usually by sticking interesting characters into ordinary situations, or by putting ordinary characters into extraordinary situations, it helps the audience to see life from another angle and get another, often amusing, view of the world we might not normally see.

A typical slice-of-life story might be structured like this:

- **Setup**- The characters are introduced.
- **Problem** – Interesting characters are presented with a mundane task, or mundane characters are presented with an interesting task.
- **Interesting Events** – Interesting things (to the audience, at least) happen while the character tries to do that task, either because the person or the task itself is interesting.
- **Climax** – The character(s) accomplish their mundane task, often in a way which puts a twist or surprise on the task or situation.
- **Ending** - Life goes on.

This isn't the only slice-of-life story structure, but it is a common one, and works because the fundamentals of story (action + results) are still present. A character has a goal, and then sets out to accomplish that goal, even if the goal is extremely mundane or vague. For example, a character is bored and decides to go to the store to buy something to drink. The character is trying to relieve their boredom and buying something to drink is a method to solving that issue because it gives them something to do. Along the way, they see some interesting things, and so when they reach the store, they're no longer feeling bored. They were bored and solved it by going out (achieving a result).

This story structure will still work if characters decide to be inactive. Even when characters are passive and do "nothing," they are still doing something by making the choice to do nothing. Not taking action is still an active choice, and therefore can produce results as well. By not taking out the garbage, garbage piles up, and a result is produced (a stinky place filled with garbage), or by choosing to just sit there and not move, other things they need to do (cook, clean, call their mother) will still affect them sooner or later (again, the results of inaction). Whatever we choose to do or not do produces a result, and that can be used for producing story.

Slice-of-life, then, comes from using the activities of life to produce story, no matter how simple or vague that story may be. And this may be why the Japanese have been so drawn to it, because it falls right in line with the *kishotenketsu* structure that they use to conceive of story- a structure not built on conflict but on invoking reader interest. Slice-of-life stories often don't involve conflict, which puts them at odds with the conflict-based version of the Three Act Structure that's become the fundamental story form in the West. On the other hand, Japanese kishotenketsu stories don't require conflict, and therefore slice-of-life approaches fit right into their concepts of story.

As a result, you can find slice-of-life story approaches everywhere in Japanese fiction, from their four-panel comics to their light novels. In fact, their use of the slice-of-life approach in light novels is one of the things that makes their work feel unique or different from other types of light fiction and webfiction you generally find across the Internet. It isn't unusual to find light novels (or manga) where the entire story structure is a slice-of-life approach, often mixing normal people with interesting situations or interesting people with mundane situations to produce stories.

Harem-based light novels using a slice-of-life approach are especially common, where a normal, average person suddenly finds themselves surrounded by a collection of weird and eccentric characters vying for their romantic attentions. Each of these eccentric characters brings with them complications, dramatic questions, and situations that make their interactions with the lead character and others interesting, and the story runs off the interest this generates. Whether it be that the harem members are fish out of water in this setting, or have personality issues, or needs and goals that conflict with those of the lead, it creates situations that the reader will find fascinating and/or amusing. This juxtaposition of interesting characters and mundane situations keeps readers' attention, and the story in motion until the end.

And, each time the Harem story starts to run out of energy, the writer just needs to introduce another character to spice things back up, using the new arrival to keep things lively. Of course, this has its drawbacks, as there are only so many harem members you can throw in before it gets too crowded, and so pure slice-of-life Harem stories have a limited lifespan unless the writer is very clever or the characters very interesting.

As a result, most light novel Harem stories combine some element of slice-of-life with another kind of genre or story to keep the story interesting. A good example of this is *How a Realist Hero Saved the Kingdom*, where the lead character is trying to save a fantasy kingdom in trouble, but the troubles are mostly slow-moving mundane ones like economics, agriculture, sanitation, civil engineering, etc.- so most of the chapters are just slice-of-life stories about the experiences the lead character has with his typical harem of cuties during the course of trying to save the kingdom. At the same time, the big projects are happening around them, and the story alternates between slice-of-life and actual big plot kingdom development. Most of the focus isn't on the big projects, they're a part of the main over-plot, but not a part of the main character's daily life and experiences, and move too slowly to be the focus. So, instead the story focus is on the life the main character and supporting cast lead while they try to accomplish their greater tasks.

And this is something else worth mentioning- many light novels use the approach of having a grand overall story like a quest or situation to be resolved, but then use a series of slice-of-life stories to advance that greater plot instead of having each story be about the overall story. Each individual story is a slice-of-life story about the characters and situations, but taken as a whole they tell a greater non-slice-of-life story about how the character(s) accomplish something. For example, say the story was about characters trying to build up an interstellar transport business (Mundane

Characters + Interesting Situation), and each story is a slice-of-life tale about daily life in the space freighter trade. The overall story might be about them going from nobodies to successful business owners, but that's a story playing out in the background of the slice-of-life pieces of their daily lives.

Not that a writer **must** be stuck with any particular kind of story structure (you could alternate between slice-of-life and High Adventure stories, and that would be fine too), but that's something that needs to be planned and set up from the start. The characters in a Mundane Characters + Interesting Situation type story aren't likely to be as suited to situations of high adventure as the characters in an Interesting Characters + Mundane Situation story are. The leads in *The Devil is a Part-Timer* are all exiled warriors and powerful figures from a fantasy world, and despite working at *McRonalds*, if called upon they do have a skill set for dealing with fantastical situations. On the other hand, if you put the characters from *Ascendance of the Bookworm*, who are typical peasants in a non-magical fantasy kingdom (Mundane Characters + Interesting Situation), into an adventure situation they'd be monster chow pretty fast.

Now, can slice-of-life stories be built around Interesting Characters and Interesting Situations paired together? The answer is yes they can, but the problem is that slice-of-life is about the mundane, and unless there are mundane elements to the story it isn't a slice-of-life story. So, a heroic space fleet admiral who lives the life of a glorious military officer overseeing a million worlds can still be a character and situation you can tell a slice-of-life story about, but it will mean finding the tiny mundane details in their life to focus on. (Like them trying to sneak out to get fast food when their ship's doctor has put them on a diet.) And, the more "interesting" the character and situation are, the less mundane and normal they are, and slice-of-life stories are built around the normal, which makes them more challenging to write.

At the other extreme, we have stories about normal people in normal situations, which are also perfectly good fodder for slice-of-life stories, but have much the same problems. If the character and situation are both very ordinary and not especially interesting, then you have lots of mundane, but not much to build a story that will keep the reader's attention. This too will require a lot of skill as a writer, as the interest in the story will come from adding little twists and turns of setting and circumstance to the character's otherwise dull lives. (Like two middle aged women who meet for tea every day at a coffee shop, but one day their waiter is a gorgeous man who the two very normal women begin trying to out-flirt each other with. Leading to a fight that ends when the waiter's boyfriend shows up to pick him up.) There are always situations which can turn normal people into interesting ones by bringing out their hidden sides, and normal situations can be made abnormal when the quirks of human behavior become involved.

However, the easiest type of slice-of-life setup, especially for longer stories like webfiction and light novels is an equal mix of the unusual and mundane, which by its nature generates stories that are going to hold the reader's interest and offer a lot of material for the writer to work with. Writing is already hard enough without making your life more difficult by choosing a hard to work with set of controlling ideas. Unless you're a dramatic or comedic writer who is an expert at finding the interesting in the everyday, trying to work with mundane characters and settings for the long haul might not be the best choice for you.

Which brings us to the final, significant topic to consider when writing slice-of-life stories- humor.

While slice-of-life stories don't have to be humorous in any way, humor and slice-of-life go together like icing and cake. Whether the story itself is meant to be humorous, or just the situations and the reactions of the characters involved make the reader laugh, most slice-of-life stories use some element of humor to keep their audience interested. In shorter slice-of-life stories, this is often a comedic twist at the end, and the story effectively plays out as a joke leading up that twist. In longer slice-of-life stories, the humor will often come from the character interactions and situations which appear, and there may not be any twist at all, just a resolution as the characters realize the nature of the situation they've found themselves in. Or, the twist may still be there, but serve as a reminder to the characters (and audience) some flaw of human nature. (see the above story about the tea time friends)

Many Situation Comedies (SitComs) you see on television are similar to slice-of-life stories, although they've turned up the level of humor to an extreme and are very plot and joke driven. This generally makes them funny in short bursts, but they lose much of the relatability that comes with a real slice-of-life story. In a slice-of-life story, the closer the story is to mundane reality, the better it works, but comedies like SitComs take it to another level and become another type of story altogether. Real people don't talk like that and aren't that witty. Ironically, however, the most popular SitComs of all time (*Leave it to Beaver, All in the Family, M*A*S*H, Different Strokes, FRIENDS, Seinfeld, Big Bang Theory*, etc.) have tended to be closer to slice-of-life stories than their joke-driven counterparts, and this focus on the natural humor of those characters and situations was largely responsible for their success. (As opposed to the several dozen joke-driven shows that appear each year and are cancelled and forgotten on a regular basis.)

SLOW LIFE STORIES

In recent years, there has been a special type of slice-of-life story which has popped up in Japanese light novels and webfiction which fans call "slow life stories." These are stories like *A Story About Treating a Female Knight, Who Has Never Been Treated as a Woman, as a Woman* by Kengo Matsumoto which are basically celebrations of slower and more natural ways of living.

In some of these stories, interesting characters who have led busy or adventurous lives usually either retire or are forced to move to the countryside to start new lives as members of a rural community. These fish out of water characters have to learn basic skills like farming, cooking, sewing, and other fundamental skills that humans have done for centuries, and discover the simple pleasures and spiritual calming that comes with these activities and environments.

In other stories, more average characters find themselves in unusual situations like being stuck in a fantasy world, and then begin building a new life for themselves as members of the local community. Their new life is one of simple living, despite the fantastic nature of their surroundings, and often the interest in the story comes from them discovering the simple pleasures of this new world. They might become a farmer, a local shopkeeper, or even a baker, but by pursuing these careers they find their place in the world.

And finally, there are some slow life stories which are the low-key versions of Rising Hero stories which focus on characters coming to enjoy the daily activities that happen while preparing for some greater accomplishments. Even Rising Heroes have to live normal lives most of the time, and these stories show the value of the quieter times and spiritual calm that comes with living life well.

Whatever the story idea, these slow life stories are Zen-like studies on the beauty of life well lived away from the pressures and stresses of the modern world. They are often yearnings by the writers for a more peaceful and communal way of living that they don't have in their own lives, and these desires for simple living are shared by the modern Japanese reader. They can be light comedies, dramas, task stories, romances, or combinations of all of the above, but they pay tribute to the joy of daily life well lived.

FINAL NOTES ON SLICE-OF-LIFE:

- Slice-of-life stories get their energy from interesting characters and interesting twists on daily events.
- Most often used for teen, interpersonal, Harem, and romance stories.
- Sometimes used for relationship stories where the romantic leads have a series of slice-of-life experiences together and these represent the evolution of their relationship.
- Mundane means that the story element or character is everyday in our real world. Something like Monster Hunting might be mundane in a fantasy setting, but it isn't mundane in our world so it's not going to be slice-of-life. However, if you could present the job of Monster Hunting in a way which makes it seem just like a job in our world (say being a Pest Control Expert), then it can still come across as slice-of-life.
- Slice-of-life stories often have a lead character, but they don't have to, and can be about groups instead.
- This form works very well for webcomics and short visual stories.
- Japanese slice-of-life stories are often built around routine tasks, procedures, festivals and seasons.

WRITING YOUR SERIAL

As you have seen, there are many different ways to write webfiction depending on the style, the story, and the audience.

Now it's your turn.

The following chapters are advice to help you when planning and writing your own stories, and they apply whether you're writing a short story, a novel, a serial, or anything else. They will help to guide you in shaping your stories to give you the best chances at both finishing your story and leaving your audience satisfied.

Most of the basics you needed to know to write your own webfiction were covered elsewhere in this book, so these chapters are extra things that didn't fit with the other things being covered, but are no less important. If you match them with the first chapter (What Popular Webfiction Stories Have in Common) then you have a solid beginner's guide to writing serial webfiction, and if you add in the information from the other chapters, then your personal guide will be complete.

WRITING YOUR STORY

Many people think storytelling is an art which blossoms from the soul of an artist, and a talent that you need to be born with and then nurture into full bloom by writing hundreds of thousands of words. They tell themselves this because they aren't good storytellers, and it's easier to say that they just don't have the gift than it is to actually do the hard work needed to become a good storyteller.

In other words, this is an excuse, not reality.

Reality is that storytelling is a science and a trade much more than it is an art. It is definitely an art, but that artistic ability can be developed by anyone who is willing to put the effort in to learning their craft and constantly practice it until they can't get it wrong.

Writing has more in common with building a house than it does painting, and more in common with cooking than it does singing. Painting and singing are talents that are developed by practice and experience, but building a house and cooking are trades that are a collection of skills working together to produce a final result.

In other words, if you know the fundamental skills of storytelling, you can use those skills to tell stories, whether you have some mystical talent or not. Anyone can tell a story as easily as anyone can nail two pieces of wood together or make a sandwich from two slices of bread and a bit of nut butter. It will be a simple story, and it might not be much to look at, but it is a story.

And with more knowledge, practice, and time, anyone can learn to tell better stories, and maybe even tell stories that people will pay money just to enjoy. Just like a master builder or master chef started with wood and nails, or bread and nut butter, and now today have made their trades into their careers, you can become a master storyteller.

And it all starts with knowing three simple things...

THE SHAPE OF STORIES

If you're going to write stories, the first and most important thing to understand is that all stories have the same basic parts- *setup, action and result*. Stories are about the results which come from characters taking actions (or having actions happen to them), and from top to bottom all stories will be made of these three parts.

It might be a single sentence:

Terry (setup) opened the door quickly (action), and it shattered (result).

Or it might be the Three Act Structure of a whole epic Fantasy serial:

Dong Li (setup) rose from being a peasant farmer to a powerful immortal sorcerer (action) and defeated the world's evil god emperor (result).

But everything in stories is built around the simple pattern of setup>action>result, and in fact for the human brain to consider something a story it needs all three of these parts in there someplace, either stated or implied. It doesn't matter whether it's a sentence, a paragraph, a scene, a chapter, a sequence, a story arc, an act, a book, a series, or a whole serial- they are all structured around characters doing things and getting results from their actions.

This is so important to understand because if you're going to be a good writer you not only need to make sure your stories have this structure in there someplace, but you also need to know what these pieces are so you can play with them. Even though the setup>action>result pattern is extremely simple, it is also very flexible and powerful, and during this chapter you will see how you can play with this simple structure to create stories that your audience won't want to put down.

Overall Story

Stories work on many levels, and at the very top there is the overall story. This is who and what the main story is about, and is the spine which holds everything else together. In most cases, it represents the main thing the lead character is trying to do, and gives the story a clear direction and focus that it needs to stick together.

Think of the overall story as the whole journey the character is taking in the story- Where do they start? Where do they finish? What happens in between? That's the overall story. Which is important to keep in mind in a long serial, as without an overall direction a story can get lost in the wilderness as the writer takes the story in different directions to keep the audience interested and engaged.

The Spine of Action

No matter how long or short a story is, it's based around the main character doing something. That thing can be short and simple, or it can be a huge and epic task, but there will also be one central action or idea which is holding the whole story together- and this is called the story's Spine of Action. Just like a human spine, it holds the whole story together and connects all the important parts in a way that keeps things from falling apart on the journey from beginning to end.

Basically, most characters in stories are trying to do one of three things- attain, maintain, or lose. They want to get something they don't have (attain), to keep something they do have (maintain), or to get rid of something they don't want (lose). The spine of action of stories will be based on whichever of those three things the character is trying to do.

- Bill will attain justice by solving a murder.
- Joe will to maintain his company and keep it from falling apart.
- Kelvin will lose weight by not eating anything but vegetables.
- Susan will attain love by finding mister right.
- Ali is will attain the perfect car by building it himself.

In fact, you will find the heart of most stories can be broken down into a simple formula of:

[Character] will [attain/maintain/lose] Z by [doing/not doing] Y.

Z is the thing they want (their motivation), and **Y** is how they're trying to get it.

And, once you know what your main character's goals are you know what your story's spine of action is. This will be the thing that drives the character through the story, and gives the story its focus as well.

Here is a brief list of a few common motivations that drive characters:

- Acceptance (the character wants to be accepted by others)
- Accomplishment (the character wants to achieve a particular goal or a sense of having done something worthwhile)
- Boredom (the character is easily bored and wants something interesting to do)
- Challenge (the character desires to test their skills or abilities against others)
- Compassion (the character wants to help others fill their needs)

- Curiosity (the character wants to learn more about something)
- Fame (the character wants their name to be known by others)
- Family (the character is driven by their love of their family members or the idea of family)
- Fear (the character is driven to avoid something or someone)
- Fighting (the character enjoys physical or verbal conflict)
- Food (the character desires food or eating experiences)
- Friendship (the character wants to gain or maintain close friendships)
- Greed (the character wants to acquire something)
- Guilt (the character is trying to make up for some past misdeeds, real or perceived)
- Honor (the character wants to uphold values held by their clan, group or society)
- Ideology (the character has a strong belief in an idea or system (like religion, or a code of conduct) that motivates what they do)
- Independence (the character is driven by a need for personal freedom)
- Knowledge (the character wants to gain information, skills or an experience)
- Love/Hate (the character loves/hates someone or something)
- Novelty (the character wants to have new experiences)
- Order (the character wants to create order in their life or environment)
- Physical Activity (the character wants to exercise their body)
- Power (the character wants control over others and the things that come with it)
- Responsibility (the character feels responsibility towards someone or something)
- Revenge (the character feels they been harmed or wronged, and wants to return the favor)
- Safety (the character wants to feel secure and protected)
- Savings (the character wants to accumulate something)
- Sex (the character wants to have sex with others)
- Social Status (the character wants to increase their status in society)
- Survival (the character wants to get the things they need to live)

Using this list of motivations, and the above formula, you can easily know where your story needs to start and end. It starts when they begin on the road to wanting that goal, and it ends when they either get it or no longer can.

For example:

- The character will <u>attain money</u> if they <u>do a job</u>.
- The character will <u>maintain their honor</u> if they <u>get revenge on their enemy</u>.
- The character will <u>lose social status</u> if they <u>fail to attend the ball</u>.
- The character will <u>attain love</u> if they <u>find the right romantic partner</u>.

This formula will give you big character motivations or small ones, but most importantly it makes your story's spine of action very clear. You can also use it to figure out what the character's motivations and goals are during the individual story arcs. (See below.)

THE THREE ACT STRUCTURE

Overall stories are commonly broken down into smaller and more manageable pieces to help writers when planning and creating them. At the top level, the setup>action>result pattern becomes known as the three-act structure-often taught in English classes as introduction>rising action>conclusion, or introduction>conflict>resolution. However, no matter what the three phases are called, they represent the beginning>middle>end of the story and are just a way to break the story down when writing it.

Let's look at the three-act structure in more detail to understand exactly what each part does.

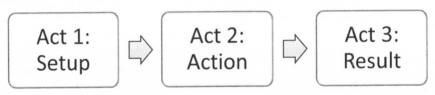

Act 1: Setup (aka the Situation, Introduction, or Beginning)

<u>Length:</u> usually between the first 10% to 35% of the story, averaging 25%.
<u>Questions Answered:</u> Who is involved? Where are they? When does this take place? What motivates them? Why are they doing what they're doing?

Details:

The first phase of any story unit exists to tell the audience everything they're going to need to know to understand the rest of the story. This doesn't just include characters, time, place, and other matters of context, but also includes the motivations and problems that the characters face. The story begins here with a character and a goal or need, and this will be the central idea that carries the story from here to the end.

Notes:

- Act One should always introduce some problem the main character has to deal with, even if it's just that they're thirsty. Whether it's a single sentence or a whole series, the character should be given a motivator like a need or goal which guides them and makes them get off their sofa, put down their phone, and take action.

- Act One doesn't have to be the "real" first part of the story, it's just the point where you drop your audience into the story. The story itself often started long before the main characters or audience get involved, and the first part is about playing catch-up while the action is already in progress. However, this is still the first part of the story you're telling because it's still performing a setup function. In cases like this, the first act might only be as long as 10% of the story because the author wants to get the characters and audience up to speed as soon as possible and get on with the action.

- Nothing should happen in the story which isn't laid out in some way during the first act. It might not be directly shown, but everything that happens should be a natural outgrowth of controlling ideas and story elements which are presented to the audience in the first part. If there's a storm in the Third Act/Result phase, clouds should be gathering in the First Act/Setup phase.

- Opponents sometimes aren't shown directly in the first Act of a longer story, but their presence is hinted at in some way or suggested by the situation.

- Think through your Setup phase carefully, and look here when you have problems writing later parts of the story.

Act 2: Action (aka the Development, Conflict, Event, or Confrontation)

Length: extremely flexible, but usually the middle 40%-80% of the story, averaging 50%.

<u>Questions Answered</u>: What happens? How does the main character try to solve the problem? What gets in their way? How do they overcome challenges?

<u>Details:</u>

The middle phase of any story is where most of the story's action is going to take place. The main character of the story tries to accomplish some goal, and may or may not make progress towards achieving that goal. They may succeed, fail, meet resistance, or discover new information which complicates the situation and changes or modifies their goal. There are many possibilities, which is why this phase is so flexible in length. The main requirements for the Act Two/Action phase are that it's interesting to the audience and that everything that happens is built around what was introduced in the Act One/Setup phase.

<u>Notes:</u>

- Typically, most stories are conflict based, which means that they're about a character in conflict with themselves, another person, society, or the world around them. In these stories, the Action phase is where the character comes into conflict with a someone or something that prevents them from accomplishing their goals. Whether they succeed or fail is left for the Result phase to decide.
- The Act Two/Action phase often ends with some kind of surprising twist or dramatic turn that changes the situation (often for the worse) and increases the level of drama going into the Result phase.
- Sometimes you will see people talk about a four-act structure- this is just the three-act structure with Act 2 broken down into two halves to make it easier to organize. Similarly, if you see five, seven, or nine-act structures, they're still just the three acts broken down into smaller bite-sized chunks.

Act 3: Result (aka the Resolution, Denouement, Climax, or Ending)

<u>Length:</u> usually the final 10%-30% of the story, averaging 25%.

<u>Questions Answered</u>: How does it all turn out? Does the main character succeed or fail? How do they accomplish (or fail to accomplish) their goals? What happens to them after the story is done? What are the consequences of the actions they took in the story?

<u>Details:</u>

The end Result phase of any story is there to bring everything to a satisfying close. It usually contains the climax, where the main character finally overcomes the last great obstacle between them and their goals, and the ending, where you see the results of everything the main character did come together.

<u>Notes:</u>

- Audiences want satisfying endings more than surprise endings, and a satisfying ending is one which is logical and earned by the main character. It is the result of the actions taken in the story, the choices they made, and feels "right" to the audience based on everything which has taken place.
- If possible, endings should also surprise the audience in some way for the best dramatic effect, but surprise is less important than satisfaction. The audience knows all along the main character will generally succeed and wants it to happen (at least at the end of the story), but they also want to know how the character does it and see it happen in an interesting way.
- There should be no major loose ends (unless the story is part of a larger one), and everything introduced in the Act One/Setup phase should be resolved in the Act Three/Result phase unless you're planning a sequel.

STORY ARCS

In serial fiction, the term "story arc" is used to refer to the smaller stories that make up the larger overall story. You can compare these to the individual novels that make up a series of books, or the individual films that would make up a movie series. A story arc has its own three act structure story with a beginning, middle, and end, and while it could be taken as a story on its own, story arcs usually work best as part of a larger tale.

Typically, after you've planned the overall story of your webfiction, you should then break it down into a series of smaller story arcs that will map out the different phases of your story's journey. These parts can be any length you want, from a three chapter visit to an old friend to a two-hundred-chapter epic battle, or anything in between. The only rules are that it must be a complete story inside itself with its own Spine of Action, and that it contributes to the overall story in some way.

Creating Arcs

Generally, when breaking stories down into arcs, you're best to think of them as the steps that the main characters must take to get to the end of the story. And, a handy way to divide them up is to write down the steps that the character(s) must take, and then figure out how to turn each step (or combination of steps) into an arc.

To give a simple example, let's say the main character of your story, Lisa, wants to become a chef and own her own Michelin Star restaurant. You would first sit down and figure out the steps that she'd have to go through to become a chef...

- Attend cooking school at local community college
- Get experience working in a local restaurant kitchen
- Get into good culinary school
- Graduate high in her class at the school to get recruited by a top restaurant
- Become an assistant chef at a top restaurant
- Become a head chef at a top restaurant
- Open up her own restaurant.
- Get her restaurant to the top of the local food scene.
- Get her first Michelin Star rating as a top restaurant.

By mapping out Lisa's journey like this, we can see the steps she'll need to go through to reach her goals, and then it just becomes a matter of turning those into story arcs. They might not all get used, or they might be combined in various ways like this...

Story Arc 1: Lisa is inspired to follow her dream of becoming a Michelin Star chef by her grandfather, who also ran a restaurant and tells her to follow her dreams before he passes. She enrolls in the culinary arts program at her local community college and works nights at a restaurant to pay for it. It's a struggle, but she graduates top of her class.

Story Arc 2: Lisa enters a prestigious culinary school and discovers that the school has a very structured pecking order where the younger chefs are treated poorly by the older students. Also, the competition here is fierce, so Lisa must fight harder than she ever has before to reach the top, since only the best graduates of the school get recruited for top restaurants. She needs an apprenticeship at a top restaurant to make a name for herself. Again, she succeeds, but only after a long struggle and a lot of heartbreak.

Story Arc 3: She is now working at La Top, a rotating restaurant literally on top of the tallest building in the capital and under a Michelin Star head chef. She quickly realizes that she's still got a lot to learn, and the head chef is like a devil to her and the other assistant chefs. She has to find a way to gain the chef's respect and survive in an insanely tough environment. It breaks her, and she quits at one point, but the other chefs convince her to try again, and she eventually rises to a high position at La Top.

Story Arc 4: Lisa is fired from La Top, but it's actually the head chef forcing her to go out and follow her dream. She opens her own restaurant, which involves many new challenges of management and finances that she's never dealt with before. It's a real struggle to get the place going, but with her new partner David helping her, she makes her new restaurant Lisa's On First, into a successful business.

Story Arc 5: Lisa's On First is doing well, but she still wants that Michelin Star. She completely revamps the restaurant, creates a new menu, and begins trying to attract attention to both her food and her establishment. She faces competition like she never has before, and it threatens her relationship with David, her business, and her health, but still she perseveres and thanks to a spot on a major restaurant review show, she gets a visit from the judges at Michelin. She gets her star, marries David, and visits her grandfather's grave to thank him for the inspiration.

As you can see in this rough example, the actual story arcs don't follow the steps exactly, and some parts are combined or split, but it still gives the story a clear direction and flow. Each arc is its own story with the main character trying to accomplish some major goal through taking action and eventually doing it after struggling through challenges.

If you are writing a webfiction serial or book series, you are advised to try using this method to at least roughly figure out the steps and possibly what happens in each arc before you start writing your stories. You can change things as you go if you get better ideas, but having a plan of some kind is very helpful for keeping your story going and for when you don't know what to write next. As long as you're moving in the direction of the story's final goals along its Spine of Action, your story will feel like it's going somewhere and your audience will be happy.

CHAPTERS

Before you start writing chapters successfully, there are two important concepts that you need to understand– *dramatic questions* and *dramatic tension*. If you master these key concepts, then you'll be well on your journey to writing chapters that your audience won't be able to stop reading. It is only once you understand these ideas that you'll be able to structure and plan your chapters in a way that keeps your audience in the palm of your hand.

Dramatic Questions

Human beings are curious creatures, and every time you present them with an incomplete piece of information, they want to know the rest. Marketers call this the "curiosity gap," and it's one of the key tools they use in advertising to get audiences to read ads online. However, it's also been a key tool in the writing of stories since the first storytellers wove tales around campfires in ancient Africa.

Storytellers use this technique in the form of dramatic questions– which are questions the events of the story create in the minds of the audience as they experience the story. Every time something interesting or surprising happens, it creates a question in the audience's heads, and they keep reading to find out the answer to those questions like a detective follows a trail of clues to solve a mystery.

It sounds complicated, but actually it's a very simple idea at heart. For example, compare the following two sentences.

1) Bob walked into his house, grabbed some cake from the kitchen, and sat down in his favorite chair to watch TV.

2) Bob walked into his house, grabbed some cake from the kitchen, and was going to sit down in his favorite chair to watch TV when he noticed someone was already in the chair.

The first sentence gives the audience a series of events, but there's nothing compelling there that makes the audience want to keep reading. On the other hand, the second sentence creates a situation and then introduces an unknown element that makes the reader start asking questions – Who was in the chair? Why are they there? Could it be a thief? Does Bob owe someone money? What's happening here?

Your reader's head is filled with questions and possible answers when they're confronted with an incomplete situation or problem, and then they keep reading to find out if they're right. Even right now, you probably have a mental itch in the back of your head to know who is in that chair just from reading that single sentence. You'll find out later.

This is the power of dramatic questions, and if you want to get good at them, then go grab stories by some of your favorite writers and look at how they're using these questions generated in the heads of the audience to keep the audience hooked and interested as the whole story plays out. You'll probably find that the writers you like are making a point of starting and ending each chapter and scene they write with a dramatic question to keep you interested.

That question might come from...

- Introducing a new problem for a character to face
- A character facing a difficult challenge
- Something surprising happening

- An unexpected result from a character's actions
- A new character being introduced

Or anything else that makes the audience curious and want to know more about what happens next and how it all turns out. Audience's aren't there to read about the ordinary and see things go as expected, they're there to read about the extraordinary and be put on an emotional ride of twists and turns that keeps them involved.

Of course, dramatic questions don't just come in one size. There are big questions and small questions, and writers make use of many different sizes and types of questions to keep their audiences going. And this leads to the other important idea that storytellers need to understand...

Dramatic Tension

There are two common situations in stories that generate dramatic tension:

1) Anticipation - an audience thinks they know what will happen and either desire it or dread it.

2) Curiosity – an audience wants to know the answer to a dramatic question and are being held in suspense waiting for it.

Both of these come from dramatic questions that the storyteller has created in the minds of the audience. In the case of anticipation, they expect something to happen, and in the case of curiosity they want to know something. Both are key parts of keeping the audience engaged, and the better you are at using them, the better a writer you will be.

Anticipation

Generating dramatic tension through anticipation is actually pretty simple- you either let the audience have information that the characters don't have, or you offer the audience the promise of something happening you know that they want to see. Either of these will create a natural feeling of dramatic tension in the audience, who will tear through pages to get the results.

If you give the audience access to knowledge the characters don't have, which is a technique called *dramatic irony*, then it can create tension by giving the audience expectations about what is about to happen in the story. The audience knows the character is going to be surprised, and so they wait to see what happens when the character receives that surprise- good or bad.

A classic example of this is used in horror stories, where the audience often knows that the killer is lurking around waiting to strike and the characters don't. This gives every moment the characters face dramatic tension, because the audience knows that at any moment these people could suddenly meet a gruesome end. Thus, when the character goes down into the dark basement with the broken light to check out the noise they heard, the tension has the audience clinging to their seats and jumping at every sound in dread of what might happen next.

This is all built around knowledge the audience has, but the characters don't, and in most stories, writers often let the audience in on the villain's plans exactly because it creates dramatic tension as to how the hero is going to deal with this trouble they might not see coming.

On the other hand, sometimes the character and audience both know what's coming, and they can't wait for it to happen! This is another type of dramatic tension- when the storyteller offers the audience something they want to see occur and then makes them wait for it. This too can come in many forms, for example...

- A sympathetic character is put in a position of power where they now have a major advantage over their enemies.
- An unsympathetic character is about to get the justice they deserve.
- Two romantic leads look like they're about to finally get together.
- A sympathetic character seems to be about to get the reward they deserve.
- A sympathetic character looks like they're about to accomplish a major story goal.

As long as the audience desires something to happen, and are made to wait for it, it creates dramatic tension that keeps them focused and builds up a feeling of excitement. Then, when that excitement reaches its peak, the storyteller finally gives them what they want, giving a sweet sense of release and happiness that the audience enjoys.

Making this work is all about setup, and it does take some effort and planning on the part of the writer, but it can also create a strong high for the audience when it finally pays off.

Curiosity

The other (and easier) way to create dramatic tension is to use the audience's own curiosity. As was mentioned above, curious audiences want to know the answers to their questions and they will keep reading to find out those answers. So, storytellers use that desire to know against the audience to build tension into their stories and keep the audience interested.

This is done using the pattern of tension and release.

All you need to do is introduce something into the story that creates a dramatic question, and then delay giving them the answer to that question. This is one of the most basic skills of showmanship that is used by performers everywhere- public speakers, singers, musicians, salesmen, magicians, teachers, comedians, film & TV directors, and everyone else who needs to hold an audience interested uses this basic technique as part of their craft.

In fact, a common writer's saying is, "When the audience wants something, don't give it to them. Let them have it when they're not expecting it or in a way they don't expect."

Therefore, one of the most important skills for storytellers to develop is to make audiences want something, and then hold back on delivering it just long enough that they can't wait anymore. This creates tension, and makes the audience want it even more, and thus when they finally get it, they feel a sense of relief and joy at getting what they want.

In fact, making the audience wait for something makes them want it even more, even if it was something they didn't care that much about in the first place. Some small thing that didn't seem all that important at the time can become the most important thing in the world if the audience wants it but can't have it. For example, how many of you are still reading to see who was waiting in Bob's chair? (Just a little longer, folks!)

And then, when they get it, especially if they get something even better or more interesting than they were expecting, it means all that much more to them and generates stronger emotion than it might if they were given it right away. This both makes the audience happy, and makes them want to read more because they know this writer has the ability to make them happy, and will continue to do so as they keep reading the story.

Thus, good writing makes constant use of dramatic tension generated by curiosity, turning simple dramatic questions into hooks that pull the audience along and use them to build tension and then release those hooks one by one to make the audience feel happy. This creates a rhythm of tension and release in stories that makes them compelling and interesting, and it's the presence or absence of this dramatic tension that decides which stories are hits and which ones are flops.

However, there are two major things every storyteller needs to know about using dramatic tension based on curiosity- 1) it only works if the audience cares, and 2) the audience will only wait so long to get what they want.

First, if the audience doesn't want to know the answer to a question, then this technique doesn't work. A good storyteller needs to make sure that they give the audience questions that they'll want to know the answer to, and preferably that they **must** know the answers to.

The easiest way to do this is by having a sympathetic lead character whose goals the audience cares about, which means that everything that seriously threatens those goals becomes a dramatic question the audience will be interested in. The more emotionally invested the audience is in the characters and their success, the more important each dramatic question that stands in the way of their success becomes.

This is why it's so crucial that audiences and lead characters connect, and that audiences can feel sympathetic towards the main character, their goals, and the end of the story. If the audience doesn't care about these things, there's no way to really generate strong dramatic tension, and the story will be boring and flat instead of compelling and lively.

And second, each dramatic question only has enough dramatic power to keep audiences going for so long before they give up trying to find the answer. Dramatic questions come in many shapes and sizes, and while some can only get readers to the next sentence, others can keep readers going right until the end of an epic serial.

For example, the question of who is in Bob's chair wouldn't really have enough power to keep someone reading this far unless they were also reading to find out something else. (Like how to write a great story!) It would probably only keep most readers interested for another paragraph or two beyond the introduction of the question, and then they'd get bored of it and quit. This is because you have no investment in Bob, his situation, or the results of who might be in that chair.

On the other hand, if we reveal that it's his wife, but she's holding a gun pointed right at Bob, that would probably keep the audience interested for a little bit longer than a paragraph. It might even get the audience to read the next chapter to find out why she's doing this because it's such an unexpected surprise and they want to know more about this odd situation.

However, the audience still won't read several chapters to find out the answer, unless they're really invested in Bob. His life is at stake, which does seem to make things more interesting, but since you don't care about Bob or his goals, whether he lives or dies is a minor curiosity not a major question. So, this dramatic question couldn't drive a whole novel or film from beginning to end the way it is.

On the other hand, if this is a scene in a story about how Bob is a doctor trying to cure the plague that has left his daughter with hours to live and threatens to kill millions if he doesn't stop it, then that could be a question that could drive a greater story. A situation where a sympathetic person with sympathetic goals is against steep or impossible odds naturally creates a huge dramatic question which can make audiences read through dozens or even hundreds of chapters.

Now, suddenly Bob's wife holding a gun to him and threatening his life isn't just about him, it's about the goal he and the audience share, and their daughter, and the potentially millions of people who will die if she shoots him. And, why is she threatening to shoot him anyways? What possible motive could she have for threatening his life here and now at such a precious time, and when their daughter's life is on the line?

All dramatic questions a good storyteller will make the audience wait to find out the answers to...

Thus, understanding dramatic questions and dramatic tension are a must if you're going to keep audiences reading and your readership growing. They are easy to understand, but can take a lifetime to master, and many great writers struggle with them their entire careers. But, if you can start to use them in your own work, you will be a huge step forward in being able to write powerful dramatic chapters that keep your readers on the hook.

Structuring Your Chapters - Blocking

Chapters in webfiction should be looked at as mini-stories. They start with something happening that is going to make the reader want to read the chapter, give the reader an interesting experience as events play out, and then finish up with something important occurring. However, the trick with chapters as opposed to overall stories is that chapters often start and end in an incomplete way.

Sticking with the principle of dramatic tension, the first rule of structuring webfiction chapters is *never end a chapter with a finished scene* (unless it's the end of the story or story arc). Each chapter should always end with an unfinished scene that continues over into the next chapter, which forces the reader to keep reading to find out what happens next. This saves on having to constantly come up with contrived cliffhangers to end each chapter with, although you still need each chapter to end at a dramatic question of some kind.

Even within chapters, you should be starting with a dramatic question that makes the reader want to read the rest of the chapter and then presenting a series of smaller dramatic questions that you then delay the answer to in order to create the tension and release pattern. This might happen within scenes, between paragraphs, and even between scenes. The most popular method being to introduce a dramatic question, then jump to another viewpoint to give background information or another perspective, and then when the tension is high, jump back to show the result/answer to the dramatic question that was introduced. (See Writing Battles for more on this.)

Thus, chapters in a webfiction serial are generally composed of 1-5 "blocks," with each of these blocks representing a shift in viewpoints or situations to build dramatic tension. Calling them "scenes" isn't quite right, since while they can be scenes, they can also be just changes in viewpoint within a single scene to prolong suspense.

Here are some common ways webfiction chapters block out the scenes happening inside them:

One-Block Incomplete Scene Chapter
Block 1: A new scene starts, or a scene which started in a previous chapter continues in this one, and then ends unfinished at the end of the chapter.

Two-Block Scene Change Chapter
Block 1: The second half of a scene which started in the previous chapter.
Block 2: The first half of a scene which ends partway through on a dramatic moment, to be continued in the next chapter.

Three-Block Scene Change Chapter
Block 1: A short scene finishing a scene that started in the previous chapter.
Block 2: A cut-away scene to show things happening elsewhere, or maybe reactions to the results of that previous scene from other points of view.
Block 3: The start of a new scene which is left unfinished at the end of the chapter on a dramatic moment.

Four-Block Scene Change Chapter
Block 1: A short scene finishing a scene that started in the previous chapter.
Block 2: The start of a new scene.
Block 3: A cut-away to another scene or location to present something happening.
Block 4: The continuation of the new scene from Block 2, but it is left unfinished at the end of the chapter on a dramatic moment.

Five-Block Scene Change Chapter
Block 1: Short scene finishing a scene that started in the previous chapter.
Block 2: A cut-away to another scene or location to present something happening.
Block 3: The start of a new scene.
Block 4: A cut-away to another scene or location to present something happening.
Block 5: The continuation of the new scene from Block 3, but it is left unfinished at the end of the chapter on a dramatic moment.

SCENES

Scenes in stories tell what happens at a particular place and time in the story, and most stories are made up of collection of scenes which link together to form the larger story. Writers use scenes to cut out all the boring stuff that happens during the story and just focus on the interesting parts. Scenes represent the major events of the story playing out, and what happens during those events.

Scenes in stories also follow the same basic pattern as the other levels of story- they usually involve characters with goals trying to accomplish those goals and getting results of one kind or another. This follows the standard setup>action>results pattern that you are already familiar with, and most scenes should be thought of as mini-stories which make up a larger story.

Typically, the scene will start by introducing the important details the audience needs to know...

- Who is in the scene?
- When is it?
- Where are they?
- What do they want?
- Why do they want it?

And then, following that the scene will play out as the central character or characters try to accomplish their scene goals, and reach one of three possible results- success, failure, or a draw.

If the scene ends in success, then the character is now in a position to start another goal, which will lead to another scene. Successful scenes are needed to keep the story moving along, but they are usually smaller successes which lead towards the final bigger success at the end of the story. To keep things moving, scenes which end in successes usually actually end in a dramatic hook that naturally leads to another scene. ("We have the weapon, now we can go defeat the demon lord!" or "We won the contract, but now the client wants us to deliver it by next Tuesday! There's no way we can do it!")

If the scene ends in failure, then it forces the character to deal with the result of that failure. The following scenes will usually give details as to the effects of that failure and then lay out how the character handles it. For example, they may need to recover from the failure, find a new approach and try again. Or, they may no longer be able to do what they did before and now have to find a new way to achieve their greater goals.

If, as happens occasionally, the scene ends with a draw, then the character was unable to achieve their goals completely, but did have some partial success, partial failure, or both. These situations also lead to further scenes where the character needs to build on what they achieved in the scene and/or overcomes the problems which resulted.

In any case, try not to let any single scene end without a dramatic question hook of some kind that makes the reader want to read the next scene which is linked to this one. Also, don't be afraid to break scenes into smaller pieces which can be intercut with other scenes happening at the same time or which are related to the current scene. You'll see examples of this in the chapter on Writing Battles which involves jumping between points of view as the scene plays out to draw out the natural dramatic tension of the scene.

DIALOG

For some people, dialog comes easily, while others find it very difficult to write dialog. Most people fall into the "dialog is difficult" camp, and even the people for whom it comes easily are usually writing it on instinct rather than knowledge, so it's good for them to understand dialog better so they can write it well.

The first thing you need to remember about dialog is that it isn't real. Dialog is a creation by the writer as much as the plot, setting, characters, and everything else about the story. It exists to serve the purposes of the story like a servant serving a master. A servant without a master has no direction, and dialog without direction is just random noise.

So, when you are writing dialog, you aren't trying to create reality, you're trying to make something fake that looks and sounds like reality. Real dialog always serves the story by moving the plot forward, expressing character, showing character's states of mind, and giving the audience information they need to know, and words which don't do at least one of these three things aren't dialog.

The second thing to know is that dialog is a natural combination of two things—situation and character.

What characters say is often based on what they are trying to accomplish in a particular scene. Characters in stories don't speak randomly, but to accomplish goals of some kind. Everything they say is based on what's happening in that scene and how they are acting or reacting to the events which are playing out.

So, if two characters are discussing how to kill a dragon, the things they are saying represent the shared goal of killing a dragon and the scene goal about is finding a solution to their dragon-slaying problems. Similarly, if a character is talking to the people who just kidnapped them and wants to escape, then the words they say will be based around their attempts to get free, find out information, and avoid the situation getting worse.

However, while situation drives dialog, who the characters are is equally (or more) important because everything the characters say reflects those characters in some way. The words they choose reflect their upbringing, history, mood, goals, feelings about the other people, and a host of other small things that make up who that character is. Different characters not only approach different situations in different ways, but they also use different language to achieve those goals which reflect who they are.

Thus, you need to make sure that when you are writing you understand what each character's unique voice is, and how it reflects who that character is. The simplest way to do this is the interview method, which is to come up with a list of general and story-related questions and then write the answers to those questions in the role of the character. Put yourself in the position of the character, think about how they would talk and express themselves, and then become an actor taking on the role of that character and answering how you think they would answer.

Usually only a few pages of interview answers are needed for you to understand how a character speaks and behaves, and it will save you a lot of time. If you don't do this, you'll often find the character's voice changes as you write the story and the character evolves in your head, which means you have to go back and change the story later to be consistent with your new idea of the character. It's much faster to just search for a sheet of "character interview questions" online, and then spend a few hours interviewing each of your main characters.

If you've done your job, by the time you're done the characters will literally write themselves once you put them into a situation in the story, and the whole story will be much more lively and interesting for it. So, don't skip this step!

FINAL THOUGHTS ON WRITING YOUR STORY

As was stated at the start of this chapter, storytelling is a skill like bricklaying or writing computer code. First you pick your overall goal, then you break down the task into smaller and smaller pieces, and once you have those pieces laid out you start to put the story together one piece at a time. Anyone who can write a simple sentence can write a paragraph. Anyone who can write a paragraph can write a scene. Anyone who can write a scene can write a chapter. Anyone who can write chapters can write a story arc (or book). And, anyone who can write a story arc can write a long serial story.

All it takes is thinking like a crafter who has a big project before them. The ability to make beautiful art comes with constant practice, and the basic skills can be developed one step at a time.

So, get out there and take your first steps!

WRITING WEBFICTION BATTLES

A major part of webfiction is often the cool and interesting conflicts between characters and groups, and knowing how to write battle exciting battles is a must for a non-romance webfiction writer. However, many webfiction writers struggle with how to turn their conflict-driven stories into interesting battles that audiences can't get enough of.

Writing combat is also both an art and a skill, and while both parts take time to master, knowing a few key principles can let you write conflict situations from criminal trials, to space battle, to cooking competitions with style. With a little knowledge and work anyone can write page turning conflicts, it just means you have to understand a few key ideas.

Let's begin.

WHERE ART AND FICTION MEET

The first thing you need to understand is that fights and battles in webfiction are almost nothing like violent conflicts in real life. In real life, battles are short, quick, and brutal events that are over almost before anyone knows what's happened (including the people involved). Martial artists and other fighters train their whole lives to make their bodies react without thinking because they know when the moment comes there will be no time to think, and the fight will be over before they know it.

Even boxing and mixed martial arts events are mostly about the two opponents sizing each other up and testing their opponents, and when they find a weakness they can exploit, they dive right in and the fight ends in a brief burst of violence.

Hardly cinematic, and not very useful to someone who gets paid by the word.

Thus, webfiction battles aren't realistic- they're stylized and drawn-out conflicts which are designed to get maximum drama (and word counts) from the fight. Just like how a Jackie Chan kung-fu battle looks nothing like a mixed martial arts fight, a webfiction fight won't look much like a real battle would either. It will be longer, with more breaks and pauses to enhance the tension, drama, and suspense and keep the reader intensely focused on what's happening.

From the beginning to the end, the writer's goal is to keep the reader's attention and build suspense about who is going to win the fight. Everything else is there to serve that purpose, and once the fight is done the whole thing should be wrapped up quickly and the story should move on, preparing for the next conflict.

However, there is one area where webfiction fights and real fights do overlap-battles are about preparation, and the victor of most fights is decided long before the actual fight ever happens. This is true for both the writer and the characters in the story.

For the writer, the success or failure of a battle as a dramatic exercise will be determined by how they've set up the battle in the minds of the audience.

- Does the audience care about the battle's results?
- Are they attached to the main character?
- Do they hate the opponent?
- Are there real stakes to the battle's results for the main character?
- Does the audience understand the rules of the battle?
- Do they know who has the advantage?
- Do they know the possible moves that each side can make?
- Do they know each side's readiness for the battle?
- Has the writer foreshadowed any tricks/surprises the characters could use?
- Do they know where the battle is taking place?
- Do they understand how the environment could affect the battle?
- Do they need to know who the audience is?
- Are there any special audience members they need to be familiar with?
- Are any "surprise" events foreshadowed or otherwise set up beforehand?

The audience should know all of these things before the first punch is even thrown, or at least the ones which are most important to what's happening at the start of the fight. Sometimes these things can be slipped in during breaks in the action (see Duels below), and some things might not be foreshadowed on purpose, but all of this is important information to making the audience both appreciate and enjoy a good battle in a story.

The more the audience knows, the more engaged in the battle they will be, because they understand the situation and want to see the results. They should also care about the results if the writer has done their job, as a good fight is even more about emotion than it is action, and the audience want to feel thrilled, worried, excited and overjoyed as they watch the battle play out.

On the other hand, the characters also need to be prepared for any fight.

A fight is a story, and the actual battle is the result of a story of preparation. Whether the character themselves wins the fight or battle will be determined by everything they did before hand to prepare, just like the martial artists who train their whole lives for a few seconds of conflict here and there. Everything the character brings to the fight is part of their background and preparations to be ready when the time comes.

In actual story terms, this means that the character must have done their homework and gotten the things they need ready to face the battle. This can be anything from physical training to having gotten the resources or knowledge they need to face their opponent. They may also have planned or worked out their options, and gotten all of their equipment in place, or even prepared the environment where the battle will take place.

The winner in most battles is decided long before the battle itself ever happens, and both the character and writer should have laid out the battle before the first blow is even struck.

WRITING BATTLES: DUELS VS. SMACKDOWNS

Battles in webfiction generally come in two basic flavors- duels and smackdowns.

A duel is a battle between two sides which are at least somewhat matched with each other, and where either side has a realistic chance of winning or at least achieving some victory conditions. This can be a direct duel between two people at marbles, debating, cooking, fighting, spellcasting, or whatever form the duel takes, or it can be conflicts between spies, armies or space fleets under the guidance of a commander who is directing their forces against another commander. Either way, a duel is a battle between near-equals.

A smackdown, on the other hand, is a battle in name only where one side has an overwhelming advantage over the other. It is a battle of sailboats versus battleships or ants versus elephants, where one side is so clearly outclassed by the other that there is never a chance of victory from the start. The battle itself is just one side teaching the other a cold, hard lesson in reality.

Each of these, duels and smackdowns, has their own place in stories, and each is written differently depending on the effects that the writer wants to achieve. Read the rules for each carefully in order to achieve maximum effect when writing these kinds of conflicts in your stories.

Duels

A duel in webfiction is a long, drawn-out affair where two roughly equal opponents first test each other, then try their best to defeat their opponent, and then go all-out if they can't actually defeat them easily. It is a back and forth play, like a game of chess, where each side is unleashing a series of moves against their foe and looking for the right chance to strike and finish the battle.

To write duels well, you need to understand a few basic principles first:

1) The elements of action
2) The principle of closure

Each of these comes together to make duels exciting in different ways.

First, the most fundamental idea you need to understand to write action is that everything characters do can be broken down into at least three parts- the action, the description of the action, and the result.

For example, let's say a character takes a book off a shelf...

1. The action – the character reaches up to take a book
2. The description – the character pulls the book off the shelf and takes it down to look at
3. The result – the character has the book in their hands

Or, let's say a mage casts a fireball at a tree...
1. The action – the mage casts a magic spell
2. The description – a ball of fire appears, hits the tree, and explodes
3. The result – the tree is left a pile of burnt toothpicks

Or, one character kisses another...
1. The action – one character leans in and kisses the other
2. The description – the two character's lips press against each other in a lingering kiss
3. The result – the receiver of the kiss is left flustered and surprised, but happy

So, as you can see from these three examples, you can break any action down into three parts.

Why is this useful to know?

Because if you can break an action down into smaller parts like this, you can use it to create drama and tension. Thanks to the principle of closure, once an action starts in a story, the audience naturally wants to see the results of that action so they can see what happens. Thus, since the audience always wants to know the results of an action, if you don't give it to them right away, you can use that to create tension and suspense. They want to know what happens, and you just need to make them wait for it - instant tension.

Here's how it works.

Duels in webfiction are actually made up of a number of parts which can be used in many different ways and combinations to produce interesting battles. By using them effectively, a writer can control both the pace and the presentation of the battle, and use that rhythm to make what might otherwise be a straightforward fight into a fascinating duel.

The parts of a duel are...

- **Character actions** (what did they do?)
- **Description of the action** (what looks like it happened?)
- **Results of the character's action** (what actually happens?)
- **Audience reaction to the action** (how do they feel about it?)
- **Opponents reaction to the action** (how do they feel about it?)
- **Opponent's response to the action** (what are they going to do about it?)
- **General commentary on the action** (what do people think about the results? (as opposed to feeling about them)
- **Reactions to the results** (how do characters feel about the results?)
- **Context information** (why is what happened important?)
- **Interludes to other events** (what's going on elsewhere?)
- **Flash-backs and Flash-forwards** (what already happened or will happen?)
- **Expectations** (what do the participants or audience think will happen?)

And, by alternating the three core elements of an action (action, description, result) with the other parts of the duel, you can add tension and variety to the final result.

Here is a sample fight to show you this principle in action, one to ten are a single action>description>result pattern with extra things added to boost dramatic effect:

Ninja Bob is fighting evil Samurai Ed in a duel during a big battle where the ninja are trying to rescue a princess Ed kidnapped.

1) Ninja Bob unleashes his special move- "Ninja Fire" (*Character action*)
2) A great flaming bird leaps out and attacks Samurai Ed (*Description of the effects of the action*)
3) The fighters around them stop, shocked to see Bob can do such an amazing legendary move. (*Audience reaction*)

4) Bob's master cries tears of joy, and when asked he explains that Bob has tried to master this move his whole life. It was passed down by their ancestors and feared lost for generations. (*Reaction + Context information*)

5) Samurai Ed tries to jump out of the way, but the fire bird follows him and strikes his chest armor, setting him on fire. (*Description of the results*)

6) Ed screams in pain. (The actual *results*)

7) Ed's servants cry that their master is done for and search for water to put out the blazing samurai warlord. (*Audience reaction*)

8) Bob says that the fire bird is powered by the rage in his soul, and no water can put it out- Ed is doomed. (*General commentary*)

9) Suddenly Ed bursts from the inferno, singed and without his armor, but still able to fight. (*Opponents' response to the results.*)

10) Ed's servant comments that the ancestral armor took the fire for Ed, saving him! (*Audience reaction + General Commentary*)

11) Ed attacks Bob with his sword, and the hunter is now the hunted. (*Character action*)

12) The fight continues...

Think of it like a multi-layer sandwich, where the top bread is the action, the meat is the effects, and the bottom bread is the results. In between the bread and the meat, you can put a lot of extra things which will make the sandwich tastier, more filling, or more nutritious. The audience wants the whole bite thanks to the principle of closure, so they'll keep biting until they get a whole mouthful, and you can use this to turn what would just be two slices of bread and a thin piece of meat into a delicious feast.

Now, if you just pile several of these "layered action sandwiches" on top of each other, you have a long, drawn-out battle with tension and drama which the audience will happily work their way through.

This is the art of writing webfiction duels, and webfiction action in general.

Smackdowns

On the other hand, sometimes the battle is so one-sided you can't even really call it a battle. It's not a fight, it's an object lesson in who is stronger. Sometimes, one side thinks that they're fighting a duel, while the other is fully aware that this isn't a contest and for their own reasons is taking their time in letting their opponent realize the harsh truth. While other times both sides know the truth, but the weaker side is determined to try anyway, usually in a vain effort to buy time or achieve some other victory condition besides defeating their opponent. (Although, this too may fail.)

Either way, this is a hopeless battle, and you might think it would be dull or heartbreaking to watch, but in reality, this is one of the most popular types of situations in webfiction and audiences can't get enough of smackdowns.

Why?

Recall that webfiction stories are actually power fantasies, and that they're about the audience getting their thrills by watching a character they feel connected to doing powerful things. So, there is nothing they enjoy more than watching a powerful "hero" lay a beating on a "villain" who really deserves it, especially if the villain can't actually fight back. This gives them a sense of power that they can't get in their own lives, and they can imagine what it would be like to deliver righteous vengeance on the people who anger them in real life.

On the other hand, stories about heroic last stands also make audience's blood run hot, because they're about characters they deeply care about and respect going out in a blaze of glory- something the audience can only dream of doing. Their own lives aren't likely to include giving it all for a cause, but they can enjoy characters who don't give up no matter the odds, and even if the characters lose terribly, it was still a glorious battle.

So, as you can see, there's actually a lot to like about smackdown stories.

But they have to be written correctly in order to have maximum effect, otherwise they can very easily go off the rails and leave the audience unhappy. Let's look at how to handle them.

Power Fantasies

In order to write a good power fantasy smackdown where the hero delivers justice on the villain, you need to remember two simple rules:

1) The more the audience hates the villain, the more satisfying it will be.
2) The power fantasy smackdown should never be told from the hero's point of view.

First, like any battle, power fantasy smackdowns are all about setup. They take a lot of effort to make the audience hate the villain as much as possible so that when the curb stomping occurs the audience feels happy and that justice has been served. If the audience is ambivalent about the villain, then they will hate the hero instead for being unjustly cruel. They must **hate** the villain for this situation to work.

Writing this type of story usually follows a fairly simple pattern-- the villain does bad things to others and gets away with it, or it seems like they're getting away with it, and then just when the villain reaches "peak evil" the hero shows up and mops the floor with them. The villain then unleashes all their best moves, which might seem to have an effect, but really are doing nothing but delaying the inevitable, and then the hero proceeds to beat them to death or something close to it.

And, in order to make it work, you need to follow the second rule- the event can't be told from the hero's point of view.

If you tell this scene from the hero's point of view, then the hero who knows they're much more powerful than the villain won't be a bringer of justice, they'll be a bully. They know the villain is no match for them, and they could probably easily defeat them without seriously hurting them, so they're the strong picking on the weak. Even worse, they might be enjoying it, so that makes them a sadistic bully, who the audience will like even less. This will completely kill the audience's power fantasy fun and ruin the thrill.

Thus, this type of scene can only be told well from two points of view- the victim, and the villain.

If the scene is told from the person who has been suffering at the hands of the villain, then the audience knows just how bad the villain is, and when the hero shows up, they'll happily cheer the hero on in whatever they do. Seeing the victim suffer has raised the audience's emotions to maximum bloodlust (if you've done it right) and the audience only wants to see the villain suffer as much as they've seen the victim suffer. It's primal "eye for an eye" justice, and the hero is a hero to both the audience and the victim alike if they deliver it to the villain in kind. (Regardless of whether the "hero" is actually heroic at all.)

On the other hand, if the scene is told from the villain's point of view, it's another kind of intense experience. First, the audience has seen what the villain has done, but now they're seeing things from the villain's perspective, so they also know why the villain did these things. They know that the villain is irredeemably evil, and is someone who deserves punishment because they're enjoying the suffering of others. And second, the audience gets to enjoy the villain going from thinking they're the one in charge to the slow realization that they've got no chance. They get a ringside seat to the villain's suffering and the payback they receive for what they have done.

So, by making sure that the audience is screaming for the villain's head, and then delivering it in a way that takes most of the responsibility away from the hero, smackdowns can become a fun exercise in seeing justice delivered. Chinese xianxia audiences especially love these situations, where haughty, rich "young masters" are literally smacked around by the more powerful main character after acting like jerks and abusing others. However, you can find it in plenty of Japanese and Korean stories too, and some American comic book anti-heroes like Batman make use of this type of presentation as well.

Heroic Last Stands

The other way a smackdown can become a thrilling situation is if the main characters are fighting a hopeless battle they know is hopeless, but are doing it anyway for some greater cause than themselves. These situations tend to also play out in two different ways:

1) A learning moment
2) Actual Last Stands

If the "heroic last stand" happens earlier on in the story, it usually isn't actually a last stand but the writer teaching the main character (and audience) a lesson about the balance of power in the setting. In these cases, the encounter is actually a type of flash-forward, where the lead is getting a taste of what lays ahead of them if they keep going on the path they're on. The unbeatable foe is their future giving them a lesson in just how hard they will need to fight if they want to achieve their story goals, and how much work and personal growth they have ahead of them.

Naturally, the main character will survive this encounter, usually thanks to outside help or the unbeatable foe deciding that the main character isn't worth the time to finish off, but they will be left a physical or spiritual wreck. Their confidence or their body will be shattered, and it will take time for them to recover from this experience and regain their momentum. The audience too, now appreciates just how hard the character's goals are, and it creates tension over how the main character could possibly defeat such a terrible opponent.

Of course, usually the main character (with a little help from their friends) will spring back into action, and begin moving at a more realistic pace towards another encounter with the unbeatable foe. They know the height they need to reach, and can realistically begin planning ways to reach it so that the results are different next time.

Then again, sometimes there are actual last stands, or situations where the characters know they will die fighting for what they believe in. In these cases, the characters are usually fighting for some other goal besides defeating their enemy, and have another victory condition in mind. That way, when they die, they still win if they accomplish their goal, so it turns what would be a tragic moment into something that is bittersweet instead, and the audience can console themselves with the hero's partial victory.

Typically, these are not situations that the main character of a story finds themselves in, because it would make it pretty hard to reach the end if they did. Usually, this is the actual last stand of supporting characters who are dying to help the main character accomplish their goals, and whose deaths the audience feels deeply. They are paying a noble price so that the main character can reach their target, or sometimes be in a position to defeat the otherwise unbeatable foe.

While they hate to see favorite supporting characters go, there is nothing audiences love more than to see characters meet their end in glorious ways for a worthy cause. If done properly, the character has gone on a full character arc from when they were first introduced until now, and their end is the final exclamation point on their transformation into someone who achieved their life's purpose. Naturally, this takes a bit of setup, and you can't expect characters introduced two chapters before to have much of an effect on the audience, but with a little work and planning you can get amazing results.

Final Thoughts on Smackdowns

If you intend to write a smackdown, just remember that one-sided battles need to be carefully timed. If you make them too short the audience won't get their emotional high from them, but if you make them too long the audience will become bored and lose interest.

Just remember that the best drama comes from duels and close battles, so you need to maintain the illusion that a battle is at least winnable (whatever that means) in some way to keep the drama going. As soon as it's clear that there can be no other outcome, the battle is over, and everything that comes afterwards is just cleanup.

Once the battle is decided in the minds of the audience, finish it, drop the curtain, and move on to setting up your next conflict. That's going to keep the audience much more interested than dragging on a needless struggle.

FINAL NOTES:

Writing battles can be a fun exercise, and is one of the more enjoyable parts of webfiction when you get the hang of it. Some people have a natural talent for it, while others need a lot of practice, but as you can see in this chapter it's as much skill as it is art. With study and practice anyone can write interesting conflicts into their story and get maximum suspense from them.

It should also be noted that duels often turn into unexpected smackdowns, and what seems like a smackdown sometimes turns into a duel. As always, a writer should be keeping their audience on their toes, and mixing the types of stories and events up to keep the audience interested. This is only a basic set of principles for writing dramatic combat, and you should experiment to find your own style of writing fights and battles that you feel brings out the best in your work.

If you are not comfortable with writing combat like this, then by all means do it however works for you. However, you will find that webfiction writers from around the world are using these techniques to great success, and you might find it worth at least trying before you decide it isn't for you.

This isn't the only way to do it, just one way, and in the end, you should always do whatever keeps your audience coming back for more.

PLANNING YOUR WEBFICTION SERIAL

In theory, you can just sit down and start writing your webfiction serial based on your current interests and then see how it goes. This has worked for some people, and there's no question that it feels lot more fun than doing a whole bunch of planning work before you get to the fun part of writing your story.

But there is one problem with that approach- people who don't plan ahead don't usually finish.

Writing based on passion and enthusiasm comes to a very sharp end the moment that it stops being fun and transforms into hard work, which is usually just about the time the story finishes its introductory arc. Suddenly, a long hard road stretches out before the writer, and they're not sure what path to take or where to go, so they get overwhelmed and they quit. Or, they get distracted by another story idea or character idea that catches their attention, so they put their old story "on hiatus" to start a new one, and never get back to it. (Or finish the new one either, in most cases.)

This creates an even bigger problem – a writer can only quit writing so many stories before the audience loses faith in them, and they lose faith in themselves. If the audience thinks a writer is just going to quit on them, why should they commit to reading it? On the other hand, with a series of failures in their past, the writer eventually just gives up on writing, deciding it just isn't for them.

All problems that could be avoided with just a little planning right at the start.

Legendary science fiction writer Robert A. Heinlein once said, "to be a writer, you must write, and you must finish what you write." And, while people love to focus on the "just write and you'll be a writer" part, they always seem to forget that the finishing part is just as important.

If you want to be a successful writer, you need to finish your stories. Even bad endings are better than no ending at all, and the best way to avoid both bad endings and not finishing is to plan ahead. It might not be a detailed plan, and there might be a lot of fuzziness in the middle, but in the end, a good plan will see you through many rough patches and keep you from stopping when you need to keep grinding on. You will know where the story is going, and how cool that ending will be, so you can just focus on getting across that finish line.

So, take the time, and plan your story out- your future self will thank you for it.

STEP 1: THREE STARTING POINTS

The initial seed for your story can come from almost anything- a place you visited, a piece of dialog you heard, a dream you had, or game you played. However, when it comes to planning webfiction, there are three things you need to know right at the start, and you can decide on them in any order.

- Who is the story's main character?
- What is the story's webfiction genre?
- What is the system/cheat of the story?

Everything that comes later is determined by these three things, so you need to make sure you have them clearly decided upon before you move on to more fully developing your story.

Who is the Story's Main Character?

Webfiction stories are almost always character-driven stories- they are about an interesting character trying to accomplish some clear big goal. So naturally, the story's main character, and what they're like, is super important to determining whether the story is going to work or not.

While most webfiction main characters are fantasy versions of the story's writer, there are a number of standard character types which pop up in webfiction over and over again. These are archetypes which the audience knows and likes, and you can use them to help shape what your own main character is going to be like.

Common Webfiction Archetypes:

1. **The Lucky Loser**
   - *Against the Gods, Arifuretta*
   - A barely competent character who stumbles across an endless supply of power boosts, equipment, or opportunities that turn them into a massive kick-butt fighter. They often have an incredible ability to withstand pain and suffering, which is how they earn the respect of the reader. However, they're not that bright, so in the end

their main tactic is still just overwhelming their opponents with force.

2. **The Conqueror**
   - o *Overlord, Dungeon Defense, That Time I Got Reincarnated as a Slime*
   - o This character starts the story with a big advantage and then proceeds to use it to build an empire of some kind, crushing everyone who stands in their way like roadkill.

3. **The Everyman**
   - o *Konosuba, Re: Zero, GATE, In Another World with My Smartphone*
   - o This character is a very average guy or girl who is stuck in an unusual situation and manages to use their personal strengths, knowledge, and common sense to build a collection of powerful allies who help them accomplish their goals.

4. **The Master Gamer**
   - o *Legendary Moonlight Sculptor, Praise the Orc, No Game No Life, Sword Art Online*
   - o This character is an above average character who has a godly talent for playing a game. Usually they're similar to the everyman, except for their gaming talents, which make them demigods when playing their games of choice.

5. **The Strategist**
   - o *How a Realist Hero Saved the Kingdom, The Saga of Tanya the Evil, Classroom of the Elite*
   - o A super-smart and observant character who plans all of their moves in advance and who gets joy from outwitting others and being the smartest one in the room.

6. **The Hero Who Hides His Strength**
   - o *The Lazy Swordmaster*
   - o A superman like character who is massively powerful in some way, but for personal or social reasons hides his abilities and usually tries to live a low-key life.

7. **The Hero**
   - o *Is it Wrong to Pick Up Girls in a Dungeon?, Isekai Cheat Magician*
   - o This character is a noble every-person character who does the right thing because it's the right thing to do. They're too good to be true, and dedicate themselves to working towards the greater good out of an overdeveloped sense of responsibility and a desire to make others happy.

8. **The Survivalist**
   - *So I'm a Spider, So What? Rising of the Shield Hero, .hack//SIGN*
   - A character who is put into a bad situation and quickly adapts and does whatever they need to do to survive. Usually they start or quickly become ruthlessly practical, and shut down their feelings and emotions with one simple goal- to make sure they're the one that makes it out alive.

9. **The Faker**
   - *How NOT to Summon a Demon Lord*
   - A character who finds themselves in the body of another person, and then pretends to be that person in order to figure out what's going on.

10. **The Old Soul**
    - *While Killing Slimes for 300 Years, I Became the MAX Level Unknowingly*
    - An old and powerful being trying to live a life of seclusion who is brought back into worldly affairs, usually by the arrival of a young person on their doorstep.

Naturally, there are others, and this isn't a complete list, but a great many webfiction lead characters fall into one of these categories. In fact, some of them even fall into more than one category, or start as one type of character and slowly change into another, and that's okay too. The point isn't to lock in the character, but have a clear idea of what the character's main focus as a character is going to be.

Once you have this simple idea which the audience knows and understands, you can then start to flesh them out and add to them to make them more unique. Just never forget what the character's core idea is, because that will be your guide to keeping the character consistent in your mind and the minds of your audience.

After you pick your story's main character, write up a profile of the character which should include the following top ten things:

1. **Basic biographical information**- age, sex, height, weight, hair color(s), job, family members, close friends, education, skills, work history, hobbies.
2. **What is the character's role in this story?** Main Character, Opponent, Ally, Motivator, Resource, Comic Relief, Love Interest, etc. Pick one or more.
3. **What are they best at and what are they worst at?** Characters are often defined by their flaws more than their strengths, so make sure your character is bad at something for everything they're good at.

4. **What are the first things people notice about this character when they meet them?** Appearance, style of dress, style of grooming, manner of speech, body language, etc.

5. **What are two Paradoxes about them?** This is a fast way to make characters unique in the minds of readers- give them details that seem to contradict each other in the minds of the reader. It also adds depth and interest to the character. For example, they're big and strong but very timid, they're a leader who is afraid of talking to people, they dress very conservatively but wear a brightly colored watch, or their personality changes when they're in a different environment (Home/work/school).

6. **What is going to make the audience like or dislike this character?** What about this character is going to make the audience connect with and care about the character? Or, on the other hand, what will make the audience dislike and reject the character? How will you as a writer make that connection with the audience?

7. **What is their overall life goal?** What, if anything, do they want to achieve in their life? What would be a perfect life for this character? What would they be willing to do to get it?

8. **What is their goal in this story?** A character's story goals generally come down to one of three things: attain, maintain, or lose. They want to get something they don't have. They want to keep something they've got. Or, they want to get rid of something they have. This isn't just physical things, it can be anything- objects, people, habits, money, knowledge, love, courage, safety, security, freedom, spirituality, and so on.

9. **What is their motivation in this story?** Why are they trying to achieve the goal in the story? What reasons are getting them off the couch and keeping them from running away? Why do they endure or try to escape? What keeps them from giving up and just being a victim?

10. **How does this character connect with the main theme of the story?** This is last, but one of the most important things to know- how does the main character reflect the theme of the story? Are they a weak person who learns to be strong? Are they a strong person who inspires others to be strong? Are they trying to change the world or restore the peace? How does the character represent the life lesson the writer wants the reader to know?

What is the Story's Webfiction Genre?

Story genres exist because people like certain types of stories a lot and audiences have certain collections of story tropes and conventions that they enjoy reading about over and over again. Thus, an important part of planning a webfiction story is deciding what the main genre of the story is going to be. That way you know what your audience is expecting from your story, and have a set of tropes in mind that you can play with and mix and match, making your life as a writer much easier.

Beyond the standard genres of comedy, horror, romance, action, drama, and others, there are also the webfiction genres that are popular with readers and which many young readers can't get enough of. While their popularity changes depending on the culture, the same webfiction genres keep popping up over and over again, so you are advised to think about which one your story fits under.

Which webfiction genre you choose will determine your main character, setting, plot, target audience, themes, and many other things about your story, so it's important to know what you're writing from the start. And, while genres can be mixed, matched and combined in many different ways, even "fusion" or "cross genre" works usually have a single core genre that acts as their base, and then elements from other genres are brought in.

Here is a list of the major ones for your reference.

- Rising Hero Stories
- Fantasy Stories
- Second Life Stories (Isekai)
- LitRPGs
- Task Stories
- Conquest Stories
- Romance
- Slice-of-Life

You probably already know which of these you plan to write, but make sure you read the chapter about it before you proceed further or pick one of the other starting points.

What is the System/Cheat of the Story?

Sometimes what inspires your imagination might be a particular system or cheat, which is also a good point to start planning your story. Not all stories have systems, or cheats, and it's common for romances to have neither, but many stories do, so if your story does make sure you know them.

Systems are related with settings, so the system you choose will have a lot to do with the parts of your setting you plan to focus on. For example, let's say your story is about a fashion model rising up in the ranks of the global fashion industry. That industry with its structure and rankings becomes your system, and everything in your story will be built around that system and the culture connected to it.

Similarly, if there's a system, there are ways to cheat it, and so you should know what cheat your character has (if any) that is letting them game the system in their favor. Cheats have been covered elsewhere, but they can be things which the character has total, some, or no control over, and can come in many different forms. In the case of the fashion model above, they might come from a powerful family, have a special mentor, have a unique ability to time their body language with music, or even a special ability to copy the movements of others. Any of these would give them the leg up they need to justifiably rise quickly up in the system they're part of.

Remember that your cheat, and possibly your system, will be one of the best ways to set your particular story apart from the others in the webfiction genre you're choosing. Characters also tend to fall into types, as listed above, but systems/cheats can be almost anything, and an interesting system, cheat, or system/cheat combination can be a major selling point to readers to get them to check out your work. So, take some time and think them through carefully.

STEP 2: PICK A CORE PREMISE

A Core Premise is the central idea of your story and a seed from which the rest of the story will grow. With it, you'll know the story you're trying to tell, and have a guiding star leading the way to the end!

To find your Core Premise, you're going to use a very basic technique that writers for movies have been using for a long time. In the movie business, writers often approach producers and directors with ideas for films, but they use a very simple structured version of their idea called a Logline to get maximum effect and make the producers interested. If they can use it to sell a movie to producers, you can use it to sell a story to yourself- so let's get started!

A great Core Premise needs to describe most of the following things:

1. One or two adjectives about the main character. (to give them personality, and add sympathy when possible)
2. The main character's role or job. (Don't use a name, just their role for now.)
3. Anything that's important to know about the setting or setup for the story.
4. What the main character's clear goal is.
5. One or two adjectives about the opposition. (to make them interesting)

6. The antagonist, opposition or challenge they face. (Also, no names, use roles instead.)
7. A hint of what will happen if the protagonist loses, or the stakes involved. (to add drama)

These can be presented in any order, but usually go in the above order, and will produce one or two sentences that look like this:

A burnt-out, nerdy office worker (adjective, who) is sent into an RPG-like fantasy world (setting) where they must learn how to use their knowledge of building model kits to help a kingdom survive an attack (goal) by an evil overlord (adjective, opposition) or lose their chance to return home (stakes).

A master video game player is sentenced to prison for a crime he didn't commit and forced to play for the prison's online gaming league in order to earn his freedom and see his dying father again, but every time he fails a competition the corrupt warden adds extra time to his sentence.

A sarcastic young blind woman tries to become a French chef by going to a legendary Vermont cooking school where she faces strict teachers and bullying students. She is on a scholarship and only has one chance to make her dreams come true, or else she'll be forced to work in her family clothing shop forever.

It's actually pretty easy and fun once you get the hang of it!

Try using the ideas you brainstormed to come up with a Core Premise that follows the rules above. You don't need to use all the information you came up with, just the main ideas. Also, don't be afraid to try different versions of the premise with different details until you get one that you like.

Once you've turned at least one of your story ideas into a good-looking Core Premise, then you should ask yourself the following questions:

1. Does this story idea grab you and make you want to write it?
2. Is this story going to be one you think will interest your target audience?
3. Is this story going to make your readers feel something?

If a premise gets three solid answers of "yes!" then that's the story you need to write. If it doesn't get a "yes" for all three questions, then you need to go back and revise the premise or brainstorm some new ideas and turn those into premises that will work for you.

STEP 3: PICK A PRESENTATION FORMAT

Your story's presentation format is the way in which your audience will get your story. It can be online daily or weekly chapters on a website, a novel or series of novels, a series of readings on a podcast, or any other way you intend for this story to be presented to an audience.

You may already know your presentation format, and it might not even be optional, but if you don't know it or have a few choices, then it's good to know the advantages and disadvantages of each format before you start writing your story.

Generally speaking, the good and bad points of the major presentation formats are as follows:

Publishing on Webfiction Sites

Good: Large audience of readers, fast and easy to publish on, can make money if the story is successful.

Bad: Need to publish regularly and very often to keep an audience with so much competition. Each site also has its own rules, own strengths and weaknesses, and own audiences. A good story on the wrong website will fail to find an audience because that isn't what those readers want. Do your homework before you pick a site, then follow its rules.

Publishing on your own Website

Good: Total control of your content, can write stories when you want of any genre, length, style, or format. Can make money through advertising and donations.

Bad: Requires a lot of effort to get noticed and find an audience. Need to publish regularly to keep the audience coming back- daily or weekly is a must.

Publishing as Ebooks on Ebook Sites

Good: Total content control. Can publish at a slower pace (months/years apart). Stories are sold for money, so can make direct profit from stories. A popular book is like a money-making lottery ticket.

Bad: Lots of competition. Often need to write a series to see real success. Editing and good covers are a must. You are trading quantity for quality, so you need to deliver a quality product. Until you have many reviews, you will need to spend money for advertising and do your own marketing.

Podcasting your Fiction

Good: Total content control. Less competition (but still some). Can make some profit from donations or running ads. Can also release podcast story collections as ebooks to hit two audiences.

Bad: You need to be a good reader or find one. You need to pay for hosting. Must publish on a regular basis to build an audience. Need to spend time editing. Less money from donations or ads than running a website. Free podcast listeners and ebook buyers are two totally different audiences and success with one doesn't mean success with the other.

STEP 4: PICK A FREQUENCY AND LENGTH

Often, how frequently a story comes out, and how long it is are decided by the presentation format, with the rough guidelines going like this:

<u>Publishing on Webfiction Sites</u>: Stories are expected to run very long, typically tens, hundreds or sometimes thousands of chapters. This is because a popular serialized story is a golden ticket, and the longer it runs the more ad and donation money it will likely make and the more popular it will become. Typically, daily (M-F) or near-daily (M,W,F) chapters are expected to run 2000-3000 words per chapter, while weekly stories should run between 6000-8,000 words per installment.

<u>Publishing on Your Own Website</u>: Stories can be of any length, but again long serials are the best bet for making a profit from doing this. Chapters too can be any length, but 2000-3000 words per chapter is a good target for daily or near-daily chapters, with longer targets for weekly chapters. The more frequent the updates, the easier it is to build a following and make checking in to read the story a habit.

<u>Publishing as an Ebook</u>: A typical novel runs 50,000-90,000 words per book, but this depends on the genre as young adult and romance can run shorter per installment. Non-romance ebooks sell best in series, with a typical series being 3, 5, 8 or 10 books long, but some series run twenty books or more. Beyond eight books, it's usually better to finish the story and start a new sequel series to bring in new readers and restart the numbering from one, but that depends on the series popularity. Typically, each book in a series sells fewer copies than the one before it so a look at your sales numbers will tell you when to quit. For best success, publishing a new book every two or three months is a good target, but popular books can have longer gaps.

<u>Podcasting Your Fiction</u>: A podcast audiobook can be of any length, but the same rules as publishing on your own website apply. Typically, most podcasts are 30 or 60 minutes in length to let them fit into commutes, workouts, lunch hours, and other daily activities. Thirty minutes of audio is roughly 6000 words of text, depending on the speed of the reader. The most common release schedule for podcasts is weekly, or semi-weekly due to the extra time needed for production, so a podcast audiobook will often be done in half-hour weekly installments. Podcasts have a big advantage, because the average listener subscribes to them and the new episode goes to the listener when it's released, so you don't need to get them to keep coming back to your website. A regular release schedule is still a must, however.

In addition, each writer should consider their own writing speed and lifestyle when thinking about their story length and release schedule. If you are a slow writer, or have a busy/unstable life schedule, then publishing on webfiction sites is probably not the best fit for you because you'll end up missing a lot of releases and eventually your audience will wander off. Similarly, if you can't get a book out every two to three months, ebooks will be a challenge unless your content is very high quality.

Publishing on your own website is something anyone can do, and it gives you a flexible schedule, but you also need to find ways to drive traffic to your site, or you'll get depressed by low readership numbers and lose faith in the project. Podcasting is best for people who are able to consistently handle a weekly 6000-word schedule and have a good reading voice or lively storytelling style.

STEP 5: PICK A WRITING STYLE

Webnovels come in many different shapes, sizes and forms, and as a result there is no one particular style when it comes to writing them. If you wanted, you could write your webnovel in text messages, as a lyrical poem, or in dense expressionistic prose- it's really up to you as the creator to decide what style you want your webnovel to be written in. As long as the audience is willing to accept it, you can do it however you want.

But there, as usual, is the question that you must always consider- what will your audience accept?

Most people wanting to read webnovels are looking for fiction that will let them escape from their daily lives and wander into the world of dreams and fantasy. As a result, they want prose that is easy to read and conveys its message clearly and without interfering with their ability to enjoy the story. Sometimes called "invisible prose," its job is to tell what happens in a manner which lets the reader forget that they're reading a story and just focus on the flow of events and ideas that are playing out on the page and in their imaginations.

This is not the writing of F. Scott Fitzgerald or George Elliot, or the many other great literary figures (although their writing is wonderful too) with flowery prose and dense metaphors to be explored and pondered on, but the workmanlike writing of tens of thousands of authors who have been writing genre fiction since the first novel was printed to paper hundreds of years ago. These are words which are designed to do their job and then leave through the back door like servants, unnoticed and inconspicuous, but still very important.

So, when you are writing your webfiction, throw away any ideas you have that it needs to be in some great extravagant language before people will appreciate it. While you are welcome to slip in some nice metaphors and similes from time to time, the things your audience wants most from your writing are simplicity and clarity. Tell them what happened, what they need to know, and let their own minds and imaginations do the rest.

This is something that is common across all three of the styles that webnovels are usually written in, and if you remember it, it will make your life much easier. Think of yourself as the reader's servant who is there to give them what they need, when they need it, and without interfering with their enjoyment of the story in front of them. They want to appreciate and admire the characters and world you've built, not the language you've used to build it.

So, with that in mind, here are a few general best practices:

- Keep your language simple and direct.
- Avoid "be" and "have" verbs and use active verbs instead.
- Avoid adverbs except when necessary.
- Keep your adjectives to a bare minimum.
- When in doubt, choose a noun over a pronoun.
- Keep dialog tags to a minimum.

If you follow those, you're off to a great start. But then things get a lot more specific depending on the type of webnovel you're writing and whether it's being done in General Fiction Style, Young Adult Novel Style, or Webfiction Style. Let's take a look at each of them and what makes them special.

General Fiction Style

This is the style most modern fiction for a mature audience is written in, and exemplifies the above ideas of the writing being there to do the job first and foremost.

Usually written in third person, past tense with an over-the-shoulder perspective, this style attempts to chronicle the events which play out in the manner of a movie camera or as if the audience were there in the room with the characters.

Here is a sample of General Fiction Style:

The clock ticked a slow methodical beat in the corner as April tried not to squirm in her chair.

Across the office desk from her, the school counsellor Mr. McGivens slowly went over the report he'd been given, making little disapproving noises from time to time. He was the high school's former gym teacher, and coach of the football team in his extra time, and he still wore a fading blue cotton track suit instead of the more proper semi-formal attire the other counselors favored. He thought it made him still look vital, but the size of the tracksuit was for someone much more in shape than he was, and it bunched on him and made him look the aging man he was.

At last, Mr. McGivens sighed and threw the report on the desk, letting the sound of the folder that held it echo in the silent office.

"Ms. Deveraux, do you know why you're seeing me and not the principal?"

April swallowed. "No...sir."

"Because we care about you, Ms. Deveraux. About you, and your future." He continued, not taking his puffy eyes off her. His eyes surprised April with the amount of concern they showed. "You might consider your pranks fun and your behavior cute, but to us they're a cry for help."

April wasn't sure how hijacking the video controls for the smartboard in Mr. Lute's class to show videos of farting cows during the science lecture on gases constituted a cry for help, but if it got her out of trouble, she was willing to play along and listen.

As you can see in this example, there is a bit of storyteller voice and commentary, but it's pretty weak and the focus of the writing is on conveying the scene for the audience to parse out on their own. We're looking at it from April's perspective, so we get a bit of her thoughts and ideas, but none from Mr. McGivens, who isn't the focus of the scene.

This is good for an audience that is used to television and movies, and that's basically what this style is simulating- a cinematic style of writing with a bit more depth and sense of character than a film camera can offer.

Key Points of This Style:
- Leans towards prose over dialog. (usually only 30-40% dialog)
- Weaker storytelling voice, more matter of fact.
- More general, factual descriptions.

- Average language for a high school student- Grade 9 or 10 is target range.
- Average paragraphs (5-7 sentences max)
- Many transitions.
- Third Person Over-the-Shoulder, sometimes First.

Young Adult Style

Young Adult style is a type of writing which overflows with character and personality. Whether it's the personality and character of the main character themselves, or of the author, Young Adult style is meant to be lively and interesting from the word "go." Meant for teens, but read by people of all ages, the focus in this style is not just to have the events play out, but make the audience feel those events by filtering them through a strong character voice.

Here's the same scene, but written in a Young Adult Style:

That antique clock in McGiven's office thunked along, making April more nervous with every tick.

She knew they had her. He knew he had her. That's why she was sitting in a chair in the guidance counselor's office.

The old gym teacher was working his way through the papers in a manila envelope with her name scrawled on it in thick black marker. Every now and then he wrinkled his nose and made a little noise that showed he'd read something he didn't like. He had tells. They were easy to spot. They weren't good. For her.

"Why don't you get it over with, already?!?" She wanted to scream.

Anything to stop this silent torture April felt as she sat there nervously. Not knowing. Not sure what they were planning.

She knew it wasn't going to be anything good. This was the principal's enforcer, "Mad Dog" McGivens, coach of the football team, and April wasn't fooled by his faded, rumply blue tracksuit into thinking he just wanted a friendly chat.

The folder slapped onto the desk, making April jump a little.

"Ms. Deveraux, do you know why you're seeing me and not the principal?"

April swallowed, hard. "No...sir."

"Because we care about you, Ms. Deveraux. About you, and your future." He continued, looking at her with a concern that left her unsettled. She'd expected rage, and instead she got, "You might consider your pranks fun and your behavior cute, but to us they're a cry for help."

Hacking the whiteboard during Mr. Lute's lecture on gases to show farting cows was a cry for help?

Inside April, a little flame of hope flickered into existence. It was small, and she intended to keep it hidden until she could use it to navigate out of this mess.

For now, she would listen and play along, curious to see where this was headed.

See how the scene now hums with April's thoughts and emotions? Young Adult style practically jumps out of the page and grabs you to make you feel what the character is feeling and experience what it's like to be April in that situation. Contrast that with the more sedate language of General Fiction style and you'll see it's much more personal, more intense, and lively. You'll also notice that Mr. McGivens and how he looks is much less important in this scene compared to how he feels, because we're working from April's impressions of him, not some objective standard of the man.

Key Points of This Style:
- More balanced dialog and prose. (50-50)
- Strong author/character voice, even in exposition.
- Emphasis is on a focal character and their thoughts and emotions.
- Pithy and graphic descriptions laden with implied meaning.
- Slightly more complex language, but still pretty simple - Grade 8 or higher language.
- Short paragraphs (4-5 sentences max)
- Some transitions, usually for emphasis or style.
- First or Third Person Close.
- Sentence fragments are common and grammar is played with for dramatic effect.

Webfiction Style

Webfiction style is a style which has become the de-facto writing style for young writers across Asia and beyond. With its focus on dialog, character, and simple descriptions, it's an easy style for new, inexperienced writers to use, and is pretty flexible as well.

Here is the sample scene again in webfiction style:

"Miss Deveraux, do you know why you're here?"

April swallowed hard, looked the man across the desk in the eye and said, "No sir."

The school guidance counselor, sighed and leaned back in his chair. "April, although we haven't met before, I'm sure you know me by reputation. Since I retired from teaching, I've tried hard to be someone the students here can rely on, and know they can talk to."

Which is why they call you "Mad Dog" McGivens, **April thought, but kept a straight, innocent face.**

"My players on the football team all know that if they have a problem, they can talk to their coach." He continued, "And, I always keep my door open because I want to use my experience to help young people like you find your way in life."

And, so we can all hear you screaming at people, April nodded.

Leaning forward, the aging gym coach tapped the manila folder on his desk with a thick finger. The squeak of his chair made her wince, but she held her ground.

"Ms. Deveraux, do you know why you're seeing me and not the principal?"

April swallowed. "No...sir."

"Because we care about you, Ms. Deveraux. About you, and your future." He looked at her with a concern that left her unsettled. "You might consider your pranks fun and your behavior cute, but to us they're a cry for help."

Her hacking the whiteboard during Mr. Lute's bio lecture on gases to show farting cows was a cry for help?

Still, concern was better than screaming rage, and April was curious to see where this went.

She decided to play along.

As you can see, there is much more focus on dialog and April's thoughts in this style, but much less emotion than in Young Adult style. It's more of a matter-of-fact style, like General Audience fiction, but with an emphasis on letting the audience hear the character's internal and external thoughts as the way of conveying the exposition of the story.

Key Points of This Style:
- Mostly dialog (60-70% dialog)
- Minimal tags and prose
- Simple descriptions.
- Simple language- Grade 6 or higher language.
- Micro paragraphs. (2-3 sentences max)
- Few transitions.
- First or Third Person Close

A Note About the Above

The three styles listed above are meant to be generic examples of what a typical passage written in that style will look like. When you're writing your own work, don't get too hung up on the details and style, as your own approach will always reflect you as a writer. If your style seems to work with your audience, then keep writing that way, and develop that writer's voice which comes naturally to you.

That said, if you're a beginning writer looking to find your style, or an experienced writer looking to try a new approach, then you might consider sticking to some of the style guidelines above while you experiment with how you're going to tell your tale. Webfiction style can be great "training wheels" for new writers who are stretching their wings, and some reading audiences prefer it over more general fiction because of its fast, character-based approach.

And to those who pooh-pooh webfiction style as an inferior form, just remember that General Fiction style doesn't look anything now like it did a hundred years ago, and how we write in the future may take many forms. With an entire generation growing up reading and writing the lighter, faster styles, we're likely to see a shift towards them in general fiction in the future. Only time will tell.

A Question of Perspective

As you read through the above, you may have noticed that all three examples are written from a third person point of view. This was intentional to minimize the differences between the three passages to just those of style, not perspective. In reality, most webfiction and Young Adult fiction tends to be written from the first-person point of view.

The reasons why most webfiction and Young Adult fiction are written in the first person are many, but the main one is that the first-person perspective is the most natural perspective of them all. People live our lives in the first person, and that makes it an effortless perspective for new writers to write their stories from. It's easy, it works, and naturally focuses on the character, their thoughts and their voice from the first word. First person also reads faster than third, which makes it a natural fit for the busy modern audience.

However, as you decide what style to present your work in, take some time to decide what perspective best reflects the feeling and tone your story is looking for. Third person is more movielike, and lets you tell the story from multiple perspectives in a way that first person can't, so if you're a more visual or cinematic writer, third person might be a better way for you to go. It can be more difficult to work with than first person, but can also have a real payoff in freeing you from the limits of a single perspective. Learn your perspectives, and they can become another powerful tool in your writer's toolkit.

STEP 6: CREATE A SUPPORTING CAST

Characters in stories come in two types- major characters and minor characters.

A major character is someone who must be there or the story doesn't work. They are the ones who are driving the story, whether they're main characters, opponents, allies, love interests, mentors, or any other type of role that the story needs to function. They will typically appear in most of the scenes in that story, and their choices and actions help to drive that story to its ending.

A minor character is a character who contributes to the story in some small way, but who isn't necessary to the story as a whole. These are characters who are only in a single scene or two, and don't have a major effect on the story or plot. They are also often nameless background characters who represent the people of an organization or a place like police officers, doctors, technicians, office workers, and so on. They can also be characters who are a major character in another story arc, but in this story aren't very important and are just there as part of the setting.

Including the main character, any given story or story arc should have no more than seven major characters that the audience needs to remember, preferably as few as you can get away with. Any more than seven major characters will start to confuse the audience, who will start to lose track of who is who, especially if the story is a long-running serial with many chapters in each story arc.

There can be a nearly unlimited number of minor characters in a story, but each story arc should actually only have seven or fewer characters in it during any particular story arc. This story is about those seven people, or maybe just a few of them, and their actions are what determines the outcome of the story. In the end, most stories only need a protagonist main character and an opponent who stands in their way, and everyone else is just extras there to add complications and make the story more interesting.

If you read most webfiction, you can see this idea in action. The typical webfiction hero's supporting cast shrinks or expands in each story arc depending on the story. In one story they might have three friends and be working together against one major opponent who has a few minor supporters, while in the next story arc it's just the main character and one friend against four major opponents. The main character's two other friends being absent or off doing their own things while the lead struggles against overwhelming odds.

A good webfiction writer keeps their story arc casts as small as possible, and treats each major character like an actor whose salary comes out of the author's own bank account. The more of them you have, the poorer you'll be until after the story arc is finished, so you keep your cast tight and limited to only the people who really need to be there.

Once you have your cast, use the same ten questions you answered about the main character in Step One to describe each of them in as much detail as you need to have a sense of who they are and what role they'll play.

STEP 7: CREATE A ROUGH OUTLINE

The next step is to take the Core Premise from Step Two and then write it out into a full paragraph, adding the main character's name and any major supporting characters who are important to the story as an overall whole. This paragraph is your story in a nutshell, and describes the beginning, middle and end of the story in very simple and general terms.

After that, many writers just sit down and turn that paragraph into a multi-page outline, letting their creativity run wild and writing out a rough synopsis of the whole story. If they have spots, they're not sure about, they leave blank space or notes, and then jump to where they do know and keep going until they get to the end in some form.

This becomes your general outline, and it should be revised until you're happy with it.

See the chapter on Writing Your Story for more details about story organization.

STEP 8: PLAN STORY ARCS

After they have a general outline most writers go back and find the points where the story needs to be divided into arcs, make those the break points. Some re-writing may be required to expand or turn a story arc into a full dramatic arc.

Story arcs in webfiction often fall into one of a number of types based on what's happening in that particular story arc. Below is a list of several common story arc plots that you can use to help build and plan the different steps of your story. This list is geared towards fantasy plots, but can work for many kinds of webfiction with a little creativity.

- **Assassination Arc**
  - o The character seeks to actively kill or otherwise eliminate another character in order to accomplish their goals.
- **Auction Arc**
  - o The character attends an auction where they bid for items and rub shoulders with dangerous and powerful people of the setting. Their goal is usually to get some item being auctioned, and they usually end up making a few enemies or allies.

- **Battle Against a Superior Foe Arc**
  - The character is being actively hunted by a powerful individual or powerful group who seek to kill/punish the character. This is usually for revenge or to maintain some social order.
- **Building Arc**
  - The character works to create or build something in order to solve some problem or achieve some story goal.
- **Challenge/Test Arc**
  - The character must overcome a series of challenges in order to prove themselves worthy for some great prize. The bigger the prize, the harder the challenge, so as to show they are worthy of it.
- **Conquest Arc**
  - The character engages in or participates in an assault on an organization, state, or group with a goal of taking it over and putting it under new leadership.
- **Deception Arc**
  - The character attempts to trick, cheat, con, or scam another character in order to achieve some story goal.
- **Dueling Arc**
  - The character has a personal competition with one or more characters to achieve some prize they need to accomplish a goal.
- **Exploration Arc**
  - The character faces challenges while exploring a new and unfamiliar environment
- **Gambling Arc**
  - The character attempts to solve their problems by making a wager or gambling with other characters, which usually does not go as expected.
- **Gathering Allies Arc**
  - The character must overcome challenges to gain the allies they need to accomplish some goal.
- **Gathering of Powerful Figures Arc**
  - The character attends an important party or other gathering of powerful figures in their setting where they are exposed to the true social order of their setting.
- **Hunting for Rare Items Arc**
  - The character faces challenges while trying to attain a rare item.
- **Hunting for Special Components Arc**

- o The character encounters challenges while trying to get rare parts or ingredients they need to create something.
- **Marriage Arc**
    - o The character faces challenges while trying to get married or avoid getting married.
- **Mystery Arc**
    - o The character needs to solve a mystery by gathering clues and information to learn the truth.
- **Personal Training Arc**
    - o The character undergoes a challenging training regime to grow stronger to accomplish some goal.
- **Protection Arc**
    - o The character must protect someone or something from an enemy who is trying to kill, attain, or destroy.
- **Rebellion Arc**
    - o The character participates in a rebellion against a government, organization, or other ruling body to overthrow it and free the people it rules over of its tyranny.
- **Relationship Arc**
    - o The character tries to start, change or renew their relationship with another character, with a goal of becoming friends or lovers.
- **Rescue Arc**
    - o The character comes to the rescue of an individual or group which is under attack by a more powerful foe.
- **Revenge Arc**
    - o The character engages in a campaign of revenge against an enemy who has harmed them or their loved ones, systematically attacking and wiping out the enemy forces.
- **Survival Arc**
    - o The character is put into a dangerous environment and must find a way to survive in a life or death situation.
- **Teaching Arc**
    - o The character attempts to train another character to overcome some challenge.
- **Tournament Arc**
    - o The character participates in a tournament against other characters of their own level for some major prize.
- **Trial Arc**

○ The character or their allies are put on trial for a crime they may or may not have committed and now need to find a way to avoid facing punishment. It usually ends with their enemies getting punished instead.

STEP 9: TURN FIRST STORY ARC INTO CHAPTERS

Take the first story arc and then begin to re-write the story arc to turn it into a series of chapters. Each chapter needs to have its own dramatic rise and fall, and a single scene often takes more than one chapter to play out, so the key is presenting and organizing the chapters in such a way to keep the reader always wanting more until the very end.

Just remember the golden rule of never ending a chapter on a completed scene, unless that completed scene creates a huge dramatic question that the reader can't wait to find the answer to.

See "Chapters" in Writing Your Story for more details.

STEP 10: WRITE THE FIRST STORY ARC

Take the first story arc and begin writing it out, chapter by chapter, as quickly as possible. Don't worry about mistakes or grammar, just worry about telling the story and getting it out. This can be done anytime, but if you're writing in the Autumn consider doing this as part of a NaNoWriMo challenge, with the goal of producing a complete rough draft of the first arc in 30 days or less.

Do not publish it as you go!

This is a rough draft for your own use, and nobody else should see it until you are finished. You will be editing this in the next step before others are allowed to look at it. They can see the edited version, but the rough draft should only be for you because you might make big changes before you let it out into the world.

For many writers, this might be the hardest step on this list. Not because they can't do it, but because they want to jump right in and start publishing once they have an outline. They're in love with their story and characters, and can't wait to share them with the world and get feedback from their audience about how much they love the story.

However, there are several major advantages to writing the first arc completely before releasing it.

1. It will teach you a lot about your writing speed, and how difficult (or easy) it's going to be for you to produce the regular work you'll need to be a webfiction author.

2. It will help you to find the voices of the characters, decide what works and what doesn't, and make major changes before the story goes live.

3. It will improve the quality of your work a lot, since you will be editing and releasing, not writing and releasing. That extra step and time will let you fix a lot of issues before they happen.

4. It will give you a big buffer of finished chapters so that if life stuff happens, you won't be forced to go on hiatus or miss releases, both of which will cost you readers. You can be writing the second arc while the first is being released, and the third while the second is being released.

5. Even if you aren't planning to publish daily, you can open with a "release blitz" where you release a chapter a day to get people's attention and build an audience fast.

STEP 11: REVISE AND EDIT YOUR FIRST STORY ARC

When you have a complete rough draft of your first story arc, set it aside for a little while and go do something else. If you're on a tight schedule, then start writing the second story arc, but definitely wait a minimum of two weeks after you finish it before you try editing it to let yourself forget about the story. A month or two is better, but two weeks can be good enough.

After that time has passed, take the rough draft out and read it from beginning to end without editing it. You should now be able to start to see your flaws and mistakes, and feel free to take notes as you go about what will need to be changed, but don't edit it yet. If you edit it now, you'll be wasting time, since you may make major changes and your edits would be thrown out.

Once you've read it through, use your notes and ideas to begin revising and changing the first story arc to make it better. Don't be afraid to re-write whole sections, combine characters, take the story in new directions, and look for places where you can build better tension and suspense. The point is to make your story the best it can be.

When you have it revised, then you can show it to other people you trust and ask their opinions. If they don't like things, find out why, and look for the things they do like, so you can possibly focus more on those elements of the story. Revise again accordingly.

Once you have a revised version, you're happy with, do an editing pass to fix any grammar, spelling, or continuity issues you find. If you have people who will help you edit (or want to pay them), then have them go through and hunt for issues. If you don't have anyone to edit, go find some text-to-speech software or website and have it read the story to you as you follow along in your text. Hearing your story read to you will highlight a lot of things that need to be fixed, and you can edit as you go.

People make fast judgements about whether to stick with a story based on the first chapters and story arc, so the higher the quality of your first releases, the faster it will build up an audience. If there's a lot of issues, people won't hesitate to go read something else.

So, polish those first chapters until they shine!

STEP 12: RELEASE YOUR FIRST STORY ARC

If you plan to publish on a webfiction site, or on your own blog, then begin releasing your story. You may want to release two or three chapters together on your first day so that your audience can get a real taste of your story and start to get into the rhythm of reading it. After that, follow your planned release schedule, and see what happens.

Just be sure to give each chapter one last editing read before you hit "publish" to avoid embarrassing missed typos or other issues. If you don't find them, your readers will, and will post comments about them to let everyone know you didn't edit properly. Doing it right the first time saves a whole lot of embarrassment later on, and you don't have the luxury of hiding behind it being a translated work from another language.

If you plan to publish it as ebooks, then always do a total proof edit before releasing each book in the series. Writerly wisdom says that the best day to release a book is Tuesday because it takes a few days to go through the system and be ready for discovery by the weekend. Also, planning ahead allows you to make use of the many marketing services and options available to schedule marketing campaigns and let people know it's out.

Finally, podcasters are advised to start with a double-length first episode, or at least two episodes released the first day to make sure people get a good taste when they discover the book. After that, drop to a normal release schedule, whatever that may be. As for editing, you will find all your mistakes when you read it aloud for the audio recordings. Although to speed things up, it's better to do a quick editing read before you record.

THE LUNCHTIME WRITER

Most people who want to write use the excuse they have no time.

They are too busy.

Too much to do.

But everyone has to eat lunch.

Everyone has half-an-hour they could find in their day...

And half-an-hour turns into five hundred words...

Five hundred words turns into 3,500 words in a week...

Fifty-two weeks turns into 182,000 words a year...

And that's ninety-one webfiction chapters of 2000 words a piece...

Or, four 45,000-word light novels, if you prefer to write books.

All from five hundred words a day.

All from thirty minutes at lunch.

During breaks. During class. During meetings. Commuting. Waiting for friends.

Time anyone has.

Time you have.

According to *Wattpad*, 53% of their users have written a story on their phone.

They turned those tiny gaps of life into creative moments when they could share their imaginations and creativity with the world.

Making friends. Making fans. Making money.

You can do it too.

Put your phone in Airplane Mode, set your timer for 30 minutes, pull up a text editor, and write.

Be a lunchtime writer.

Show the world who you are.

You won't regret it if you do.

You'll only regret it if you don't.

Have fun!

R.A. Paterson, August 2019

DID YOU ENJOY THIS BOOK?

If you want to know more about me, you can check out my blog at Robynpaterson.com where I post about my stories, writing, art, podcasting, culture, history, and whatever I think is interesting. You can also subscribe to my blog, which will let you hear about the latest posts.

Also, sign up for my newsletter at Robynpaterson.com/newsletter-signups/ to get access to special offers, writing tips, and worksheets to use when crafting your masterpiece.

You can also find my author page on Facebook as Robyn Paterson.

Thanks for reading!

RECOMMENDED READINGS

On Writing

All the Write Moves by R.A. Paterson
How to Write Manga by R.A. Paterson
Save the Cat! by Blake Snyder
The Anatomy of Story by John Truby
Wired for Story by Lisa Cron

Japanese Light Novels

English Sources:

J-Novel Club
Yen Press
Seven Seas Entertainment

Titles:

Arifureta (fantasy, rising hero, pseudo-litRPG)
Classroom of the Elite (school drama, advancement)
Grimgar of Fantasy and Ash (litRPG)
Haruhi Suzumiya (school drama, comedy)
How a Realist Hero Rebuilt the Kingdom (fantasy, task story, war)
Is it Wrong to Try to Pick Up Girls in a Dungeon? (fantasy, pseudo-litRPG)
Konosuba: God's Blessing on This Wonderful World (fantasy, comedy)
My Next Life as a Villainess: All Routes Lead to Doom! (fantasy, comedy, romance, pseudo-litRPG)
No Game, No Life (fantasy, pseudo-litRPG)
Overlord (fantasy, pseudo-litRPG, conquest)
Spice and Wolf (fantasy, task story)
That Time I Got Reincarnated as a Slime (fantasy, rising hero, conquest, pseudo-litRPG)

The Ascension of the Bookworm (fantasy, task story)
The Death Mage Who Doesn't Want a Fourth Time (fantasy, pseudo-litRPG, conquest)
The Rising of the Shield Hero (fantasy, pseudo-litRPG)

Chinese Webnovels

Sources:
Wuxiaworld.com
Webnovel.com

Titles:
Against the Gods (xianxia)
Battle Through the Heavens (xianxia)
Coiling Dragon (xianxia, xihuan)
Consort of a Thousand Faces (romance)
Demon Wang's Favorite Fei (romance)
Fields of Gold (romance)
I Shall Seal the Heavens (xianxia)
Tales of Demons and Gods (xianxia)
The King's Avatar (e-sports)
Warlock of the Magus World (xianxia)

Korean Webnovels

Dungeon Defense (pseudo-litRPG, conquest, task story)
I Alone Level (modern fantasy, pseudo-litRPG)
Overgeared (litRPG)
Praise the Orc! (litRPG)
Seoul Station's Necromancer (modern fantasy, pseudo-litRPG)
The Legendary Moonlight Sculptor (litRPG)
Trash of the Count's Family (litRPG, conquest)

Other Books

The Count of Monte Christo by Alexandre Dumas *(the OG of serialized novels!)*
The Three Musketeers by Alexandre Dumas *(another can't-miss original serialized novel)*
The White-Haired Demoness by Liang Yusheng (wuxia)
The Condor Heroes Trilogy by Jin Yong (aka Louis Cha) (wuxia)

The Adventures of Lu Xiao Feng by Gu Long (wuxia)
Little Li's Flying Dagger by Gu Long (wuxia)

Other Media

Justus R. Stone's *Light Novel Reviews* YouTube Channel (light novel news and reviews)

Deathblade's YouTube Channel (Chinese novel translator)

The Light Novel Podcast (Japanese light novel reviews)

tReading the Path of Heaven Podcast (Korean and Chinese webnovel reviews)

ALL THE Write MOVES

Your Essential
Guide to
Creating
**GREAT
FICTION**

by R.A. PATERSON